D0984705

Neuroscience of
Cognitive Development

Neuroscience of Cognitive Development

The Role of Experience and the Developing Brain

Charles A. Nelson

Michelle de Haan

Kathleen M. Thomas

WILEY

John Wiley & Sons, Inc.

Published by John Wiley & Sons, Inc., Hoboken, New Jersey.
Published simultaneously in Canada.

Portions of this book originally appeared in W. Damon (Series Editor) and R. Lerner, D. Kuhn, and R. Siegler (Volume Editors), *Handbook of Child Psychology: Vol. 2. Cognitive, Perception, and Language,* sixth edition, Hoboken, NJ: Wiley.

For general information on our other products and services please contact our Customer Care Department within the United States at (800) 762-2974, outside the United States at (317) 572-3993 or fax (317) 572-4002.

Wiley also publishes its books in a variety of electronic formats. Some content that appears in print may not be available in electronic books. For more information about Wiley products, visit our web site at www.wiley.com.

Library of Congress Cataloging-in-Publication Data:

Nelson, Charles A. (Charles Alexander)
 Neuroscience of cognitive development: the role of experience and the developing brain / by Charles A. Nelson, Michelle de Haan, Kathleen M. Thomas.
        p.   cm.
  ISBN-13: 978-0-471-74586-0 (cloth)
  ISBN-10: 0-471-74586-3 (cloth)
1. Cognitive neuroscience.   2. Developmental psychology.   3. Experience.
  [DNLM: 1. Cognition—physiology.   2. Brain—growth & development.   3. Child Development—physiology.   4. Adolescent Development—physiology. WS 105.5.C7 N425n 2006]   I. De Haan, Michelle, 1969–   II. Thomas, Kathleen M., 1970–   III. Title.
  QP360.5.N45   2006
  612.8′233—dc22

                                                                                                    2005021552

Printed in the United States of America.

10   9   8   7   6   5   4   3   2   1

Contents

Preface

Our goal in writing this book is to introduce the reader to what is currently known about the neural bases of cognitive development. We begin by introducing a number of reasons why developmental psychologists might be interested in the neural bases of behavior (with particular reference to cognitive development). Having established the value of viewing child development through the lens of the developmental neurosciences, we provide an overview of brain development. This is followed by a discussion of how experience influences the developing—and when appropriate, developed—brain. Within this discussion on experience-dependent changes in brain development, we briefly touch on two issues we consider to be essential for all developmental psychologists: whether the mechanisms that underlie developmental plasticity differ from those that underlie adult plasticity, and more fundamentally, what distinguishes plasticity from development.

With this basic neuroscience background behind us, we next turn our attention to how one examines the neural bases of cognitive development—this will essentially be a tutorial on the methods employed by those working in developmental cognitive neuroscience. We begin this section with a brief historical tour, then move the discussion to behavioral (i.e., neuropsychological), anatomic (e.g., structural MRI), metabolic (e.g., functional MRI, functional Near Infrared Spectroscopy), and electrophysiological methods (e.g., event-related potentials).

Once we have concluded our discussion of methods, we turn our attention to specific content areas, limiting ourselves to domains in which there is a corpus of knowledge about the neural underpinnings of cognitive development. We include discussions of declarative and nondeclarative memory and learning, spatial cognition, object recognition, social cognition, speech and language development, executive functions, and attention. We conclude the book with a brief discussion of the future of developmental cognitive neuroscience.

ACKNOWLEDGMENTS

We thank Robert Shannon for assistance in developing many of the figures for this book, Eric Hart and Trisha Dasgupta for editorial assistance, and the members of the Developmental Cognitive Neuroscience Laboratory, who offered valuable feedback on an earlier version of this book.

Why Should Developmental Psychologists Be Interested in the Brain?

Historical Background

Prior to the ascendancy of Piagetian theory, the field of cognitive development was dominated by behaviorism (for discussion, see Goldman-Rakic, 1987; Nelson & Bloom, 1997). Behaviorism eschewed the nonobservable, and therefore, the study of the neural bases of behavior, for the simple reason that neural processes could not be observed. (With the benefit of hindsight, this view always struck us as faulty logic because it failed to recognize that behavior was a product of physiology, and without understanding what *caused* behavior, the interpretation of the behavior itself would be incomplete.) Through the 1950s and 1960s, Piagetian theory gradually came to replace behaviorism as the dominant theory of cognitive development. However, despite a background in biology, Piaget and, subsequently, his followers primarily concerned themselves with developing a richly detailed cognitive architecture of the mind—albeit a brainless mind. We do not mean this in the pejorative sense, but rather, to reflect that the zeitgeist of the time was to develop elegant models of cognitive structures, with little regard for (a) whether such structures were biologically plausible, or (b) the neurobiological

1

underpinnings of such structures. (And, of course, at this time there was no way to observe the living child's brain directly.) Throughout the late 1970s and into the last decade of the twentieth century, neo- and non-Piagetian approaches came into favor. Curiously, a prominent theme of a number of investigators writing during this time was that of nativism. We say curiously because inherent in nativism is the notion of biological determinism, yet those touting a nativist perspective rarely if ever grounded their models and data in any kind of biological reality. It was not until the mid-1990s that neurobiology began to be inserted into a discussion of cognitive development, as reflected, for example, in Mark Johnson's eloquent contribution to the fifth edition of the *Handbook of Child Psychology* (Johnson, 1998). This perspective has become more commonplace, although the field of developmental cognitive neuroscience is still in its infancy. (For recent overviews of this field generally, see de Haan & Johnson, 2003, and Nelson & Luciana, 2001.) Moreover, our personal experience is that it is still not clear to many developmental psychologists why they should be interested in the brain. This is the topic to which we first direct our attention.

Our understanding of cognitive development will be improved as the mechanisms that underlie development are elucidated. This, in turn, should permit us to move beyond the descriptive, black box level to the level at which the actual cellular, physiologic, and eventually, genetic machinery will be understood—that is, the mechanisms that underlie development.

For example, a number of distinguished cognitive developmentalists and cognitive theorists have proposed or at least implied that elements of number concept (Wynn, 1992; Wynn, Bloom, & Chiang, 2002), object permanence (Baillargeon, 1987; Baillargeon, Spelke, & Wasserman, 1985; Spelke, 2000), and perhaps face recognition (Farah, Rabinowitz, Quinn, & Liu, 2000) reflect what we refer to as *experience-independent functions;* that is, they reflect inborn "traits" (presumably coded in the genome) that require little if any experience in order to emerge. We see several problems with this perspective. First, these arguments seem biologically implausible. Such sophisticated cognitive abilities, if they were coded in the genome, would surely involve polygenic traits rather than reflect the action of a single gene. Given that we now know the human genome consists of approximately 30,000 genes, it seems highly unlikely that we could spare the genes to code for number concept, object permanence, or face recognition; after all, our existing complement of genes must be involved in a myriad of other events of more basic importance than subserving these aspects of cognitive development (such as the general operation of the body as a whole).

A second concern about this nativist perspective is that it is not particularly developmental. To say that something is "innate" essentially closes the door to any discussion of mechanism. More problematic is that genes do not "cause" behaviors; rather, genes express proteins that in turn work their magic through the brain. And, it seems unlikely that behaviors that are not absolutely essential to survival (of the species, not the individual) have been coded for in the genome, given the limited number of genes that are known to exist in the genome. Far more likely is that these behaviors are subserved by discrete or distributed neural circuits in the brain, and, these circuits, in turn, likely vary in the extent to which they depend on experience or activity for their subsequent elaboration (a topic we discuss in detail in Chapter 3).

Collectively, we wish to make three points. First, the value added by thinking of behavior in the context of neurobiology is that doing so provides a form of biological plausibility to our models of behavior (a point that we elaborate on later). Second, viewing behavioral development through the lens of neuroscience may shed new light on the mechanism(s) that underlie behavior and behavioral development, thereby moving us beyond the level of description to the level of process. Third, when we insert the molecular biology of brain development into the equation, a more synthetic view of the child becomes possible—genes, brain, and behavior. This broader view permits us to move beyond simplistic notions of *gene-environment* interactions and instead talk about the ways that specific experiences influence specific neural circuits, which influence the expression of particular genes, which influence how the brain functions and how the child behaves.

1

Brain Development and Neural Plasticity
A Précis to Brain Development

Before discussing the details of neural development, it is important to understand that brain development, at the species level, has been shaped over many thousands of generations by selective pressures that drive evolution. According to Knudsen (2003a), this portion of biological inheritance is responsible for nearly all of the genetic influences that shape the development and function of the nervous system, the majority of which have proven to be adaptive for the success of any given species. These influences determine both the properties of individual neurons and the patterns of neural connections. As a result, these selective pressures delimit an individual's cognitive, emotional, sensory, and motor capabilities.

There is, however, a small portion of biological inheritance that is unique to the individual and results from the novel combination of genes that the child receives from the parents. Because there is no history to this gene pattern, any new phenotype that is produced has never been subjected to the forces of natural selection and is unlikely to confer any selective advantage for that individual. However, this small portion of biological inheritance is particularly important for driving evolutionary change, as novel combinations of genes or mutations that do confer a selective advantage will increase in the gene pool, while those that result in maladaptive phenotypes will die out (Knudsen, personal communication).

The brain develops according to a complex array of genetically programmed influences. These include both molecular and electrical signals that arise spontaneously in growing neural networks. By "spontaneously," we mean signals that are inherent in the circuitry and are entirely independent of any outside influence. These molecular and electrical signals establish neural pathways and patterns of connections that are remarkably precise, and that make it possible for animals to carry out discrete behaviors beginning immediately after birth. They also underlie instinctive behaviors that may appear much later in life, often associated with emotional responses, foraging, reproduction (sex would fall under a social interaction), and social interactions. Beyond the scope of this chapter, but certainly worth investigating, is a consideration of which human behaviors fall into this category of "instinctive." Our bias is that these are most likely going to be behaviors that have enormous implications for survival or reproductive fitness, such as the ability to experience fear in order to recognize a predator or to experience pleasure and, conversely, the reduction of displeasure in order to become attached to a caregiver. We should also acknowledge that it is extraordinarily difficult to study such behaviors in humans because the experimental manipulations that would need to be performed would be unethical (they would generally require selective deprivation). Hence our reluctance to claim that certain behaviors are "innate."

To return to our discussion of nativism, there is no question that our genetic makeup has an enormous influence over who we are. To a large extent, human characteristics reflect evolutionary learning, which is exhibited in patterns of neural connections and interactions that have been shaped adaptively by evolution over thousands of generations. In addition to adaptive capacities, however, genetic mutations also can lead to *deficits* in brain function, such as impairments of sensation, cognition, emotion, and/or movement. We provide examples of both in subsequent sections of this chapter.

5

Genes specify the properties of neurons and neural connections to different degrees in different pathways and at different levels of processing. On the one hand, the extent of genetic determination reflects the degree to which the information processed at a particular connection is predictable from one generation to the next. On the other hand, because many aspects of an individual's world are not predictable, the brain's circuitry must rely on experience to customize connections to serve the needs of the individual. Experience shapes these neural connections and interactions but always within the constraints imposed by genetics.

BRAIN DEVELOPMENT

The construction and development of the human brain occurs over a very protracted period of time, beginning shortly after conception and depending on how we view the end of development, continuing through at least the end of adolescence (for overviews, see Figure 1.1 and Table 1.1). Before discussing brain development

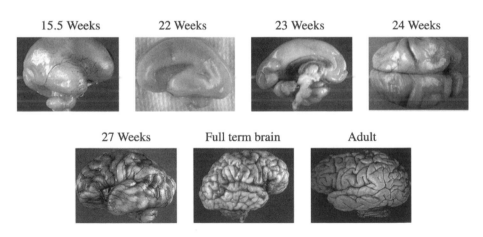

| 15.5 Weeks | 22 Weeks | 23 Weeks | 24 Weeks |

| 27 Weeks | Full term brain | Adult |

Figure 1.1   Overview to human brain development, beginning the 15th prenatal week and continuing to term and then the adult. This figure illustrates the dramatic changes (in surface structure) the brain undergoes during the 9 months of gestation. Source: From Central Nervous System, by O. E. Millhouse and S. Stensaas, n.d. Retrieved June 6, 2005, from http://www.medlib.med.utah.edu/kw/sol/sss/subj2.html.

Table 1.1 Neurodevelopmental Timeline from Conception through Adolescence

Developmental Event	Timeline	Overview of Developmental Event
Neurulation	18–24 prenatal days	Cells differentiate into one of three layers: endoderm, mesoderm and ectoderm, which then form the various organs in the body. The neural tube (from which the CNS is derived) develops from the ectoderm cells; the neural crest (from which the ANS is derived) lies between the ectodermal wall and the neural tube.
Neuronal migration	6–24 prenatal weeks	Neurons migrate at the ventricular zone along radial glial cells to the cerebral cortex. The Neurons migrate in an inside-out manner, with later generations of cells migrating through previously developed cells. The cortex develops into six layers.
Synaptogenesis	3rd trimester– adolescence	Neurons migrate into the cortical plate and extend apical and basilar dendrites. Chemical signals guide the developing dendrites toward their final location, where synapses are formed with projections from subcortical structures. These connections are strengthened through neuronal activity, and connections with very little activity are pruned.
Postnatal neurogenesis	Birth–adulthood	The development of new cells in several brain regions, including: —Dentate gyrus of the hippocampus —Olfactory bulb —Possibly cingulated gyrus; regions of parietal cortex
Myelination	3rd trimester– middle age	Neurons are enclosed in a myelin sheath, resulting in an increased speed of action potentials.
Gyrification	3rd trimester– adulthood	The smooth tissue of the brain folds to form gyri and sulci.

(continued)

Source: From "Neurobiological Development during Childhood and Adolescence," by T. White and C. A. Nelson, in *Schizophrenia in Adolescents and Children: Assessment, Neurobiology, and Treatment*, R. Findling and S. C. Schulz (Eds.), 2004, Baltimore, MD: Johns Hopkins University Press.

Table 1.1   Continued

Developmental Event	Timeline	Overview of Developmental Event
Structural development of the prefrontal cortex	Birth–late adulthood	The prefrontal cortex is the last structure to undergo gyrification during uterine life. The synaptic density reaches its peak at 12 months, however, myclination of this structure continues into adulthood.
Neurochemical development of the prefrontal cortex	Uterine life–adolescence	All major neurotransmitter systems undergo initial development during uterine life and are present at birth. Systems do not reach full maturity until late adulthood.

per se, we must first provide some background to embryology in general.

Embryonic Origins of Brain Tissue

Immediately after conception the two-celled zygote rapidly begins to divide into a many-celled organism. Approximately 1 week after conception has occurred, 100 cells have been formed (this clump of cells is referred to as a blastocyst). A series of molecular changes occur that lead to the rearrangement of these cells, with the subsequent creation of an inner and an outer cell mass. The inner mass (embryoblast) will give rise to the embryo itself, whereas the outer mass (trophoblast) will eventually give rise to all of the supporting tissues, such as the amniotic sac, placenta, and umbilical cord (see Figure 1.2).

Over the course of the next weeks, the cells comprising the embryo itself undergo a transformation, forming inner, middle, and outer layers. The inner layer of the embryo will go on to develop into the epithelial lining of the gastrointestinal and respiratory tracts; the parenchyma (outside portion) of the tonsils, thyroid gland, parathyroid glands, thymus, liver, and pancreas; the epithe-

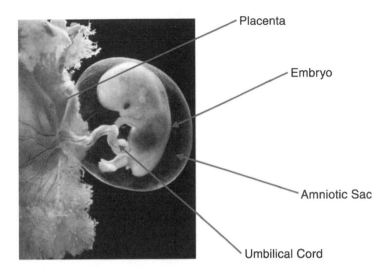

Placenta

Embryo

Amniotic Sac

Umbilical Cord

Figure 1.2   As described in the text, the blastocyst is created by the mitotic process the zygote undergoes following conception. The blastocyst proper divides into an inner and outer layer, with the latter giving rise to the support structures (e.g., amniotic sac, umbilical cord, and placenta), whereas the former give rise to the embryo itself. Source: *From* Introduction to Child Development *(6th ed.), by J. P. Dworetzky, 1996, St. Paul, MN: West Publishing Company.*

lial lining of the urinary bladder and most of the urethra; and the epithelial lining of the tympanic cavity, tympanic antrum, and auditory tube. Among others, the middle layer gives rise to cartilage, bone, connective tissue; striated and smooth muscles; heart, blood and lymph vessels, and cells; kidneys; gonads (ovaries and testes), and genital ducts; the membranes lining the body cavities (e.g., pericardial); and spleen. Finally, the outer layer of the embryo gives rise to the central (brain and spinal cord) and peripheral nervous system; the sensory epithelia of eye, ear, and nose; epidermis (or skin) and its appendages (hair and nails); mammary glands; pituitary gland and subcutaneous glands; enamel of the teeth; spinal, cranial, and autonomic ganglia; pigment cells of the dermis; the membranes covering the brain and spinal cord (meninges). The outer-most layer is the focus of attention in this book.

STAGES OF BRAIN DEVELOPMENT

Neural Induction and Neurulation

The process of transforming the undifferentiated tissue lining the dorsal side of the ectoderm (the outermost layer of the embryo) into nervous system tissue is referred to as neural *induction*. In contrast, the dual processes called primary and secondary *neurulation* further differentiate of this neural tissue into the brain and the spinal cord respectively (for recent review of neural induction and neurulation, see Lumsden & Kintner, 2003).

As Figures 1.3 and 1.4 illustrate, a thin layer of undifferentiated tissue is gradually transformed into an increasingly thick layer of tissue that will become the *neural plate*. Chemical agents collectively referred to as *transforming growth factors* are responsible for the subsequent transformation of this undifferentiated tissue into nervous system tissue (Murloz-Sanjuan & Brivanfou, 2002). Morphologically this is marked by a shift from the neural plate to the neural tube. The neural plate buckles, forming a crease down its longitudinal axis. The tissue then folds inward, the edges rise up, and a tube is formed. This process begins on approximately day 22

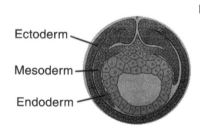

Ectoderm

Mesoderm

Endoderm

Days 18–24:
- Dorsal region of ectoderm thickens and forms neural plate
- Neural plate forms a groove
- Neural tube forms
- Tube closes at rostral, then caudal ends
- Cells trapped inside tube form CNS, those outside tube form ANS

Figure 1.3   As discussed in the text, the inner cell mass gives rise to the embryo, which in turn differentiates into inner, middle, and outer layers. The central nervous system (CNS) is derived from the outer layer (ectoderm). Source: From The Development of Children, *(3rd ed.), by M. Cole and S. R. Cole, 1996, New York: W.H. Freeman and Company.*

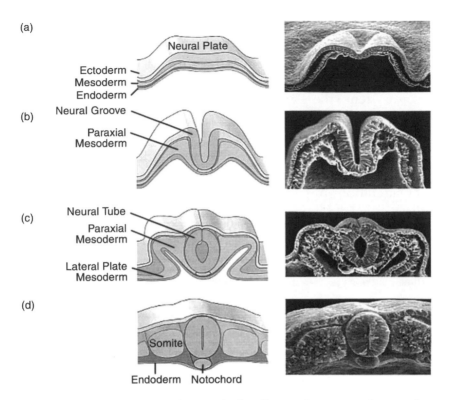

Figure 1.4   The formation of the neural tube, illustrated in cartoon form on the left side of the page and an electron micrograph on the right. Moving from top to bottom shows the initial formation of the neural plate followed by the neural groove followed by the closure of the grove to form the neural tube. Source: *From "Induction and Patterning of the Nervous System" (p. 1020), by T. M. Jessell and J. R. Sanes, in* Principles of Neuroscience, *4th ed., E. R. Kandel, J. H. Schwartz, and T. M. Jessell (Eds.), 2000, New York: McGraw-Hill.*

of gestation (Keith, 1948), with the tube fusing first at the midsection and progressing outward in either direction until approximately day 26 (Sidman & Rakic, 1982). The rostral portion of the tube eventually forms the brain and the caudal portion develops into the spinal cord (see Figure 1.4).

It is the cells trapped inside the tube that typically go on to comprise the central nervous system; however, there is a cluster of cells trapped between the outside of the neural tube and the dorsal portion of the ectodermal wall (see Figure 1.5) that is referred to as the neural crest. Neural crest cells also contribute to the central nervous system; these cells typically go on to develop into the autonomic nervous system (the elements of the nervous system that regulate autonomic functions such as respiration, heart rate, and so on).

A fair amount is now known about the genes that regulate many aspects of brain development, including neurulation. Much of this knowledge is based on studies of invertebrates and vertebrates, in which alterations in morphogenesis are observed after genes are selectively deleted ("knock-out") or in a more recently developed method, added ("knock-in"). Because humans share more than

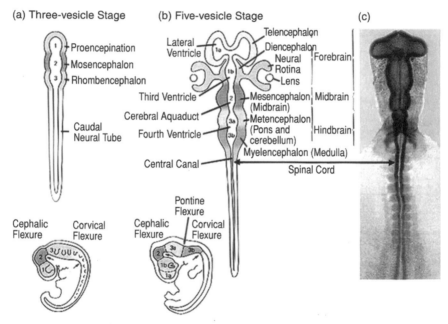

Figure 1.5   As described in the text, once the neural tube has closed, three vesicles form—the forebrain, midbrain and hindbrain. Each of these vesicles is subsequently elaborated, as is illustrated in panels B and C. Source: From "Induction and Patterning of the Nervous System" (p. 1021), by T. M. Jessell and J. R. Sanes, in Principles of Neuroscience, *4th ed., E. R. Kandel, J. H. Schwartz, and T. M. Jessell (Eds.), 2000, New York: McGraw-Hill.*

61% of their genes with fruit flies and 81% with mice, there is some basis for generalization of this information. Of course, not everything we know is based on animal models: Increasingly our knowledge of the molecular biology of brain development is based on careful genetic analysis of nervous system tissue that has failed to develop correctly.

The patterning of the neuroaxis (i.e., head to tail) is for the most part completed by about the 5th prenatal week in humans. Based on mouse studies, many of the transcription factors[1] responsible for this process are now known. As reviewed by Levitt (2003), some of the genes involved in dorsal patterning include members of the *emx*, *pax*, and *ihx* families of genes, whereas *nkx* and *dlx* gene families may play a role in ventral patterning.

Atypical Development. Unfortunately, errors do occur in neural induction and neurulation. *Neural tube defects* are disorders of primary neurulation, which means that in one way or another the tube has failed to close as it should. Such failure can be complete or partial. An example of a complete failure is *Craniorachischisis Totalis*, which is incompatible with life. Examples of partial failure include *anencephaly* (when the anterior portion of the neural tube fails to close completely), *holoprosencephaly* (when a single, undifferentiated forebrain develops, rather than a forebrain that has two halves), and most commonly, *Myelomeningocele* or *spina bifida* (where the posterior portion of the neural tube fails to close normally). Holoprosencephaly appears to be due to mutations in a transcription factor called sonic hedgehog (*ZIC2* genes; e.g., Brown et al., 1998), whereas Myelomeningocele may be due to mutations in the *Pax1* gene (Hof et al., 1996). Importantly, neural tube defects generally have been associated with a deficiency of folic acid, and indeed, supplementing the diet of women with this nutrient before and during pregnancy appears to have reduced the incidence of these disorders in the general population.

---

[1] Transcription factors refer to the regulation of the proteins involved in the transcription of other genes.

Proliferation

Once the neural tube has closed, cell division leads to a massive proliferation of new neurons (*neurogenesis*), generally beginning in the 5th prenatal week and peaking between the 3rd and 4th prenatal months (Volpe, 2000; for review, see Bronner-Fraser & Hatten, 2003). The term *massive* barely captures this process. It has been estimated, for example, that at its peak, several hundred thousand new nerve cells are generated *each minute* (Brown, Keynes, & Lumsden, 2001). Proliferation begins in the innermost portion of the neural tube, referred to as the ventricular zone (Chenn & McConnell, 1995), a region that is derived from the subependeymal location that lines the neural tube. In a process called *interkinetic nuclear migration*, new neural cells travel back and forth between the inner and outer portions of the ventricular zone. During the so-called S phase of cell division (mitosis), the new cell first travels toward the outer portion of the ventricular zone where DNA is synthesized, creating a duplicate copy of the cell. Once the S phase has been completed, the cell migrates downward toward the innermost portion of the ventricular zone where it divides into two cells (for a generally accessible description of these phases, see Takahashi, Nowakowski, & Caviness, 2001). Each of these new cells then begins the process again. As cells divide, a new zone is created, the marginal zone, which contains processes (axons and dendrites) from the cells of the ventricular zone. During the second phase of proliferation, neurons actually begin to form. However, for each dividing cell, only one daughter cell will continue to divide; it is the nondividing cell that goes on to migrate to its final destination (Rakic, 1988; see discussion that follows).

Before turning to disorders of proliferation, we wish to make three final points. First, with the exception of cells that comprise the olfactory bulb, the dentate region of the hippocampus, and possibly regions of the neocortex, virtually every one of the estimated 100 billion neurons we possess (Naegele & Lombroso, 2001) are of prenatal origin (see section on postnatal neurogenesis); glia follow this same general pattern, although the development of glia (with

14

the exception of radial glial cells; see section on migration) lags somewhat behind neuronal development. What needs to be under-scored about this observation is its importance in the context of plasticity: specifically, unlike all other cells in the body, the brain does not make new neurons after birth (with the exceptions noted previously, and subsequently, when we talk about postnatal neuro-genesis), which means that the brain does not repair itself in re-sponse to injury or disease by making new neurons.

Second, as cells continue to proliferate, the general shape of the neural tube undergoes a dramatic transformation. As seen in Figure 1.5, three distinct vesicles are formed: the *prosencephalon* (forebrain), *mesencephalon* (midbrain), and *rhombencephalon* (hindbrain). Fur-ther proliferation leads the prosencephalon to split into two portions, the *telencephalon* (which will give rise to the cerebral hemispheres), and the *diencephalon* (which gives rise to the thalamus and hypothal-amus). The rhombencephalon in turn will give rise to the *meten-cephalon* (from which the pons and cerebellum are derived) and the *myelencephalon* (which will give rise to the medulla). The mesen-cephalon gives rise to the midbrain.

Third, our knowledge of the molecular biology behind cell prolif-eration is gradually advancing. However, we know much less about these processes than we do about the morphological changes that result from them. The *Foxg1* gene has been implicated in the pro-cess of cell proliferation (Hanashima, Li, Shen, Lai, & Fishell, 2004), but undoubtedly we will find that many other genes are in-volved as well.

Disorders of Neurogenesis

There are a number of examples of errors of cell proliferation, al-though most fall into two categories: *microcephaly* (small brain) and *macrocephaly* (large brain; see Volpe, 2000). Microcephaly is generally thought to occur during the asymmetric period of cell division, generally the 6th through 18th week of gestation. The cause of the microcephalies can be either genetic or environmental; examples of the latter include rubella, irradiation, maternal alcoholism, excessive vitamin A, and human immunodeficiency virus (e.g., Kozlowski et al., 1997; Warkany, Lemire, & Choen, 1981). Macrocephaly is generally thought to be due to an underlying genetic disorder; for example, if genes that regulate normal cellular proliferation do not turn off, this failure could lead to an overproduction of new cells. Assuming survival, both micro- and macrocephaly generally lead to varying degrees of mental and physical retardation/impairment.

Postnatal Neurogenesis

With the exception of cells in the olfactory bulb, it was assumed until recently that the nervous system contained at birth virtually all the neurons it would ever have, and that no new neurons were added later in development. Like many aspects of neuroscience, we have now had to revise this view, due in part to the advent of new methods—specifically, the use of new staining techniques for examining DNA turnover (e.g., 5′-Bromo-2-deoxyuridine [BrdU], which permits the visualization of cells undergoing mitosis). Based on work with both human (e.g., Gage, 2000) and nonhuman primates (e.g., Bernier, Bédard, Vinet, Lévesque, & Parent, 2002; Gould, Beylin, Tanapat, Reeves, & Shors 1999; Kornack & Rakic, 1999) and rodents (Gould et al., 1999), there is now widespread agreement that in certain regions of the brain new cells are added for many years after birth. Where this agreement breaks down is in determining precisely which regions experience this postnatal birth of new neurons. There is little controversy that the olfactory bulb and the dentate gyrus of the hippocampus both show postnatal neurogenesis; where controversy exists, however, concerns regions of the neocortex, such as the cingulate gyrus (part of the prefrontal cortex) and segments of the parietal cortex (for review and discussion, see Gould & Gross, 2002). There have also been reports of postnatal neurogenesis in the amygdala, piriform cortex, and inferior temporal cortex in nonhuman primates (Bernier et al., 2002), although to date these findings have not been replicated (for a highly readable review of postnatal neurogenesis generally, see Barinaga, 2003).

16

Particularly relevant to this chapter is the observation that the addition of such cells can be influenced by experience (e.g., Gould et al., 1999). For example, the number of cells produced in the rodent dentate gyrus is increased when rats are placed in contexts in which demands are placed on learning and memory. Similarly, the presence of the hormone prolactin (a hormone produced by the pituitary gland, which stimulates milk production) in pregnant rats appears to increase the number of new cells in the forebrain subventricular zone. Because this zone gives rise to olfactory neurons, it has been assumed that this adaptive response may facilitate olfactory recognition of offspring (see Shingo et al., 2003). In contrast, stress in adulthood (such as the presence of novel odors, such as the smell of a fox) appears to down-regulate neurogenesis in the rat dentate gyrus. Moreover, when rodents are housed together, dominance hierarchies develop, and the dominant animals produce more new neurons than the nondominant animals (Gould, 2003). Interestingly, if these same animals are then housed in complex environments (see Chapter 3), there is an upregulation of neurogenesis in the dentate, although the dominant animals continue to fare better than the nondominant animals. Finally, inflammation (which commonly occurs following brain injury) can lead to a down-regulation of dentate hippocampal cells (Ekdahl, Claasen, Bonde, Kokaia, & Lindvall, 2003). Collectively, experience appears to have an important influence on postnatal neurogenesis.

It is important to note that postnatally derived cells may differ in several respects from prenatally derived cells. For example, the former differentiate and appear to be normal in all respects, although these cells may have a relatively short half-life (Gould, Vail, Wagers, & Gross, 2001). Furthermore, it is not yet clear whether these cells function differently, although Gage and colleagues (e.g., van Praag et al., 2002) have reported that newly generated cells in the adult mouse hippocampus show many similarities to mature dentate granule cells (e.g., display action potentials). In addition, Song, Stevens, and Gage (2002) have demonstrated that postnatally derived cells both express neurotransmitter and form synaptic connections.

What remains unknown, however, is how such cells might work their way into existing synaptic circuits. Finally, this revised view of neurogenesis is not without its critics (e.g., Rakic, 2002a, 2002b). For an enlightened discussion of this topic, see the special issue of the *Journal of Neuroscience*, 2002, *22*(3). Resolution of this matter will prove vitally important to our understanding of plasticity and to the development of interventions and theraputics; regarding the latter, for example, there is strong evidence that exercise (in rodents) leads to an upregulation of neurogenesis in the dentate gyrus of the hippocampus. If such findings prove robust, it may well be the case that exercise becomes an inexpensive and widely available treatment for certain disorders (with multiple secondary benefits as well). (For a general discussion of the possible link between postnatal neurogenesis and theraputics, see Lie, Song, Colamarino, Ming, & Gage, 2004.)

Cell Migration

As discussed by Brown et al. (2001), the ventricular zone (the epithelium that lines the lateral ventricular cavities) gives rise to cells that undergo cell division, with the postmitotic cell migrating through the intermediate zone to its final point of destination. The cells born first take up residence in the preplate (the first layer of cortical neurons), which subsequently divides into the subplate and the marginal zone, both of which are derived from the cortical plate (see Figure 1.6).

The postmitotic cells move in an inside-out (ventricular-to-pial) direction, such that the earliest migrating cells occupy the deepest layer of the cortex (and play an important role in the establishment of cortical connections), with subsequent migrations passing through the previously formed layer(s) (note that this rule applies only to the cortex; the dentate gyrus and the cerebellum are formed in an outside-in pattern). At approximately 20 weeks gestation, the cortical plate consists of three layers, and by the 7th prenatal month the mature contingent of six layers can be seen (Marin-Padilla, 1978; see Figures 1.7 and 1.8).

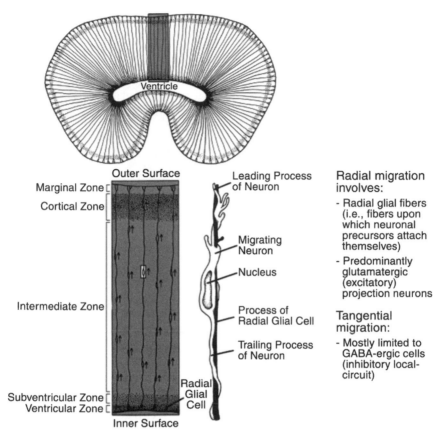

Figure 1.6   Cell migration occurs through two processes—radial and tangential migration (see text for details). Source: *From* Brain, Mind, and Behavior *(3rd ed.), by F. Bloom, C. A. Nelson and A. Lazerson, 2001, New York: Worth Publishers.*

There are two types of migratory patterns for neuronal cells—radial and tangential. Pyramidal neurons, the major projection neurons in the brain, along with oligodendrocytes and astrocytes enlist radial glial cells to migrate through the layers of cortex (Kriegstein & Götz, 2003), whereas cortical interneurons (for local connections) migrate via tangential migration within a cortical layer (Nadarajah & Parnavelas, 2002). Radial migration is particularly noteworthy given its broad importance in migration, and is observed in many forms.

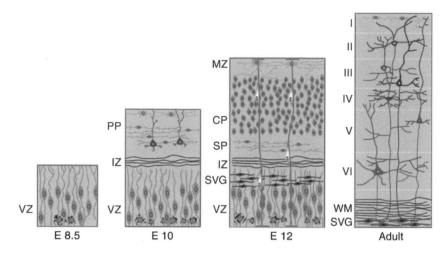

Figure 1.7   The six layers of the cortex form in an inside-out fashion, primarily through the process of radial migration. This figure illustrates the gradual differentiation of each layer. Source: From "Neurogenesis and Migration" (pp. 391–416), by M. Bronner-Fraser and M. B. Hatten, in Fundamental Neuroscience (2nd ed.), L. R. Squire, F. E. Bloom, S. K. McConnell, J. L. Roberts, N. C. Spitzer, and M. J. Zigmond (Eds.), 2003, New York: Academic Press.

Locomotion is characterized by migration along a radial glial fiber. In somal translocation, the cell body (soma) of a cell advances toward the pial surface by way of a leading process. Finally, cells that move from the Intermediate Zone (IZ) to the Subventricular (SVZ) zone appear to migrate using multipolar migration (Tabata & Nakajima, 2003). These migratory processes are thought to be regulated by a number of genes, including the Minibrain (Mnb) gene, the unc-6/Netrin1 gene, the reeler gene, and Ephrin B1, a receptor tyrosine kinease (Kriegstein & Götz, 2003). (For good overviews of the molecular biology of cell migration, see Hatten, 2002, and Ridley et al., 2003.)

Disorders of Cell Migration

There are many examples of disorders of cell migration (for review, see Naegele & Lombroso, 2001; Volpe, 2000). Subcortical band heterotopia (also known as x-linked lissencephaly), in which neural tis-

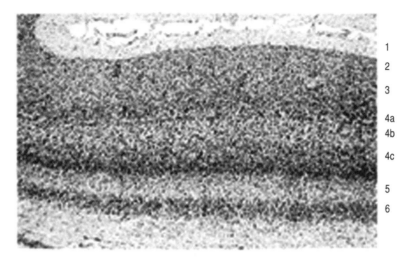

1
2
3
4a
4b
4c
5
6

Figure 1.8   The six layers of the cortex begins with migration of cells from ventricular zone into future Layer I of cortex. These cells express the protein reelin, which mediates the cell's detachment from its glial fiber when the cell reaches its final destination. Once Layer I is formed, a layer of cells between it and the ventricular zone forms a transient subplate. Newly created cells migrate through the subplate to form the cortical plate. Source: *From* Eye, Brain, and Vision, *by D. Hubel, n.d. Retrieved June 6, 2005, from http://neuro.med.harvard.edu/site/dh/b24.htm.*

sue is misplaced (e.g., cell bodies where only axons should exist) has been associated with mental retardation and epilepsy, and with the *DCX* gene. *Schizencephaly*, in which there is a cleft in the frontal cortex, has been associated with the EMX2 gene, and *holoprosencephaly*, in which the telencephalon fails to cleave resulting in one undifferentiated hemisphere, has been associated with a number of different genes (e.g., *Sonic Hedgehog*, or *SHH*; *ZInc finger cerebellar expressed 2*, or *ZIC2*).[2] Perhaps the best-known disorder of migration is agenesis of the corpus callosum, in which the corpus callosum (the major bundle of fibers that connect the two hemispheres) is partially or entirely absent. As a class, disorders of cell migration

---

[2] By "associated with" we simply mean that there is a correlation between a given disorder and a particular gene, such that, for example, the absence of that gene or a misexpression of that gene seems to be the underlying cause of the disorder.

generally result in varying degrees of behavioral or psychological disturbance; a case in point may be the psychiatric disorder schizophrenia, which has been hypothesized to result from a migrational disorder (see Elvevåg & Weinberger, 2001).

The Growth and Development of Processes
Axons and Dendrites

Once a neuron has completed its migratory journey, it generally proceeds along one of two roads: The cell can differentiate and develop axons and dendrites (the topic of this section), or it can be retracted through the normative process of *apoptosis* (programmed cell death), a phenomenon that is widespread (e.g., 40% to 60% of all neurons may die; for review, see Oppenheim & Johnson, 2003).

The Development of Axons

The *growth cone,* a small structure that sits on top of an axon, appear to play a key role in both the development of the axon itself and in guiding the axon to its target (e.g., for review, see Raper & Tessier-Lavigne, 2003). Using cues from the extracellular matrix surrounding the neuron and possibly local gene expression (Condron, 2002), the growth cone directs the axon toward some targets and away from others.

As Raper and Tessier-Lavigne (1999) discuss, *lamellipodia* and *filopodia* play primary roles in axon guidance (see Figure 1.9). Lamellipodia are thin fan-shaped structures, whereas filopodia are long, thin spikes that radiate forward. In both cases these structures provide the axon with the ability to move through parenchymal (brain) tissue micrometer by micrometer until the axon is within synapse range of a neighboring neuron. They do so by sampling the local environment for molecular cues; such cues include aminin, tenascin, collagen, fibronectin, slit, netrins, semaphorins, and proteoglycans (Bixby & Harris, 1991; de Castro, 2003). And, the receptors that bind to these molecules include integrins, immunoglobulin superfamily members, neogenin, DCC, neuropilins, plexins, robos, and proteoglycans (Hynes & Lander, 1992).

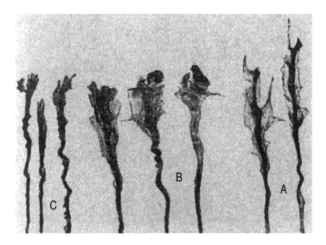

Figure 1.9   Growth cones play an essential role in guiding an axon to its target destination. Source: *From "Growth Cones and Axon Pathfinding" (pp. 449–467), by M. T. Tessier-Lavigne, in* Fundamental Neuroscience *(2nd ed.), L. R. Squire, F. E. Bloom, S. K. McConnell, J. L. Roberts, N. C. Spitzer, and M. J. Zigmond (Eds.), 2003, New York: Academic Press.*

Over and above these molecular cues, there are also molecules that sit on the surface of established axons and act as guides. An example is cell adhesion molecules (CAMs; Rutishauser, 1993; Takeichi, 1995). Whether the molecules reside in the extracelluar matrix or on the axon proper, axons are guided toward (attractant cues) or away from (repellant cues) neighboring neurons (Tessier-Lavigne & Goodman, 1996).

The Development of Dendrites

Recent work has indicated that the gene *calcium-regulated transcriptional activator (CREST)* plays an important role in the development of dendrites (Aizawa et al., 2004). The earliest dendrites make their appearance as thick processes extending from the cell body and generally have few spines (small protuberances). As dendrites mature, spine number and density increase, thereby increasing the chance of making contact with a neighboring axon. Not surprisingly, dendrites grow and develop in conjunction with axons. Dendritic sprouting begins to occur at approximately 15 weeks, about the same time that axons reach the cortical plate. Between the 25th and 27th weeks of gestation dendritic spines begin appearing on both pyramidal and nonpyramidal neurons. This sprouting continues to expand through the 24th postnatal month in some cortical regions (Mrzljack, Uylings, VanEden, & Judas, 1990).

While the production of neurons appears to occur primarily during prenatal development, the production of many axons and dendrites continues postnatally. For example, dendrites of pyramidal neurons reach peak number in the 2nd year of life (Mrzljak et al., 1990). Additionally, there appears to be an overproduction of both axons and dendrites during development with the final number achieved through a process of competitive elimination.

Disorders of Axon and Dendrite Development

A number of environmental agents have been associated with errors in axonal and dendritic development, including oxygen deprivation, toxins, malnutrition, or genetic anomalies (Webb, Monk, & Nelson, 2001). In addition, genetic disorders such as Angelman syndrome, fragile X syndrome, autism and Duchenne muscular dystrophy show possible errors in dendritic development (Volpe, 1995).

Synaptogenesis

Synapses, the point of contact between two neurons, generally come in two forms: electrical and chemical. Electrical synapses, such as gap junctions, provide for rapid transmssion of information by passing electric current from one neuron to the next (e.g., Ahmad, Martin, & Evans, 2001). In contrast, chemical synapses transmit electrical signals arriving at the axon terminal of one neuron by signaling the release of chemical messengers (e.g., neurotransmitters). Depending on the receiving neuron, the resulting action can be excitatory (promoting an action potential) or inhibitory (reducing the likelihood of an action potential).

Development. The first synapses are generally observed by about the 23rd week of gestation (Molliver, Kostovic, & Van der Loos, 1973), although the peak of production does not occur until some time in the 1st year of life (for review, see Webb et al., 2001). It is now well known that there is massive overproduction of synapses distributed across broad regions of the brain, followed by a gradual reduction in synapses; indeed, it has been estimated that 40% more synapses are produced than exist in the final (adult) complement of synapses (see Levitt, 2003). The timing of the peak of overproduction varies by brain area. For example, in the visual cortex, a peak in number of synapses is reached between roughly the 4th and 8th postnatal month (Huttenlocher & de Courten, 1987), whereas in the middle frontal gyrus (in prefrontal cortex) the peak synaptic density is not obtained until after 15 postnatal months (Huttenlocher & Dabholkar, 1997).

There is evidence that the overproduction of synapses is largely under genetic control, although little is known about the genes that regulate synaptogenesis. For example, Bourgeois and colleagues (Bourgeois, Reboff, & Rakic, 1989) have reported that being born prematurely or even removing the eyes of monkeys prior to birth has little effect on the overproduction of synapses in the monkey visual cortex. Thus, in both cases, the absolute number of synapses is the same as if the monkey experienced a typical, full-term birth. This suggests a highly regularized process with little influence of experience. As we shall demonstrate, however, the same cannot be said for synaptic pruning and the cultivating of synaptic circuits, both of which are strongly influenced by the environment.

Synaptic Pruning. The process of retracting synapses until some final (and presumably optimal) number has been reached is dependent in part on the communication among neurons. Pruning appears to follow the Hebbian principle of use/disuse: thus, more active synapses tend to be strengthened and less active synapses tend to be weakened or even eliminated (Chechik, Meilijson, Ruppin, 1999). Neurons organize and support synaptic contact through neurotransmitter receptors (both excitatory and inhibitory) on the presynaptic cell (the cell attempting to make contact) and through neurotrophins expressed by the postsynaptic cell (the cell on which contact is made). Synapses are modulated and stabilized by the distribution of excitatory and inhibitory inputs (Kostovic, 1990). The adjustments that are made in the pruning of synapses can either be quantitative (reducing the overall number of synapses), or qualitative (refining connections such that incorrect or abnormal connections are eliminated; for review, see Wong & Lichtman, 2003).

As has been thoroughly reported in both the lay and scientific press, the pruning of synapses appears to vary by region. As seen in Figure 1.10, synapse numbers in the human occipital cortex peak between 4 and 8 months of age, and are reduced to adult numbers by 4 to 6 years of age. In contrast, synapses in the middle frontal gyrus of the human prefrontal cortex reach their peak closer to one to 1.5 years of age, but are not reduced to adult numbers until mid to late adolescence. Unfortunately, these data are based on relatively few brains (thus leaving open the question of the range of individual differences) and relatively old methods (i.e., density of synapses

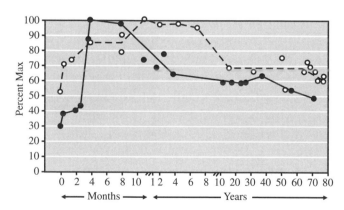

Figure 1.10 Synapse overproduction and elimination in the occipital (solid line) and frontal (dashed line) cortices. Source: *From "Synaptogenesis, Synapse Elimination, and Neural Plasticity in Human Cerebral Cortex" (pp. 35–54, Figure 2.1), by P. R. Huttenlocher, in* Minnesota Symposium on Child Psychology, 27: Threats to Optimal Development—Integrating Biological, Psychological, and Social Risk Factors, C. A. *Nelson (Ed.), 1994, NJ: Erlbaum.*

per unit area, which increases the risk that nonsynaptic and even nonneuronal elements may be counted, such as glial cells). We should expect improved figures in the years to come with advances in new methods—a point that applies to much of the literature reviewed thus far.

Synaptic Plasticity. The initial development of synapses is generally quite tenuous. Thus, it is only after a synapse has been activated repeatedly that it becomes stabilized; frequently, synapses that do not receive confirmation are eliminated or reabsorbed (Changeux & Danchin, 1976). Moreover, synapse stabilization also depends on chemical communication, such as the local release of neurotrophins by postsynaptic cells (Huang & Reichardt, 2001) or the activation of receptors such as glutamate that in turn mediate postsynaptic activation of cortical cells. Finally, even in the mature brain, synaptic plasticity is driven by synaptic activity. For example, reducing activity in a given neuron *before* a synapse has been formed leads to a reduction in functional inputs to that neuron; in contrast, reducing activity to a given neuron *after* a synapse has been established leads to an increase in synaptic input and a restoration of neuronal activity to normal levels (Burrone, O'Byrne, & Murthy, 2002).

Disorders of Synaptogenesis

There are a number of disorders of synaptogenesis, with Fragile X syndrome being perhaps the best known (Fragile X is also a very common form of mental retardation). In Fragile X, it appears that the disruption in the transcription of the FMR1 gene may be responsible for the abnormality in synapses, perhaps due in part to an exuberance in dendritic spines (e.g., Churchill, Beckel-Mitchener, Weiler, & Greenough, 2002; Churchill et al., 2002a).

Myelination

Myelin is a lipid/protein substance that wraps itself around an axon as a form of insulation, and as a result, increases conduction velocity. *Oligodendroglia* produce myelin in the CNS, whereas *schwann* cells produce myelin in the ANS. Myelination occurs in waves beginning prenatally and ending in young adulthood (and in some regions, as "late" as middle age; see Benes, 2001). Historically, myelin was examined in postmortem tissue using staining methods. From such work, it was revealed that myelination begins prenatally with the peripheral nervous system, motor roots, sensory roots, somesthetic cortex, and the primary visual and auditory cortices (in this chronological order). During the first postnatal year, regions of the brain stem myelinate, as does the cerebellum and splenium of corpus callosum; by 1 year myelination of all regions of the corpus callosum is underway.

Although staining for myelin is undoubtedly the most sensitive metric for examining the course of myelination, an obvious disadvantage to this procedure is that it can only be done on a relatively small number of postmortem brains; in addition, as is the case with human synaptogenesis, it is also of concern how representative these brains are to the general population. Fortunately, advances in magnetic resonance imaging (MRI; a method we discuss in detail in Chapter 4) have now made it possible to acquire detailed information about myelination in living children; importantly, there are now a number of longitudinal studies that have examined the course of myelination from early childhood through early adulthood (Giedd, Snell, et al., 1996; Giedd, Vatuzis, et al., 1996; Giedd et al., 1999; Jernigan, Trauner, Hesselink, & Tallal, 1991; Paus et al., 1999; Sowell et al., 1999; Sowell, Thompson, Holmes, Jernigan, & Toga, 2000). The results of this work paint the following picture: the pre- through postadolescent period witness an increase in gray matter volume, followed by a decrease, whereas white matter shows first a decrease and then an increase. The decrease in gray matter is thought to be due to apoptosis (loss of cells bodies and glia), whereas the increase in white is thought to be due to increasing myelination. During this same age period (pre-post adolescence), particular changes of note occur in the dorsal, medial, and lateral regions of the frontal lobes, whereas relatively smaller changes are observed in the parietal, temporal, and occipital lobes. This suggests, not surprisingly, that the most dramatic changes in myelination occur in the frontal lobes through the adolescent period (for a general overview, see Durston et al., 2001).

SUMMARY

Overall, brain development begins within weeks of conception, and continues through the adolescent period. This general statement does not do justice to the age-specific changes that occur during the first 2 decades of life. Thus, the assembly of basic architecture occurs during the first two trimesters of fetal life, with the last trimester and the first few postnatal years reserved for changes in connectivity and function. The most prolonged changes occur in the wiring of the brain (synaptogenesis) and in making the brain work more efficiently (myelination), both of which show dramatic, nonlinear changes from the preschool period through the end of adolescence.

2

Neural Plasticity
Background

Having established how the anatomical and physiological proper-ties of the brain are laid down over the first 2 decades of life, we may have inadvertently created the impression that these events simply unfold of their own accord—that is, are largely maturational in nature. Although that is true to a great extent prenatally, it vastly under-represents the powerful role of experience in sculpting the fine architecture of the brain. Before providing specific examples of experience-induced changes in brain development and brain func-tion, we must first provide some background.

It is important to understand that experiences don't just happen to the brain; rather, experience is the product of an ongoing, recip-rocal interaction between the environment and the brain. Second, experience has typically been defined by the properties of the envi-ronment in which an individual lives—for example, the language one is exposed to, the kind of caregiving experiences one has, the kinds of cognitive challenges that are supported by the environment, and so on. Here it must be stressed that experience is not simply a function of the environment per se, but is the result of a complex, bidirectional interaction between that environment and the devel-oping brain. Third, experience interacts importantly with genetics. Two examples suffice, one from the rodent literature, one from the human literature. Regarding the former, Francis, Szegda, Campbell, Martin, and Insel (2003) cross-fostered two strains of mice with one another, either prenatally (in which hours-old embryos from one strain were implanted in the mothers of the other strain) and post-natally (in which newborn pups from one strain were placed with the mothers of the other strain). The offspring of the two original (noncross-fostered) strains served as controls. All animals were tested at 3 months of age. As expected, the control animals differed reliably from one another on four dimensions: (1) differences in ex-ploration of an open field (a test of anxiety or wariness of novelty); (2) relative time on the open arms of a plus maze (another metric of anxiety coupled with spatial navigation skill); (3) latency to find a hidden platform in the Morris water maze (a metric of spatial mem-ory); and (4) acoustic startle prepulse inhibition (an index of anxi-ety). Animals that had been cross-fostered prenatally *or* postnatally did not exert any effects on the expected phenotype. However, mice that had been prenatally *and* postnatally cross-fostered exhibited the same behavioral phenotype as the adopted strain, despite differing genetically from the adopted strain. The fact that mice that had been cross-fostered prenatally did not show this effect supported the authors' contention that the effects of the combined cross-fostering must be due to nongenetic factors, and instead reflects the powerful role of experience on gene expression.

Moving to the human, Turkheimer, Haley, Waldron, D'Onofrio, and Gottesman (2003) examined IQ in 7-year-old twins, a substan-tial number of whom were drawn from families living at or below the poverty level. The authors reported that the heritability of IQ varied nonlinearly as a function of socioeconomic status (SES). Thus, among twins living in impoverished environments, a substan-tial portion of the variance was accounted for by environmental fac-tors, with relatively little variance accounted for by genetics; in contrast, this effect was nearly completely reversed among twins liv-ing in affluent families.

Collectively, these two studies demonstrate the powerful role of the environment in moderating and mediating effects of genes on behavior. Animal studies, adopting both knock-out and knock-in molecular tools, coupled with careful rearing studies will undoubtedly shed light on the pattern of gene expression and nongenetic inheritance patterns.

Within this context, any given experience can vary enormously under identical environmental conditions, depending on the history, maturation, and state of the individual's brain. This principle, which is so obvious when considered in the context of complex experiences, applies equally to simple experiences. Even the experience that results from a simple physical manipulation, for example, may vary widely depending on the background and state of the individual involved. The opportunity to exercise may be an example of this.

The relative maturity of the brain also has an enormous impact on experience. Different areas of the central nervous system mature at different rates. A young child who is exposed to information before his or her brain is capable of processing that information will not have the same experience as an older child who has more advanced capability. A less mature brain is affected largely by more fundamental features of the environment, such as patterned light or the speech train. As the brain matures and changes with experience, more detailed and possibly more specific aspects of the environment influence it. Thus, as an individual's brain changes, particularly during the early developmental periods, the same physical environment can result in very different experiences.

Certain properties of the brain differ dramatically across individuals and within individuals over time. Therefore, because experience is defined as the interaction of the brain with the environment, a scientific description of an experience must include a description of the background, developmental stage, and state of the brain as well as a description of the specific experience to which the individual is exposed. By the same token, an analysis of the effect of an experience also must take into account variability in those same variables.

The impact of experience on the brain is not constant throughout life. As the brain passes through its different developmental stages, its sensitivity to experience varies accordingly—hence the concept of *sensitive periods* (see Knudsen, 2003a). Early experience often exerts a particularly strong influence in shaping the functional properties of the immature brain. Many neural connections pass through a period during development when the capacity for experience-driven modification is greater than it is in adulthood. Thus, individual capabilities reflect the combined influences of both evolutionary learning and personal experience.

In the sections that follow, we deconstruct plasticity into two types: developmental and adult. By this we simply mean plastic processes that operate during the time of brain *development* (presumably the first 2 decades of life) versus the post-developmental period (when the brain is certainly capable of *changing* but not in the same fashion as the child's brain; that is, it is not developing *qua* developing). We revisit this simplistic view at the end of this section by discussing whether the plastic processes that operate during development are the same or different as those that operate during adulthood.

We, and others, have provided overviews to the myriad of ways experience influences the developing and developed brain (Black, Jones, Nelson, & Greenough, 1998; Cline, 2003; Grossman, Churchill, Bates, Kleim, & Greenough, 2002; Huttenlocher, 2002; Knudsen 2003b, 2004; Nelson, 1999, 2000a, 2002; Nelson & Bloom, 1997). Our purpose here is to provide a brief overview to this topic, beginning with a discussion of developmental plasticity and proceeding to a discussion of adult plasticity. Within each of these sections, we draw on a range of species, although we focus most on rodents, monkeys, and humans. Finally, we limit our discussion to perceptual and cognitive functions, and do not discuss aspects of plasticity from social emotional development.

DEVELOPMENTAL PLASTICITY

A rather amazing example of plasticity in the auditory system was published a number of years ago by Sur and Leamey (2001). Normal retinal inputs pass through the lateral geniculate nucleus (LGN) of the thalamus on their way to the visual cortex, whereas normal auditory inputs pass through the medial geniculate nucleus (MGN) on their way to the auditory cortex. In this study, retinal projections in the young ferret were surgically rerouted through the MGN. When electrophysiological recordings were made from the auditory cortex, normal *visual* responses were observed; for example, these "auditory" cells showed orientation selectivity to visual stimuli.

Recently, Cheng and Merzenich (2003) reported that infant rats reared in continuous, moderate-level noise showed a delay in the organization of the auditory cortex; specifically, the auditory receptive fields differed from what would be expected under normal auditory rearing conditions. When these rats reached young adulthood, the auditory cortex appeared to be very similar to infants—that is, the auditory receptive fields had not yet crystallized into the adult pattern and had retained their juvenile appearance. To test the hypothesis that rearing the rats in continuous noise from birth delayed the closing of the critical period for organizing the auditory cortex, the authors exposed some of the same rats to a 7 kHz tone train for 2 weeks. This led to a reorganization of the auditory cortex, supporting the hypothesis that degraded acoustic inputs early in life delayed the organizational maturation of the auditory cortex. This delay might not necessarily be adaptive; indeed, the authors speculate that early exposure to abnormal auditory inputs (e.g., loud noise) could contribute to some auditory and/or linguistic delays in human children.

Visual Function

The development of stereoscopic depth perception is made possible by the development of ocular dominance columns, which represent the connections between each eye and layer IV of the visual cortex. If the two eyes are not aligned properly, or can't move together (vergence movements), then the ocular dominance columns that support normal stereoscopic depth perception fail to develop normally. If this situation is not corrected by 4 to 5 years of age (when the number of synapses begins to reach adult values), the child will not develop normal stereoscopic vision. Thus, normal visual input to an intact visual system during a sensitive period is necessary for the development of binocular vision.

Another example of sensitive periods for visual development can be found in an elegant series of studies by Maurer and colleagues who have reported on a longitudinal study of children with cataracts. A particularly attractive feature to this work is that some infants are born with cataracts, and others acquire them a few years after birth; moreover, some have their cataracts removed in the first months of life, others undergo this procedure a few years later. The authors reported that among infants born with cataracts that are removed and new lenses placed within months of birth, even just a few *minutes* of visual experience can lead to a dramatic change in visual acuity. The longer the cataracts are left untreated, reducing the amount of early visual experience, the less favorable the outcome. Note, however, that although most visual functions undergo dramatic improvements following early cataract removal, some aspects of *face* processing remain impaired for years (Le Grand, Mondloch, Maurer, & Brent, 2001). From this observation comes the idea of a differential sensitive period: specifically, the sensitive period for visual acuity may differ from that for face processing.

Learning and Memory Function

Hormones have long been thought to mediate cognitive differences between males and females due to their organizing effect on the brain. This association can even be observed prenatally. For example, Shors and Miesegaes (2002) capitalized on previous findings in which exposure to stressful and traumatic events enhances new learning in adult male rats, but impairs new learning in adult female rats. In this study, the authors performed two experiments. In the first, male rats were castrated at birth, whereas female rats were injected with testosterone; both groups were then tested on a hippocampal-dependent learning task (trace eyeblink conditioning). The castrated male rats still exhibited enhanced learning, *as did the testosterone-injected females* (opposite the normal pattern of response, in which reduced learning is typically observed for females). In the second experiment, pregnant female rats were injected with a testosterone antagonist, thereby depriving the offspring of testosterone. The male and female offspring were subsequently tested as adults on the same learning task following exposure to a stressor (loud noise bursts). Male *and* female rats now both exhibited reduced learning, pointing to the powerful role of early experience with testosterone.

Summary

The literature reviewed here most likely confirms what most readers assumed when they started to read this section: The developing brain is very plastic. Although clearly true, it is important to stress that the degree of plasticity varies by domain (e.g., visual function versus cognitive function), by timing (e.g., the length of sensitive or critical periods varies across domains), and very likely, by the individual. This last component has proven most elusive, as most investigations deal with groups, not individuals. When examining such studies, it is readily apparent that there is variability between and among individuals. The nature of such individual differences will likely serve as an opportunity to refine our views of plasticity in the coming years.

ADULT PLASTICITY

For many years, it was commonly believed that once the brain was fully developed (thought to be the end of adolescence), its ability to be molded by experience and to recover from injury was greatly limited. This view has been turned on its head in recent years; indeed, research on so-called "adult plasticity" is currently receiving a great deal of attention in the field of neuroscience. In this section, we provide an overview to several domains in which the adult brain is now known to be plastic.

Motor Learning

There are countless examples that could be offered with regard to the plasticity of motor functions, many of which have been reviewed elsewhere (e.g., Nelson & Bloom, 1997; Nelson, 1999, 2000a). Three will suffice. First, Elbert and colleagues (Elbert, Pantev, Wienbruch, Rockstroh, & Taub, 1995) reported (using magnetoencephalography, or MEG) that the somatosensory cortex representing the fingers of the left hand (used for fine finger board movements) in highly proficient stringed instrument players is larger than (a) the analogous area in the opposite hemisphere representing the right hand (used to bow), and (b) than nonmusicians. Similarly, Stewart et al. (2003) reported a study in which musically naive subjects were scanned using functional magnetic resonance imagery (fMRI) before and after they had been taught to read music and play keyboard. When subjects played melodies from musical notation after training, activation was seen in a cluster of voxels within the right superior parietal cortex consistent with the view that music reading involves spatial sensorimotor mapping. Third, Draganski et al. (2004) have recently reported that in individuals who had been given 3 months to learn to juggle showed increased neural activation (as revealed by fMRI) bilaterally in the midtemporal area and in the left posterior intraparietal sulcus; importantly, 3 months after this group of jugglers stopped juggling, there was a decrease in activation. There was a dose/response effect between juggling performance and changes in brain activity. Finally, nonjugglers over the 6-month period showed no changes in brain activation.

Visual and Auditory Function

As was the case for motor functions, just a few examples will be provided for adult visual plasticity. First, it has been well established that congenitally blind individuals show activation of the visual cortex when reading Braille or performing other tactile discrimination functions (Lanzenberger et al., 2001; Sadato, Pascual-Leone,

Grafman, & Deiber, 1998; Uhl, Franzen, Lindinger, Lang, & Deecke, 1991). Interestingly, a Braille-reading woman blind since birth who subsequently suffered a bilateral stroke of the visual cortex in adulthood lost the ability to read Braille although other somatosensory functions remained intact (Hamilton, Keenan, Catala, & Pascual-Leone, 2000). And, Sadato, Okada, Honda, and Yonekura (2002) have now reported that among Braille-reading individuals who lost their sight *after* age 16, activation of V1 cortex was absent, whereas such activation was present among those who lost their sight *before* age 16. Such findings are consistent with a sensitive period for visual function. Finally, Finney, Fine, and Dobkins (2001) have reported that deaf individuals show activation of the auditory cortex to visual stimuli.

Collectively, it appears that the somatosensory, visual, and auditory cortices are capable of reorganizing well into adulthood, although there is some hint that there may still be a sensitive period for such reorganization.

Learning and Memory Function

No domain of plasticity has received more attention in the neuroscience literature than that of learning and memory. It has been known for over 30 years, for example, that rats raised in complex laboratory environments (i.e., those containing lots of toys and social contacts, and sometimes erroneously referred to as "enriched" environments) perform certain cognitive tasks better than rats reared in isolation (e.g., Greenough, Madden, & Fleischmann, 1972). Looking closely at the brains of animals raised in the complex environments reveals that (1) several regions of the dorsal neocortex are heavier and thicker and have more synapses per neuron; (2) dendritic spines and branching patterns increase in number and length; and (3) there is increased capillary branching, thereby increasing blood and oxygen volume (for examples of both original findings and overviews, see Black et al., 1998; Greenough, Juraska, & Volkmar, 1979; Kolb, Gibb, & Robinson, 2003; Kolb & Whishaw, 1998).

Moving up from the cellular to the systems level of the nervous system, Erickson, Jagadeesh, and Desimone (2000) have reported a study in which multicolored complex stimuli (some familiar, some novel) were presented to monkeys. Neuronal activity was recorded from the perirhinal cortex, an area known to be strongly involved in episodic memory (see later section on declarative memory). After only 1 day of experience viewing the stimuli, performance of neighboring neurons became highly correlated during viewing of familiar stimuli, whereas viewing novel stimuli revealed little correlated neuronal activity. These findings suggest that visual experience leads to functional changes in an area of the brain known to be involved in memory.

Perhaps the most dramatic example of experience-induced changes in the neural architecture underlying memory is the now well-known "London cab driver study." Here structural MRI scans were obtained from London cab drivers, all highly expert at navigating the streets of London. Maguire et al. (2000) reported that the posterior hippocampus (hypothesized to serve as the storage location for spatial representations) of these drivers was larger than in a comparison group. Not surprisingly, there was also a positive correlation between hippocampal volume and the amount of experience the driver had. (Unfortunately, this study suffers from selective sampling—specifically, whether individuals who choose to be cab drivers already have a larger hippocampus or possess more plasticity than noncab drivers, thus making them more likely to show anatomical changes in response to experience.)

Overall, there are now ample data to suggest that learning and memory are correlated with changes in the brain at multiple levels, from changes in pre- and postsynaptic functioning mediated by glutamate receptors to the molar changes at the level of anatomy. There is little or no evidence to suggest a sensitive period for learning and memory to occur (for a tutorial on the *development* of learning and memory, see Nelson, 1995, 2000b). Indeed, there is some sense that activities that engage the learning and memory system may confer some protection on lifelong learning and memory function (see Nelson, 2000b, and the following section for a discussion).

What Are the Effects of Enriched Environments on Brain Development and Function?

Although a great deal is known about the effects of deprivation on brain development and function, very little is known about enrichment. Indeed, in the work on complex environments discussed earlier, such environments, while enriched relative to typical laboratory conditions, are still impoverished relative to real-world environments. Over and above the challenge of defining what is meant by enrichment (e.g., what may be considered enriched in one context may be impoverished in another), there is also the challenge of employing measures that possess the sensitivity to detect such effects. One example of enrichment effects on human brain function can be found in a recent study by Colcombe et al. (2004). These authors reported that highly aerobically fit older adults or previously unfit older adults who were provided aerobic training demonstrated improved performance on a test of executive function and showed increases in task-related activity in the superior and middle frontal gyrus and the superior parietal lobule, and reduced activity in the anterior cingulate cortex, regions all associated with attentional control. This not only speaks to the plasticity of these cortical regions well into the life span, but also demonstrates that enrichment confers benefits on brain function over and above typical living conditions (in which many older Americans lack cardiovascular fitness).

What Is the Difference between Development versus Plasticity?

At a very molecular level, we might argue that the processes that underlie plasticity—for example, changes in the neurochemical profile of a synapse, anatomic changes such as growth of an axon or sprouting new dendritic spines, and so forth—are no different in the developing brain than they are in the mature brain. Specifically, once the cellular machinery is in place, it pretty much operates the same regardless of the age of its container. Similarly, the sprouting of new dendritic spines in response to complex environments may be the same regardless of the age of the brain involved—and the molecular events that underlie changes in dendritic function are also likely the same or vastly similar. However, there are still a number of fundamental differences in the way plastic processes might work in the developing brain than in the developed brain.

First, the local cellular, anatomic, and metabolic environment in which plastic processes operate are vastly different early in the life span versus later in the life span. Thus, the newborn brain has countless more neurons and synapses than an adult brain, and many of these are not yet committed to particular circuits or functions. Thus, an axon that is growing toward its target has a very different terrain to negotiate in the newborn brain than in the adult brain. Similarly, modifying already-committed synapses (i.e., rewiring the brain) is quite different than committing synapses to a particular circuit for the first time (i.e., wiring the brain).

An example of this point can be found in a recent paper. Carleton, Petreanu, Lansford, Alvarez-Buylla, and Lledo (2003) report that the development of the electrophysiological properties of neurons born in adulthood (i.e., postnatally derived neurons; see Chapter 1) differ from those born pre- or perinatally. For example, spiking activity (i.e., the excitability of the cell) was delayed in late-born versus early-born cells; that is, this was not observed until the cell was nearly fully mature. The authors argue that this could be due to the need to make sure the late-born new cell does not interrupt the existing circuit until it is ready to be part of that circuit. Suffice to say, this illustrates a fundamental difference between neurogenesis in the developing brain versus the developed brain.

A second example of this point can be found in the work on postnatal neurogenesis. For example, Gould (2003) has reported that the number of prenatally derived cells tends to be fairly stable across development, with only a slight reduction with aging. In contrast, cells derived in adulthood (see earlier section on postnatal neurogenesis) tend to be massively produced but relatively short lived (e.g., the adult rodent dentate gyrus may contain a total of 1.5 million cells, with 250,000 of these being generated anew each month).

Another way to illustrate the difference between developmental versus adult plasticity can be found more at a systems or behavioral level. For example, a primary goal of infancy is to develop neural circuits in the service of some behavior. However, in the adult, these systems are already in place, and must simply be reconfigured for a different, albeit related purpose; for example, acquiring a second or third language. Thus, second language learning may, in fact, be fundamentally different than first language learning by virtue of the fact that in the former case there is already a scaffold on which to build whereas in the latter case there is not (leaving aside whatever preparedness for acquiring language exists at birth). Naturally, this example builds on our first point, as second language learning may involve either rewiring or extending existing neural circuits to a new albeit related domain, whereas learning a first language surely involves new wiring.

Finally, it may be necessary to consider as a third point whether there is a difference between development and plasticity. Developmental psychologists are familiar with the principles that underlie behavioral change across age. Yet, neuroscientists are also aware that there are likely molecular, anatomic, physiologic, and neurochemical changes operating in the background that underlie changes in behavior. Thus, if at the cellular/anatomic level the processes that mediate changes in behavior in general are the same as those that mediate changes across age, then what is the difference between development and plasticity? We would contend that these terms are fundamentally the same; the difference, however, is that we view plasticity as lifelong, whereas we view development as something that happens over the first 2 (or so) decades of life. If this is true, then this raises the possibility that the plastic processes that exist throughout life may be different than those operating to direct development during the first 2 decades of life (and surely there are differences within this developmental plastic processes within these first 2 decades).

Admittedly our answer to the question of whether developmental and adult plasticity are different is not fully satisfying. It is our hope that a more complete answer to this question will be found over the coming years, as research into neural plasticity increases. But, it is important to ponder this question as developmental theory gradually comes to be more neurobiological in its orientation.

CHAPTER

3

Methods of
Cognitive Neuroscience

Having established how the brain is assembled and subsequently
modified by experience, we next turn our attention to how we
can image (or in some cases, infer) the function of the brain in vivo
in the developing child. This tutorial sets the stage for the sections
that follow in which we discuss what is known about the neural
basis of cognitive function.

LESION METHOD

Predating all current methods of direction visualization of the brain
is the *lesion method* in which we examine the perturbation in behavior following accidental (e.g., head trauma) or intentional injury
to the brain (generally in animals but also in elective surgery in humans; for a review, see Moses & Stiles, 2002). This approach to
structure/function relations dates back several centuries but was
perhaps most manifestly brought to our attention in the 1800s by
Broca and then by the famous patient Phineas Gage (see Bloom
et al., 2001, for an overview). In the latter case, dramatic changes in
cognitive and emotional behavior were observed following injuries
to different regions of the frontal cortex.

The lesion approach is attractive in part because the costs of conducting the research are relatively minimal; typically behavioral as-
says are performed, thus avoiding the expense of neuroimaging tools

(discussed later). However, a number of shortcomings to this approach must be acknowledged. First, this approach is typically applied to only one or a small number of patients, and thus generalizability must be considered. Second, in the case of humans, we often have little control over the size and extent of the lesion, particularly when the lesion results from an accident (e.g., head injury). Similarly, in animals, a consideration is whether fibers of passage (i.e., those axons carrying information from one structure to another) have been violated when lesioning a particular site (although more recent lesion tools, such as musimol or lidocaine, spare fibers of passage). Third, since the lesion approach is most widely used in animals, we must question the generalizability to humans (e.g., structure/function relations might be different across species). Fourth, in both humans and animals, we must question whether the structure lesioned is the only structure that affects function; for example, it is entirely possible that another brain region is more heavily involved in a given behavior, but because this structure is connected to the lesioned structure, the functioning of both is affected. Perhaps most important in the context of this chapter are developmental considerations. For example, a lesion to a particular area in the adult brain may not lead to the same consequence as a lesion to a developing brain. Examples that most readily come to mind are the effects of perinatally acquired focal lesions on spatial relations and language (see Stiles, 2001, and Bates & Roe, 2001, respectively).

ELECTROPHYSIOLOGICAL PROCEDURES

Electrophysiological procedures provide one method for examining brain function online as cognition is occurring. Active neurons generate electrical signals that can be measured locally by electrodes placed directly in the brain (animals) or, in humans, distally by electrodes placed on the scalp surface. While some indwelling electrodes are capable of measuring signal cell firing, scalp-recorded activity is thought to reflect the intermittent synchronization of small populations of neurons, predominantly cortical neurons on the gyral surfaces (Andreassi, 1989). Electrical voltage is measured at multiple scalp locations relative to background noise, with the signal measured at each electrode presumably reflecting neuronal activity close to that electrode location or from especially activated brain regions. Since any given neuronal signal propagates throughout the brain through the principle of volume conduction and can be recorded at multiple scalp locations, it is difficult to determine the precise anatomical source of the activity from scalp-recorded methods. However, using a large number of scalp electrodes (socalled high-density arrays) provides a more sensitive measure of the surface distribution of the voltage and allows the use of mathematical techniques for modeling the brain generators of the observed signal (dipole source localization). The noninvasive nature of electroencephalogram (EEG) makes this technique particularly amenable for use across the life span, from infancy through late adulthood (for a review, see DeBoer, Scott, & Nelson, 2004).

To understand the brain electrical activity associated with cognitive processes, investigators have typically examined the event-related potential (ERP) that reflects EEG activity time-locked to particular sensory and/or cognitive events. The ERP reflects the average response to an event over multiple presentations and provides a very fine scale for determining the timing and temporal sequencing of particular neural events. Specific sensory modalities (e.g., visual or auditory) or basic cognitive processes produce unique components in the event-related waveform. These components traditionally are labeled according to their polarity (positive peak or negative peak) and timing with respect to the stimulus, either in order of appearance (e.g., P1, P2, P3) or in milliseconds (e.g., N200, P300) (see Polich, 1993). The average waveforms can be compared across multiple stimulus types or cognitive events, and across study groups, and then analyzed for changes in the amplitude, latency, or scalp distribution of these identified components. Figure 3.1 illustrates the various ways many labs now record ERPs from infants and children. Figure 3.2 illustrates the average ERP waveform elicited for 8-year-old children (left panel) and adults (right panel) at a single electrode location in response to a particular visual stimulus. The large positive peak, labeled the P300 or P3b component, is thought to reflect updating of working memory

Figure 3.1   The different methods of recording event-related potentials from infants. Starting from the far right, a newborn outfitted with disposable electrodes; a 6-month-old wearing individually placed electrodes held in place with adhesive foam (not seen) and a headband; a 6-month-old wearing an electrode cap; a 6-month-old wearing an elastic net of 64 electrodes; and a 10-year-old boy wearing a 128-channel net. Pictures taken from Nelson Lab Server.

following the presentation of a stimulus. As evident from the brief time scale, the onset and peak magnitude of individual components can be reliably timed to within tens of milliseconds. Individual components demonstrate unique scalp topography and response characteristics. For example, the P300 component is largest at parietal

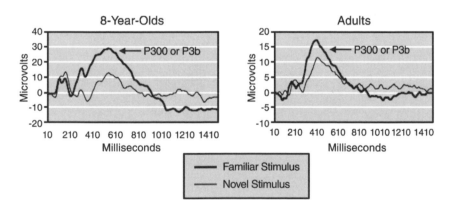

Figure 3.2   Examples of ERP responses to familiar and novel stimuli in children (left panel) and adults (right panel). The P300 component indicated by the black arrow is typical of rare, target, task-relevant stimuli (stimuli to which the participant makes some response) and tends to show maximal amplitude at electrode locations over central and posterior scalp regions. As demonstrated in these data, the majority of ERP responses are broader (of longer duration) for children as compared to adults. Source: From "Assessing Brain Development Using Neurophysiologic and Behavioral Measures," by K. M. Thomas, 2003, Journal of Pediatrics, 143, pp. s46–s53.

compared to frontal or temporal electrode locations. The amplitude of the P300 component is larger for visual stimuli that require a behavioral response (targets) than for those that do not (nontargets), and is larger for rare stimuli than for frequently repeating stimuli. Not all components are evident at all points in development. For example, the P300 response changes in shape (morphology) across early childhood and does not reach its adult form until early adolescence. In fact, the P300 component for visual stimuli is not evident in infant ERP waveforms. It is unclear to what degree the change in morphology reflects structural and physiological brain development or development of the cognitive functions producing the response. In addition to these traditional methods of viewing voltage at a single electrode over time, ERP data can be viewed as a map of the scalp surface at a single point in time. These voltage plots, or their mathematically transformed cousin the current source density map, provide further information regarding the spatial distribution of electrical activity. However, this improved spatial information should not be confused with brain localization. Both temporal and spatial voltage plots reflect only the scalp-recorded distribution of the generated activity, and sophisticated analysis techniques are required to infer information regarding the brain systems generating this activity. To date, only a few investigators have attempted dipole source localization techniques to estimate the neural generators of electrophysiological data from infants or children (e.g., Johnson et al., 2001; Richards, 2004; in press). Such techniques require a large number of behavioral trials and very low noise levels, both of which tend to be more difficult to obtain with young subjects.

ERP methods are particularly useful for examining very brief cognitive events and for identifying the temporal order of cognitive processes, but they are limited in their ability to identify the precise brain regions generating the measured signal. ERP methods have been particularly useful with very young subjects, including infants, given the relatively robust signal in the face of motion artifact (for recent reviews, see Nelson & Monk, 2001; DeBoer et al., 2004). Other neuroimaging techniques, particularly the magnetic resonance imaging (MRI) methods, described later, are less appropriate for cognitive imaging in very young children who cannot remain completely still on command. When used in combination with structural and functional MRI methods, electrophysiological measures may provide an additional layer of information regarding the temporal dynamics of brain activity. Currently, ERP recordings remain one of the few methods available for assessing online cognitive function in infants and very young children.

ERP methods have proven useful in examining group differences in specific cognitive domains such as covert attention, recognition memory, or long-term recall (e.g., Carver, Bauer, & Nelson, 2000; Nelson et al., 2000; Richards, 2001). In addition, physiological measures can sometimes provide an index of functional brain differences despite an absence of behavioral difference or impairment (e.g., Nelson et al., 2000).

METABOLIC PROCEDURES (fMRI)

One of the most widely used measures of online brain function in human adults is functional magnetic resonance imaging (fMRI; see Figures 3.3 and 3.4). Both structural and functional MRI techniques rely on the fact that protons behave differently in the presence of a strong magnetic field. That is, the constantly spinning and moving protons in the body tend to become aligned with the magnetic field. MRI images are generated by applying a series of brief radio frequency (RF) pulses through the tissue. These pulses generate local magnetic fields that momentarily disrupt or tilt the protons out of alignment with the strong magnetic field. Structural images of body tissue are constructed based on measures of the energy released as pulsed protons relax back to their aligned state. Different tissue types demonstrate different relaxation times, with lipids (which make up the bulk of myelinated tissue) showing different relaxation times than water (Bloch, 1946; Hahn, 1950). These relaxation differences can be mapped to produce structural images of the brain, for example, emphasizing the difference between regions with different tissue properties (e.g., gray matter versus white matter).

A number of investigators have used anatomical MRI to examine brain development across the life span and in relation to cognitive

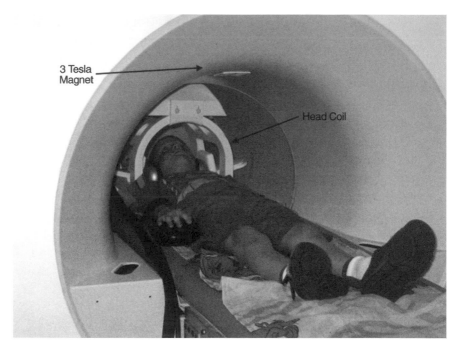

3 Tesla
Magnet

Head Coil

Figure 3.3   An 8-year-old child being studied in a 3 Tesla MRI scanner. Picture taken from Nelson Lab Server.

performance. Giedd and colleagues have published a number of papers examining normative changes in brain structure across development. For example, they report decreases in the volume of subcortical gray matter structures such as the basal ganglia during childhood (Giedd et al., 1996a, 1996b), although cortical gray matter does not appear to show volume decreases until puberty (Giedd et al., 1999; for elaboration, see earlier discussion of myelination in Chapter 2). MRI can be used to link brain structure to behavior by examining correlations among MRI-based anatomical or morphometric measures and measures of behavior. For example, Casey and colleagues reported that the volume of the anterior cingulate gyrus (a midline region of the prefrontal cortex) was significantly related to measures of executive attention in children 5 to 16 years of age (Casey et al., 1997a).

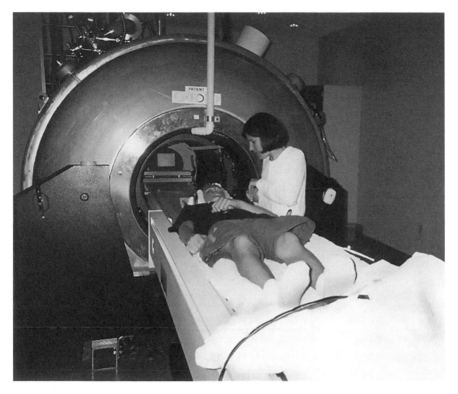

Figure 3.4   A 10-year-old child being studied in a high-field 4 Tesla scanner (shown alongside a graduate student). Picture taken from Nelson Lab Server.

Similar to electrophysiological methods, MRI techniques can also be used to record brain activity or function online and noninvasively. Neuronal activity is assumed to produce local increases in blood flow and oxygenation near the source of activity (Kwong et al., 1992; Ogawa, Lee, Nayak, & Glynn, 1990; Turner, Le Bihan, Moonen, Despres, & Frank, 1991). The most common type of functional MRI, blood oxygenation level dependent (BOLD) imaging, relies on the observation that oxygenated and deoxygenated hemoglobin behave differently when pulsed by the RF magnetic field. Deoxygenated hemoglobin is paramagnetic and causes distortions in the local magnetic field, leading the spinning protons in that region to drop out of phase with one another. This change in energy state from the in-phase to the out-of-phase spin states (called T2* relaxation) can be mapped to indicate the relative neuronal activity, as measured by changes in blood oxygenation, across the brain. This hemodynamic change is not instantaneous. In fact, the peak observed signal change would be expected to occur as late as 5 to 6 seconds after the presumed neuronal response.

Unlike the electrophysiological methods discussed earlier, MRI methods can precisely localize the brain regions showing structural and/or functional change between groups or between behavioral conditions. Like structural MRI, functional MRI measures can be used to identity group differences in the location or extent of activation. For example, Casey et al. (1995) demonstrated that children activated both dorsal and ventral regions of the prefrontal cortex during a verbal working-memory task, whereas activity was limited to dorsal prefrontal regions for adults. Correlations between measures of functional brain activity and behavioral performance can be used to assess whether activity varies parametrically with task performance. For example, Braver and colleagues (1997) have demonstrated that activity in the prefrontal cortex correlates with accuracy on a working-memory task. Similar relations can be assessed between functional activation and measures of individual difference, such as age or aspects of temperament or personality. In a study of amygdala response to facial expressions of emotion, Thomas et al. (2001a, 2001b) observed a positive correlation between the amygdala response to fearful facial expressions and children's self-reported level of everyday anxiety.

The ability to acquire both structural and functional measures of brain development within the same session is certainly an advantage of MRI methods. However, functional MRI measures have relatively poor temporal resolution (on the order of seconds) compared to electrophysiological measures, making it more difficult to capture very rapid changes in activity or to determine the sequential order of cognitive events, for example. In addition, the cost of MR imaging is still quite high at most institutions, and MR imaging is not ideal for every study population. Participants must lie in a loud, confined space and remain still for the duration of the scan (as long as 1 hour, in the case of functional MRI). Even minor head motion (on the order of 3 to 5 mm) can result in significant blurring of the images. These parameters may be too restrictive for certain groups, particularly those who are unable to stay sufficiently still to acquire artifact-free images (e.g., awake infants or toddlers).

OPTICAL IMAGING

Optical imaging, first used in animals, shares certain principles with functional MRI. As with fMRI, optical imaging entails examining the transition from oxygenated hemoglobin to deoxygenated hemoglobin. In the human, this is accomplished by placing a laser diode on the subject's head, along with a detector (see Figure 3.5). The laser illuminates the vessels on top of the head, and the detector examines their light frequency band (for a review, see Meek, 2002). The frequency of the emitted light permits the determination of whether the blood is oxygenated or deoxygenated. As seen in Figure 3.5, the procedure is entirely noninvasive, similar to wearing a cap. Like fMRI, optical imaging has excellent spatial resolution but relatively poor temporal resolution. That said, there are two major drawbacks to the procedure. First, an investigator can peer into the brain but a few millimeters, thereby limiting the procedure to examining functions that reside in a nearby gyrus. Second, because of the difficulty in sampling the entire brain (due to the limited number of sensors), mapping the cortical surface can prove to be a painstaking process. At present, this procedure has been used successfully to map various sensory functions (see Meek, 2002, for a review), with infants engaged in speech perception tasks (Peña et al., 2003), and in tasks purported to involve spatial working memory (Baird et al., 2002). For example, Peña and colleagues employed a 24-channel system to examine the newborn's response to normal speech, speech played backward, and silence. The left temporal areas showed greater activation to normal speech than to either of the two control stimuli, suggesting that the left hemisphere superiority for language (at least speech) processing develops with relatively little postnatal experience with human

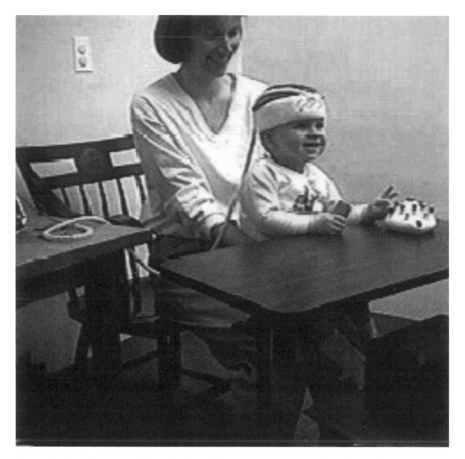

Figure 3.5   Functional Near Infrared Spectroscopy, as performed in infancy. Here a wearable head device is fitted to the infant's head, and contains both a light-emitting transmitter and a receiver. In so doing, changes in blood oxygenation can be inferred (see text for details). Picture taken from Nelson Lab Server.

speech. Baird and colleagues performed a longitudinal study with infants from 5 to 12 months of age, recording optical signals from the frontal cortex. Four different object-permanence tasks were performed. As infants gradually developed object permanence (on average, 7 months), there was a corresponding increase in total hemoglobin, consistent with models that posit involvement of the frontal cortex in object permanence.

MAGNETIC ENCEPHALOGRAPHY

The general principle underlying magnetic encephalography (MEG) is that small magnetic fields arise with every bioelectric signal that a neuron generates. These magnetic fields develop at right angles to the flow of bioelectric signals. Because pyramidal neurons are the primary source of these signals, neurons in the sulci of the brain generate the associated magnetic potentials, which, like the EEG and ERP, can be detected from the surface of the brain. However, unlike the EEG and ERP, the current generated by these fields is infinitesimally small. Such small signals, set against the relatively larger magnetic field generated by the earth itself, requires the deployment of exquisitely sensitive detectors. This is accomplished by using high-gain magnetometers devised from superconducting quantum interference devices (SQUIDs) that operate at super-cooled temperatures using liquid helium (Figure 3.6).

The beauty of MEG is that the magnetic fields associated with any given electrical dipole flow to the scalp surface in an orderly manner, thereby making it possible to solve the inverse problem— the ability to infer the source of signals recorded at the scalp surface. Thus, unlike EEG and ERPs, the spatial resolution of MEG is excellent; moreover, unlike fMRI, the temporal resolution is also excellent. In addition, like EEG and ERPs, the procedure is entirely noninvasive, and simply entails positioning a helmet-like device over the subject's head (see Figure 3.3). However, two potential disadvantages must be acknowledged. First, it is typically possible to infer only relatively shallow sources that lie in a sulcus, making imaging of deep structures challenging. Second, because of the need to use SQUIDs and a magnetically shielded room, a typical MEG setup often requires an investment of several million dollars.

Despite the attraction of MEG, there has been surprisingly little interest in this tool by developmental cognitive neuroscientists. Leaving aside the clinical use of the tool (e.g., in epilepsy surgery; see Paetau, 2002, for a review), much of the work that has been done has been concerned with auditory processing in fetuses. For example, after identifying the fetal ear canal through ultrasound,

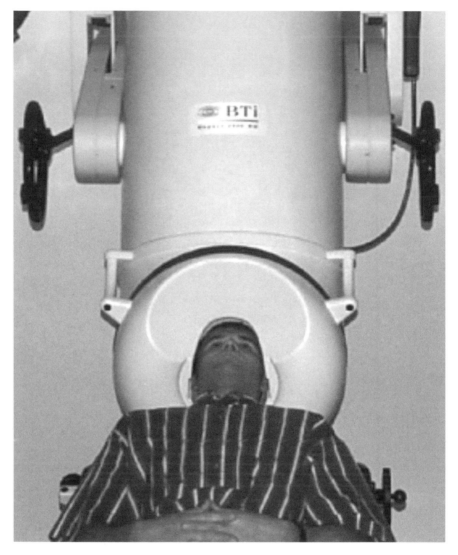

Figure 3.6   Magnetic Encephalography, as performed on an adult. Picture taken from Nelson Lab Server.

auditory stimuli are presented to the mother's abdomen, yielding an auditory evoked response from the fetus peaking at around 140 msec (in one case this was confirmed by testing the same infant immediately after birth; see Blum, Bauer, Arabin, Reckel, & Saling, 1987; Blum, Saling, & Bauer, 1984; 1985; Eswaran et al., 2002a).

More impressive, Eswaran et al. (2002b) have recorded the *visual* evoked potential from the fetal visual cortex by flashing light onto the maternal abdomen. There is also a small amount of work examining the auditory evoked response using MEG in children (e.g., Paetau, Ahonen, Salonen, & Sams, 1995). Unfortunately, MEG has not yet been used to study the development of cognitive abilities in infants or children.

SUMMARY

Tremendous strides have been made over the past decade in directly visualizing the brain at work. Unfortunately, only a relatively small handful of the procedures that have so successfully been used to study mature function have been applied to the study of development. The two most commonly used tools are ERPs, which have been used in infants, children, and adolescents, and fMRI, which with one or two exceptions have been used exclusively with children over the age of 5 or 6 years. Relatively little effort has been made to coregister these tools—that is, use more than one tool to examine different elements of brain function (e.g., combining the superb temporal resolution of ERPs with the superb spatial resolution of fMRI). Given the excitement now being generated by advances in developmental cognitive neuroscience, we anticipate greater use of these tools over the coming years, as a greater number of cognitive developmentalists become curious about the neural bases of behavior.

CHAPTER

4

The Development of Speech and Language

Having laid the foundation for how the human brain develops and how one studies such development in the living child, we now turn our attention to the neural bases of specific cognitive functions. As is the case with many of the topics targeted for review in this chapter, the reader is encouraged to consult more comprehensive treatises on particular domains of cognition (e.g., de Haan & Johnson, 2003; Johnson, 2001; Nelson & Luciana, 2001). Also note that, because the focus of our discussion is on the *neural bases* of cognitive development, we restrict our discussion to the literature that directly relates a specific cognitive ability to brain development; the basic cognitive developmental behavioral literature is thoroughly reviewed in other sources. Given the close connection between cognition and language, we open this section with a discussion of the neural bases of speech and language development.

THE NEURAL BASES OF SPEECH AND LANGUAGE DEVELOPMENT

At first glance, a chapter on speech and language development may appear out of place in a book concerned with cognitive development. Moreover, there is not a great deal known about the neural bases of speech and language development, at least relative to other domains discussed in this book. However, as will be apparent shortly, there is perhaps no better example of the role of experience in influencing behavioral and brain development than in the domain of speech and language.

We begin with a brief tutorial on what is known about the neural bases of speech perception. Understandably, given this is an ability that becomes reasonably adult-like early in life, the bulk of our review will be concerned with infants. We then turn to a discussion of word processing, followed by a discussion of sign language. Finally, keeping with our theme of plasticity, we conclude this chapter with a discussion of the effects of early focal brain lesions on language development broadly defined. We have selected these topics because they are the best investigated from a cognitive neuroscience perspective.

Speech Perception

In a recent review of the literature, Kuhl (2004) notes the remarkable pace at which infants progress from being able to discriminate speech sounds, to babbling at 6 months, to speaking in full sentences by the age of 3. Arguably the roots of language begin with the ability to discriminate elements of the speech train (e.g., one phoneme from another, one morpheme from another), and subsequently, recognizing those same elements as words and then, eventually, sentences.

Systematic study of infant speech perception arguably began in the 1970s with work by Eimas and colleagues. The original observation that so impressed most scientists occurred in 1971, when Eimas and colleagues (Eimas, Siqueland, Jsczk, & Vigorito, 1971) reported that infants could discriminate nonspeech (both pure tone and click) from speech sounds, and could discriminate among a variety of speech contrasts (e.g., the sound of "ba" versus "pa"). The latter observation was expanded, leading to the observation that infants perceived speech categorically. *Categorical speech perception* refers to the tendency to respond to a range of stimuli similarly and to respond differently to another range of stimuli (in the visual domain, an example might be distinguishing male faces from female faces). We know that the speech train exists on a continuum, and that there are boundaries on this continuum which, when crossed, leads to the perception of a different sound. Thus, the sound of "ba" differs from the sound of "pa." This important component of speech distinguishes it from nonspeech. Thus, the speech train is naturally divided into different types of sounds.

It later became apparent that categorical speech perception is a general phenomenon, occurring for most languages of the world. Reports began to appear in the literature that infants are capable of discriminating nearly all of the phonetic units that comprise the languages of the world, whereas most adults perceive only differences that are functionally relevant in their native language. Thus, American or Canadian infants being reared in English-speaking homes can discriminate speech contrasts from Czech or Thai or Swedish, whereas adults cannot (unless, of course, they speak those languages; for general discussion, see Eimas, 1975; Eimas et al., 1971; Werker & Lalonde, 1988; Werker & Tess, 1984). Importantly, some time after 6 months of age this ability begins to disappear, after which speech perception gradually becomes more adult-like and language-specific. From this observation follows the suggestion that the speech perception apparatus is very broadly tuned at birth and, with experience, the perceptual window through which speech is perceived begins to narrow, eventually encompassing only those sounds that are familiar (for review, see Kuhl, 2004; Werker & Vouloumanos, 2001).

It appears however, that the door does not shut completely on retaining the ability to discriminate nonnative contrasts; for example, Kuhl and colleagues (2003) have reported that, if before 12 months of age infants are given additional experience with speech sounds in a nonnative language, this ability is retained. Collectively, these speech data have been interpreted to suggest that the speech system remains open to experience for a certain period of time, but if experience in a particular domain (such as hearing speech contrasts in different languages) is not forthcoming, the window begins to close within the 1st year of life.

NEURAL BASES OF SPEECH PROCESSING AND SPEECH PERCEPTION

As is the case with other cognitive functions that emerge early in life, the vast majority of the literature on the neural bases of speech perception employs measures of the brain's electrical activity (event-related potentials or ERPs). Relatively fewer studies have examined magnetic activity (magnetic encephalopathy or MEG) or metabolic activity (functional near-infrared spectroscopy or fNIRS; functional magnetic resonance imaging or fMRI).

Event-Related Potentials

The ERP literature on speech perception is vast, thus, only a summary of this work will be provided.

Newborn.   The original work in this area was less concerned with speech perception per se than with the neural organization of speech processing. Molfese, for example, demonstrated that newborns' brain activity shows hemispheric differences in processing speech that are similar to those observed in adults (e.g., Molfese & Molfese, 1979, 1980, 1985; also see Cheour-Luhtanen et al., 1996), a finding recently replicated with greater precision using optical imaging (Peña et al., 2003). Thus, the left hemisphere shows more activity than the right hemisphere when listening to speech. More intriguingly, Molfese and colleagues have consistently shown that newborn ERPs collected in response to human speech predict later language proficiency (e.g., Molfese & Molfese, 1985, 1997). Collectively, this work supports the notion that the newborn brain is organized and prepared to learn language, although as we shall see in the discussion that follows, much develops beyond the newborn period.

Older Infant and Child. There is now a tremendous amount of work concerned with the neural correlates of speech perception, and several extensive reviews exist (e.g., Dehaene-Lambertz & Gliga, 2004; Werker & Vouloumanos, 2001). Similar to behavioral work in this area, this ERP work clearly demonstrates that infants in the 1st half-year of life can discriminate a variety of speech contrasts and elements of the speech train, including voice onset time and place of articulation. Indeed, although relatively few studies have been done using high-density recordings, which make possible the ability to draw inferences about underlying neural sources (see section on ERPs in Chapter 3), the consensus is that the neural bases underlying these abilities is remarkably similar in infants as in adults (for discussion, see Dehaene-Lambertz & Gliga, 2004). Far more interesting than simply discriminating one phoneme from another is the ability to discriminate words from one another, a topic discussed in a later section of this chapter.

Magnetic Encephalopathy

As we noted in our discussion of MEG in Chapter 3, this procedure has been used little in the study of development. This is most unfortunate because MEG has many of the same advantages as ERP (e.g., it is noninvasive, requires little motor or language ability, and so on), but unlike ERP, MEG has very good spatial resolution. The little work that has been done thus far has primarily been performed by Risto Näätänen and his colleagues (for recent review, see Cheour et al., 2004). For example, Kujala et al. (2004) recorded MEG activity in newborns in a Match-Mismatch Negativity (MMN) paradigm (see section on ERPs). Infants were presented with a frequently occurring steady vowel sound, and on rare trials the same vowel with a raising pitch (hence, the intonation changed). The authors reported that 6 of 10 infants showed a MMN response to the pitch change. Similarly findings have been obtained in newborns presented with a frequency change (Huotilainen et al., 2003).

Unfortunately, little work has been done with older infants and children, and it is therefore difficult to compare these newborn data with data from older participants. By the same token, however, the MMN findings observed with MEG are quite similar to those observed with ERPs, lending support to the proposition that MEG can in fact provide valuable information about the neural correlates of speech processing.

Functional Magnetic Resonance Imaging (fMRI)

In the only published study to examine speech perception in infancy using fMRI, Dehaene-Lambertz, Dehaene, and Hertz-Pannier (2002) presented forward and backward human speech (an adult female reading a children's book in French) to 2- to 3-month-old French infants while recording the BOLD response in a MRI scanner. The authors reported a large area of activation in the left temporal lobe that included the superior temporal gyrus (including Heschel's gyrus), the superior temporal sulcus and the temporal pole. In addition, the left angular gyrus and left mesial parietal lobe (precuneus) were more active during forward speech than backward speech. Interestingly, although infants who were awake versus asleep did not differ in the activation patterns in the temporal lobe, those who were awake also showed activation in the right dorsolateral prefrontal cortex, primarily in response to forward speech.

There are several noteworthy features about this study. First, the activation observed in the left temporal lobe is consistent with infant ERP studies (see earlier discussion). Second, the greater activation observed to forward versus backward speech is consistent with adult observations of speech processing. Collectively, these two observations suggest that as early as 2 to 3 months the functional neuroanatomy of the speech perception apparatus is well instantiated in the brain.

Role of Experience

Three examples suffice to reinforce the point that experience plays a prominent role in the development of speech perception. First, Cheour and colleagues (Cheour et al., 1998) recorded ERPs from Finnish and Estonian 6- and 12-month-old infants. As the authors note, Estonian and Finnish have very similar vowel structures, but there is one vowel unique to Estonian. At 6 months and again at 1 year of age, infants were presented with standard and deviant vowel sounds. The authors reported that at 1 year of age, but not at 6 months, infants' ERPs (specifically, the MMN) distinguished native from nonnative speech sounds. Thus, speech perception became more specialized over the course of the 2nd half year of life. Second, as already discussed, Kuhl and colleagues (Kuhl et al., 2003) have reported that if additional training with a nonnative language is provided before 12 months of age, infants receiving such training retain the ability to discriminate those nonnative speech sounds. Finally, Cheour, Shestakova, Alku, Ceponiene, and Näätä-nen (2002) have reported that 3- to 6-year-old Finnish children show ERP evidence of discriminating speech contrasts in French after only 2 months of emersion in a French school; in other words, with as little as 2 months experience with a nonnative language one can already observe changes in the neural organization involved in language. Collectively, these studies argue for tremendous plasticity in the speech perception apparatus. Exactly when such plasticity is lost remains unknown, although Newport and colleagues have reported that the window of opportunity appears to close (or be closing) by approximately 10 years of age.

Word Processing/Word Learning

There are a number of investigators actively exploring the development and neural bases of word processing and word learning. For example, Molfese, Wetzel, and Gill (1994) presented 12-month-old infants with known and unknown words (inferred from parental report). The authors reported that ERP activity distinguished the two word types, a finding that replicated an earlier study with 14 month old infants (Molfese, 1989). Unfortunately, since Molfese and colleagues used different analysis techniques than traditional component based ERP data analysis, it is somewhat difficult to compare their findings to those of other investigators. In addition, these studies typically have emphasized the age at which the ERP correlates of word meaning first appear rather than their subsequent elaboration, so the overall developmental picture remains incomplete.

Mills and colleagues (e.g., D. Mills, Coffey-Corina, & Neville, 1993, 1997; D. Mills et al., 2004) built on this work in two ways. First, they focused their attention on previously observed components of the ERP, typically negative components, appearing within the first 500 msec after stimulus onset. Second, they examined the progression of this ability across the age range identified in the behavioral literature as relevant for the development of word usage (e.g., Stager & Werker, 1997; Werker, Cohen, Lloyd, Cassaola, & Stager, 1998; Werker, Fennell, Corcoran, & Stager, 2002). Similar to Molfese, these authors observed that ERP activity discriminated between known and unknown words. However, this activity was typically bilaterally represented at 13 months of age, whereas by 20 months the activity was more focused over temporal and parietal scalp of the left hemisphere (as has been found in adults). Interestingly, when subgroups of infants were examined, infants with vocabularies over 150 words had more focal responses than those with smaller vocabularies (<150 words). From these latter findings the authors have concluded that vocabulary development represents an important component of the neural organization of phonetic processing. Once again, we see the prominent role of experience in speech/language development.

Second Language Learning, Including Sign Language

There has long been great controversy over the sensitive period for acquiring a second (or third or fourth) language. Dehaene et al. (1997) have reported that the neural representation of a second language is identical to that of a first language in truly bilingual individuals. However, if linguistic competence of the second language is not as strong as the first, then the functional neuroanatomy (based on PET data) is different. Since the bilinguals studied in this work had acquired their second language early in life, the initial conclusion was that the second language needed to be acquired early in order to be represented in the brain in the same location as the first language. This conclusion has recently been challenged, however. Perani et al. (1998) asked whether it was the *age* at which the second language was acquired that was the critical variable, or the *proficiency* with which this language was spoken. In this study, the age at which the second language had been mastered covaried with how well this language was spoken. The authors reported that it was the latter dimension that was most critical. Thus, regardless of when the second language was acquired, speaking this language with equal proficiency as the first language led to shared neural representation for both languages. Importantly, similar findings have been obtained with congenitally deaf individuals who are proficient in sign language; thus, the areas of the brain involved in sign are indistinguishable to those of hearing speakers using spoken language (Petitto et al., 2000).

Is there a critical period for acquiring sign language? Mayberry, Lock, and Kazmi (2002) have reported that proficiency in sign language among deaf individuals was far greater among subjects who had been exposed to either sign language early in life (among those born congenitally deaf) or individuals exposed to spoken language early in life but who subsequently lost their hearing than among congenitally deaf individuals *not* exposed to either signed or spoken language early in life. Furthermore, Newman, Bavelier, Corina, Jezzard, and Neville (2002) have reported that ASL is represented in the same location as spoken language only among individuals who acquired ASL before puberty. Thus, although there does not appear to be a sensitive period for acquiring ASL in general, there does appear to be a sensitive period for representing ASL in the same regions of the brain as spoken language, and for signing with a high level of proficiency.

Perhaps the most extensive literature examining the role of experience on the acquisition of verbal and sign language comes from Neville and colleagues' work on individuals who are born deaf. For example, Neville et al. (1998) have studied the neural organization of sign language among individuals with normal hearing who are native speakers of English; congenitally deaf individuals whose native language was sign and who learned English late in life; and normally hearing individuals who learned both verbal and sign languages early in life. High-resolution (4 Tesla) fMRI studies were performed. The authors reported that when visually processing their native language, all three groups activated regions of the left hemisphere typically associated with language (e.g., inferior frontal area, Wernicke's area, angular gyrus). In contrast, the congenitally deaf subjects did not activate these areas when they read English. From these findings the authors concluded that the areas of the brain that are committed to processing language do so regardless of the modality of the language, and that early experience with a particular modality essentially commits this area to processing language; if the language is learned later in life, other areas of the brain become involved.

Collectively, the work on sign language provides strong support for the role of experience in shaping cortical specialization, a theme we will carry forward when we discuss face processing in Chapter 9.

Effects of Early Focal Lesions on Language Development

Not surprisingly, there is a long history in studying the effects of early or late brain injury on language; after all, strokes among the elderly frequently lead to language impairments, and thus the field of neuropsychology has had a long-standing interest in brain-language associations (often in the context of language recovery). However, the work that we review briefly here, although concerned with brain injury, has another bias altogether: specifically, whether there is an innate language system or whether the neural organization of language is something that is influenced [only?] by experience.

As all students of development are aware, there is a long history to the debate over whether language represents a special modular function that is essentially hard-wired into the nervous system (as proposed by Chomsky, for example), or rather, represents a domain-general function that becomes domain-specific with experience. This debate has played out in many quarters (e.g., see Elman et al., 1996; Pinker, 1994), and there appears to be no resolution in sight.

However, there is one body of work that has weighed heavily in this debate, namely, the effect of early brain injury on the development and neural organization of language.

As Bates and colleagues note (Bates et al., 2001), it has been known for several millennia that brain damage can affect language production; similarly, it has been known since the mid- to late-nineteenth century that damage to the left hemisphere is more likely to be associated with severe language impairments than damage to the right hemisphere. These observations, coupled with early EEG work supporting the left-dominant nature of language processing and production has led many to argue for the innateness of language. However, there is a difference between a system that is innate versus one that is simply biased in a particular direction. In the former, we would expect little in the way of plasticity following early brain damage, whereas in the latter, we might expect more plasticity. It is this theme that has largely driven the work on the effects of early brain damage on language development.

Classical neuropsychology tells us that the more extensive the area of brain damage, the greater the effects on behavior. Not surprisingly, then, the early literature concerned with the effects of brain damage on language function was messy: patients enrolled in these studies were heterogenous with regard to the cause and severity of their brain injury. Thus, one patient might have suffered a closed-head injury, another an open-head injury, another a stroke, and a fourth a viral infection. To redress these limitations, a number of groups interested in language development have approached the problem quite differently. Rather than enroll patients who suffered different types of brain injury at different ages, these investigators typically study infants and young children who experienced a stroke pre- or perinatally. Although clearly there is still heterogeneity among patients, we can at least ascertain the age of the patient when the injury likely occurred (in all cases long before language developed), and with modern imaging technology, classify the nature and extent of the injury itself.

A group led by the late Elizabeth Bates has probably contributed the most to this literature by conducting a well-controlled longitudinal study of early focal brain injury. This group has published count-less journal articles and reviews (see, e.g., Bates & Roe, 2001; Bates et al., 2001). In these reports, they describe the results of a longitudi-nal study (in some cases, more than one) that included participants who had experienced a stroke immediately prior to birth or in the im-mediate postpartum period. In some cases, the stroke was limited to one hemisphere, and in others, it affected both hemispheres. In the early phases of this research program, computed tomography (CT) was used to characterize the brain damage, although MRI has gener-ally replaced CT and, as a result, there is now a much better sense of the exact extent of the damage. As the infants developed, they were studied using a battery of tasks designed to evaluate a range of both productive and receptive language functions.

These researchers consistently report that, relative to typically developing controls, children with unilateral brain damage fall within the normal range on measures of productive language, and that no differences in productive language are observed between children experiencing left versus right hemisphere damage. (Note also that children with focal lesions score within the normal range of IQ, including measures of verbal IQ.) Importantly, when com-pared to adults with left hemisphere damage, children who experi-enced focal brain injury are superior in all measures of language production. Similar findings are obtained on measures of language comprehension.

It is important to stress that these findings pertain to children who do not suffer other complicating injuries, such as seizures, pro-found prematurity, and so on. Stated differently, the sample under discussion should be considered a "clean" sample beyond their focal brain injury.

How do Bates and colleagues interpret their findings? First, the left hemisphere is initially committed to language development, and as-suming no brain injury, will in fact become specialized for language. However, if the left hemisphere is damaged, then the right hemi-sphere can subsume the functions that would otherwise have been the domain of the left hemisphere. This pattern is very different from that observed in adults and speaks to the tremendous plasticity of the developing brain. It also suggests that the neural substrate for language is not fixed, but rather, is biased in a particular direction. Should the normal pathway become impossible (due to early brain damage), other options are available to support language (notably, other brain circuits develop to take over function).

SUMMARY

Three broad conclusions can be drawn from our brief discussion of speech and language development. The first is that the brain is constructed with certain anatomical biases toward acquiring language, be it French or English, verbal or nonverbal; specifically, there are regions seemingly poised to subserve language, most of which reside in the left hemisphere (even for nonverbal language, such as ASL). The second is that these regions *become* committed based on experience. In other words, cortical specialization develops and is not prewired (what may be prewired is the potential of the brain to become specialized). Third, timing is everything: thus, in order to maintain the ability to discriminate speech sounds from multiple languages, it is necessary to be exposed to those languages early in life; the same is likely true for speaking those languages. Similarly, someone who experienced a brain injury is more likely to possess normal language if the injury occurred very early in life; if the injury occurred later in life, language is likely to be impaired.

In some ways, none of these conclusions should be surprising when considered in light of the work reviewed in Chapters 1 and 2 where we laid the groundwork for the activity-dependent nature of brain development and introduced the concept of neural plasticity. What is important to stress in the present context, however, is that, although language is unique to humans, the activity-dependent nature of language acquisition is not unique to language; as we shall see in Chapter 9, many elements of visual processing are also experience-dependent.

CHAPTER

5

The Development
of Declarative
(or Explicit) Memory
Why Is Memory Important?

We begin our discussion of brain and cognitive functions with a discourse about memory, leading with the question of why memory is important.

Memory is a cornerstone ability on which many general cognitive functions are assembled. For example, our knowledge of the world is predicated on a store of information that is acquired through acts of memory. Thus, it would seem important to delineate the developmental trajectory of this ability, particularly since our understanding of the cognitive and neural processes that underlie intelligence are not well established.

The abilities to encode and subsequently recall information are likely ones that have been conserved across species and have proven reproductively adaptive. Three examples suffice. First, in migratory birds, it is imperative that a bird return to its breeding ground in order to give birth to and provide care for the next generation. How does a bird remember the location of the breeding ground after many months? Mettke-Hofmann and Gwinner (2003) demonstrated that migrant birds can recall the location of a particular feeding site for 12 months, whereas nonmigrant birds can do so for only 2 weeks. More importantly, among migrant birds, the hippocampus increases in size from the first to the 2nd year of life (i.e., as the bird reaches sexual maturity), whereas no such increase is observed among nonmigrants. Thus, the ability of the hippocampus to adapt to the bird's environmental niche represents an example of the evolutionary significance of memory.

Second, a similar and equally impressive example of memory can be found in a report by Tomizawa et al. (2003). These authors note that the hormone oxytocin, which has typically been associated with inducing labor and facilitating caregiving behavior, has also been associated with two cognitive functions: social recognition (Ferguson, Aldag, Insel, & Young, 2001; Ferguson et al., 2000) and improved spatial memory (Kinsley et al., 1999). Tomizawa et al. (2003) demonstrated that in hippocampal slices perfused with oxytocin, long-term potentiation (LTP)[1] was facilitated, and among hippocampal slices taken from mice that had previously given birth (and in which no exogenous oxytocin was administered), CREB phosphorylation (the gene expression cascade believed to contribute to memory formation) was increased. Moreover, spatial memory could be improved in mice that had never given birth but that were treated with oxytocin, and an oxytocin antagonist administered to mice who *had* given birth impaired spatial memory.

A final example of the adaptive significance of memory may be found in the observation that the young of many species appear to have a proclivity to attend disproportionately to novelty; indeed, Nelson (2000b) has speculated that (a) this proclivity may be obligatory and serves the purpose of ensuring that the infant continually adds to his or her knowledge base and (b) this preference for novelty early in life may set the stage for the lifelong facility with which to form new memories.

In light of the ontogenetic and evolutionary importance of memory, let us turn to what is known about the neural bases of memory.

---

[1] Based on Hebbian principles, LTP is thought to reflect one of the molecular mechanisms underlying memory formation.

Before addressing this question, a brief tutorial on what we mean by memory is useful.

MEMORY SYSTEMS

Tulving (1972) opened the door to questioning the prevailing dogma that memory was a unitary trait by proposing that there are two memory systems, which he termed *semantic* and *episodic*. Tulving's argument was based on behavioral dissociations, although over the next 30 years this was augmented by experimental work with nonhuman animals and neuroimaging data from human adults. However, perhaps the turning point was the data derived from patient H. M. As Eichenbaum and colleagues discuss, H. M. (who underwent a bilateral resection of the temporal lobes for relief of intractable epilepsy; see Scoville & Milner, 1957 for original report; Corkin, 2002 for recent report, and see Figure 5.1) provided

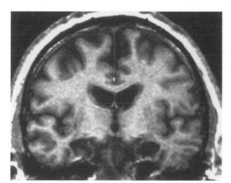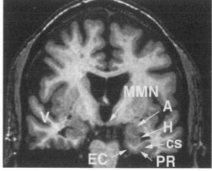

Figure 5.1   (Left) Magnetic resonance imaging scan showing the removal of medial temporal lobe structures in patient H. M. The lesion included all of the entorhinal cortex, most of the perirhinal cortex, and amygdala, and about one-half of the hippocampus. (Right) Scan of a normal control subject showing the structures removed in H. M. A, amygdala; cs, collateral sulcus; EC, entorhinal cortex; H, hippocampus; MMN, medial mammillary nucleus; PR, perirhinal cortex. Source: *From "Learning and Memory: Brain Systems," (pp. 1299–1327), by H. B. Eichenbaum, in* Fundamental Neuroscience (2nd ed.), *L. R. Squire, F. E. Bloom, S. K. McConnell, J. L. Roberts, N. C. Spitzer, and M. J. Zigmond (Eds.), 2003, New York: Academic Press.*

crucially important data to the argument in favor of multiple memory systems (Eichenbaum, 2002; Eichenbaum et al., 1999). For example, although H. M. suffered from a severe deficit in encoding new facts, he could learn new motor skills, despite having no conscious recollection of having done so.

Since Tulving's seminal paper in 1972, countless studies of rodents, monkeys, and humans have collectively pointed to a major dissociation of two types of memory: Explicit or declarative memory, on the one hand, and implicit or nondeclarative memory (also sometimes referred to as procedural memory; see Chapter 6) on the other. The standard definition of the former generally refers to memory for facts and events that can be brought to conscious awareness and that can be expressed explicitly. In contrast, implicit or nondeclarative memory generally refers to the acquisition of skills or procedures that are expressed nonconsciously through motor activity or changes in processing speed. Not surprisingly, there are different types of memory within each of these systems; thus, both recognition and recall memory fall under the rubric of explicit memory, whereas both priming and procedural learning fall under the rubric of implicit memory.

Additional evidence for the segregation of these two memory systems can be found in the neuroscience literature. At least in the adult, the explicit memory system appears to involve select neocortical areas (e.g., visual cortex for visual explicit memory), the cortical areas that surround the hippocampus (e.g., entorhinal cortex, parahippocampal gyrus), and the hippocampus proper. In contrast, nondeclarative memory involves circuits specific to the specific type of memory (although the medial temporal lobe tends not to be involved). For example, the acquisition of habits and skills appears to depend on the neostriatal system, whereas sensory-to-motor adaptations and the adjustment of reflexes appears to depend disproportionately on the cerebellum (for recent reviews, see Eichenbaum, 2003; see Figures 5.2 and 5.3).

Like many dichotomies, this distinction between memory systems is not wholly satisfying because there are many grey areas that fall between and within systems. As Cycowicz (2000) discusses, for example, the distinction between recognition memory (a type of

Perceptual memory   **Working memory**

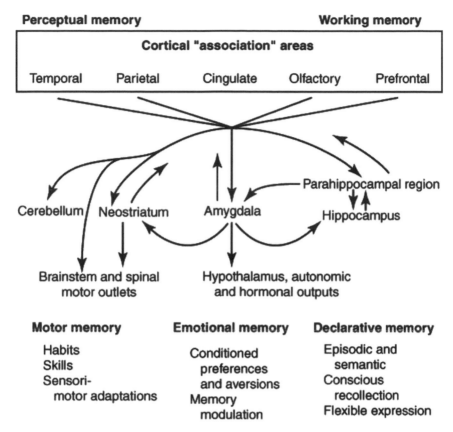

Figure 5.2   Adult configuration of memory systems as proposed by Eichenbaum.
Source: *From "Learning and Memory: Brain Systems," (pp. 1299–1327), by H.
B. Eichenbaum, in* Fundamental Neuroscience *(2nd ed.), L. R. Squire, F. E.
Bloom, S. K. McConnell, J. L. Roberts, N. C. Spitzer, and M. J. Zigmond (Eds.),
2003, New York: Academic Press.*

explicit memory) and repetition priming (a type of implicit memory) has more to do with the instructions issued to the subject than
anything inherent in memory itself. Thus, in tests of recognition
memory subjects are explicitly asked to identify previously experienced stimuli or events (e.g., by verbal response, pressing a button,
and so on), whereas in tests of repetition priming subjects are typically asked to perform an incidental task (e.g., "press button A if
the stimulus is oriented normally and button B if the stimulus is inverted"), and priming is inferred by speeded reaction times to

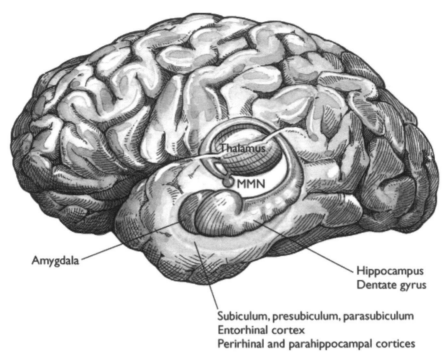

Thalamus

MMN

Amygdala

Hippocampus
Dentate gyrus

Subiculum, presubiculum, parasubiculum
Entorhinal cortex
Perirhinal and parahippocampal cortices

Figure 5.3   Diagram of the medial temporal lobe memory system. Source: From Brain, Mind, and Behavior (3rd ed.), by F. Bloom, C.A. Nelson, and A. Lazerson, 2001, New York: Worth Publishers.

previously experienced (albeit often unconsciously so) stimuli. In addition, there can also be overlap in the neural circuits that underlie each system (e.g., the visual cortex is required in both visual recognition memory and repetition priming for visual stimuli). Still, the field of memory has by and large accepted this distinction, various limitations notwithstanding.

THE DEVELOPMENT OF MEMORY SYSTEMS— SOME BACKGROUND

Drawing on data from both juvenile and mature nonhuman primates, neuropsychological and neuroimaging data with adult humans, and the small neuroimaging literature with developing humans, Nelson (1995) proposed that explicit qua explicit memory begins to develop some time after the 1st half year of life, as inferred from tasks such as deferred imitation, cross-modal recognition memory, delayed nonmatch-to-sample (DNMS), modified "oddball" designs in which event-related potentials (ERPs) are recorded, and preferential looking and habituation procedures that impose delays between familiarization (or habituation) and test. As is the case with the adult, this system depends on a distributed circuit that includes neocortical areas (such as the inferior temporal cortical area TE), the tissue surrounding the hippocampus (particularly the entorhinal cortex), and the hippocampus proper. However, Nelson also proposed that the development of explicit memory is preceded by an earlier form of memory referred to as *preexplicit* memory. What most distinguishes preexplicit from explicit memory is that the former (a) appears at or shortly after birth (b) is most evident in simple novelty preferences (often reflected in the visual paired comparison procedure), and (c) is largely dependent on the hippocampus proper.

These proposals (subsequently updated and elaborated by Nelson & Webb, 2003) were built less on direct visualization of brain-behavior relations than on the integration of data from many sources. This renders the model a useful heuristic albeit one that would benefit from more data and less speculation. The challenge, of course, is that relatively little is known about the development of the circuitry purported to be involved in different memory systems and different types of memory; similarly, there are relatively few investigators using neuroimaging tools of any sort to examine brain-memory relations. Nevertheless, advances made in testing developing nonhuman and human primates over the past decade have provided much needed additional information.

Table 5.1 summarizes our current thinking about the neural bases of memory development. We focus in this chapter on the development of explicit memory, and then turn our attention to implicit memory in Chapter 6.

Table 5.1   Current Thinking about the Neural Bases of Memory

General System	Subsystems	Tasks	Neural Systems Related to Tasks
Implicit memory (nondeclarative memory)	Procedural learning	Serial reaction time task	Striatum, supplementary motor association, motor cortex, frontal cortex
		Visual expectation paradigm	Frontal cortex, motor areas
	Conditioning	Conditioning	Cerebellum, basal ganglia
	Perceptual representation system	Perceptual priming paradigms	Modality dependent: Parietal cortex, occipital cortex, inferior temporal cortex, auditory cortex
Explicit memory system	Preexplicit memory	Novelty detection in habituation and paired comparison tasks	Hippocampus, possibly entorhinal cortex
	Semantic (generic knowledge)	Semantic retrieval, word priming, and associative priming	Left prefrontal cortex, anterior cingulated
	Episodic (autobiographical)		Hippocampal cortex
		Episodic encoding	Left prefrontal cortex, left orbitoprefrontal cortex
		Recall and recognition	Right prefrontal anterior cingulated, parahippocampal gyrus, entorhinal cortex

Current Findings—Explicit Memory in the Mature Brain

Although there is no consensus in the adult literature on the neural circuitry involved in explicit memory, Eichenbaum's model (2003) is nicely representative of the field, and of our own thinking about development.[2] According to Eichenbaum, the parahippocampal region (composed of the entorhinal, perirhinal, and parahippocampal cortices) is disproportionately involved in mediating the representation of isolated items, and is capable of holding these items in memory for short periods of time (e.g., several minutes). In contrast, the hippocampus proper appears to play a more prominent role in mediating the relational and/or representational properties of the stimuli; for example, during the time the parahippocampal region is holding individual items in memory, the hippocampus may be comparing these items to others already in memory; similarly, the hippocampus may be involved in extracting similar information across multiple exemplars or across multiple contexts. There are data from studies of human adults and developing and adult monkeys with select hippocampal lesions, that the hippocampus also mediates novelty preferences (e.g., Manns, Stark, & Squire, 2000; McKee & Squire, 1993). Finally, the neocortex is likely the storage site for long-term information, and in the case of frontal cortex, the site that facilitates storage via mnemonic strategies (e.g., chunking, and so on; for review of the neuroimaging literature on declarative memory, see Yancey & Phelps, 2001).

Current Findings—Explicit Memory in the Developing Brain

As is the case with studies of the mature organism, it is critical to consider the task being used to evaluate memory in deriving an

---

[2] Extending adult models of memory function to infants or children is problematic for many reasons, not the least of which is that we have no idea if the structure-function relations that hold in the adult will hold in the developing child. Nevertheless, we feel it is useful to begin with the adult configuration and then modify and expand accordingly, rather than to start from the ground up. As attractive as the latter is, there are currently too few studies on brain-memory relations to permit adequate model building.

understanding of what structure or circuit is involved. For example, as discussed by Nelson (1995), Nelson and Webb (2003), and most recently, Hayne (2004), the very same task, used in different ways, could impose different task demands on the subject and reflect different underlying neural circuitry. A case in point is the DNMS task, which is discussed in a later section.

There is now very good evidence from the monkey that lesions of the hippocampus lead to disruptions in visual recognition memory, at least under certain circumstances, and at least as inferred from novelty preferences. For example, Pascalis and Bachevalier (1999) reported that neonatal lesions of the hippocampus (but not amygdala; see Alvarado, Wright, & Bachevalier, 2002) impair visual recognition memory as tested in the Visual Paired Comparison (VPC) procedure, at least when the delay between familiarization and test is more than 10 seconds. And, Nemanic, Alvarado, and Bachevalier (2004) reported similar effects in adult monkeys. Specifically, lesions of the hippocampus, perirhinal cortex, and the parahippocampal cortex all impair performance on the VPC, although differentially so. Thus, lesions of the perirhinal cortex, parahippocampal cortex, and hippocampus proper lead to impairments when the delay between familiarization and test exceeds 20 seconds, 30 seconds, and 60 seconds, respectively. These findings are consistent with those from the human adult, where, for example, individuals with known damage to the hippocampus also show deficits in novelty-preferences under short delay conditions (McKee & Squire, 1993). Importantly, in the adult work, the same individuals who hours later fail to show novelty preferences *do* show intact recognition memory (Manns et al., 2000). Moreover, patient Y. R. with selective hippocampal damage shows impairments on the VPC task but relatively intact recognition memory (Pascalis, Hunkin, Holdstock, Isaac, & Mayes, 2004). Together these results suggest that recognition memory per se may be mediated by extra-hippocampal tissue (a point to which we will return), whereas novelty preferences are likely mediated by the hippocampus proper. Of course, the monkey data are only partially consistent with this view because they suggest that the hippocampus *and* surrounding cortex all play a role in novelty preferences, although differentially so . . . at least in the adult.

Further evidence for the role of the hippocampus in encoding the relations among stimuli (versus encoding individual stimuli, which may be the domain of the parahippocampal region) can be inferred from a recent paper by Robinson and Pascalis (2004). These authors tested groups of 6-, 12-, 18-, and 24-month-old infants using the VPC. Rather than evaluate memory for individually represented stimuli, the authors required infants to encode the properties of stimuli in context. Thus, during familiarization, stimuli were presented against one background, and during test the same stimulus paired with a novel stimulus was presented against the same or a different background. The authors report that although all age groups showed strong novelty preferences when the background was the same, only the 18- and 24-month-olds showed novelty preferences when the backgrounds were changed. This would suggest that this particular function of the hippocampus—studying the relations among stimuli or encoding stimuli in context—is somewhat slower to develop than recognizing stimuli in which the context was the same. Support for this claim can be found in the developmental neuroanatomy literature. Specifically, although the hippocampus proper, the entorhinal cortex, and the connections between them are known to mature early in life (e.g., Seress, 2001), it is also known that the development of dentate gyrus of the hippocampus matures more slowly (see Seress, 2001), as does the perirhinal cortex. Thus, if Pascalis and colleagues are correct that their context-dependent task is dependent on the hippocampus, then in theory the delayed maturation observed on this task reflects the delayed maturation of some specific region of the hippocampus, such as the dentate gyrus.

This last observation underscores an important point, which is that although explicit memory *emerges* sometime between 6 and 12 months of life, it is far from fully developed by this age. The fact that even very young infants (i.e., a few months of age) do quite well on standard preferential looking paradigms suggests that there is either enough hippocampal function to subserve task performance (as would be inferred from the monkey work performed by Bachevalier and colleagues) *or* that perhaps the parahippocampal region (about which virtually nothing is known developmentally) is mediating task performance. Thus, consistent with the neuroscience literature, the full, adult-like expression of explicit memory awaits the subsequent development of subregions of the hippocampus along with the connections to and from associated neocortical areas.

Novelty Preferences

Because of the prominent role novelty preferences have played in evaluating memory in infants and young children, it is worth discussing at some length the putative neural bases of such preferences. As stated previously, from monkey data we have concluded that the hippocampus plays a prominent role in novelty preferences, primarily based on the perturbations observed in such preferences when the hippocampus is lesioned. However, we need not restrict ourselves to data from monkeys. Neuroimaging studies with human adults have also reported that the hippocampus is involved in novelty preferences (see Strange, Fletcher, Hennson, Friston, & Dolan, 1999; Tulving, Markowitsch, Craik, Habib, & Houle, 1996). In contrast, Zola et al. (2000) reported that hippocampal lesions in mature monkeys did not affect novelty preferences at 1-second delays, and thus, that impairment (i.e., decline in performance) at subsequent delays was due to problems in memory, not novelty detection. Similarly, Manns et al. (2000) have shown that among intact human adults, novelty preferences and recognition memory are both intact shortly after familiarization, although with increasing delay novelty preferences disappear, and recognition memory remains intact. This work, coupled with that from Zola et al. (2000), argue for a dissociation between novelty preferences and recognition memory, and raises two questions. First, are novelty preferences truly mediated by the hippocampus or perhaps extrahippocampal tissue, and second, what does this dissociation say about the infancy literature in which recognition memory is typically inferred from novelty preferences?

First, it may be unwise to assume that all tasks that tap novelty preferences by default place the same demands on memory. For example, in tasks that require the subjects to generalize their discrimination across multiple exemplar of the same category of stimuli (e.g., to distinguish male faces from female faces), novelty preferences may depend on the ability to examine the relations among stimuli, and thus, depend disproportionately on the hippocampus. In contrast, if the task simply requires discriminating two individual exemplars (e.g., one female face from another), then perhaps the parahippocampal region is involved. Second, it may not be the case that novelty preferences and recognition memory represent the same or different processes as much as related ones. Thus, in the VPC procedure, perceptual support is provided by virtue of presenting both the familiar and novel stimuli simultaneously. In so doing, recognition may be facilitated at very short delays, perhaps due to some iconic store rather than the need to compare the novel stimulus to one stored in memory. This may occur in short-term memory and be supported by the parahippocampal region.

Whereas it is easy to dissociate novelty preferences from recognition memory in children or adults (in whom instructions can be given), the same is not true for infants, particularly when behavioral measures are employed. However, using ERPs, Nelson and Collins (1991, 1992) did appear to dissociate these processes to some degree. Four- through 8-month-old infants were initially familiarized to two stimuli and then during the test trials, one of these stimuli was presented on a random 60% of the trials (frequent-familiar), the other on a random 20% of the trials (infrequent-familiar) and on each of the remaining 20% of the trials a different novel stimulus (infrequent-novel) was presented. The authors reported that it was not until 8 months that infants responded equivalently to the two classes of familiar events and differently to the novel events. In contrast, at 6 months, infants responded differently to the two classes of familiar events and different yet again to the novel events. These findings were interpreted to reflect an improvement in memory from 6 to 8 months, specifically, the ability to ignore how often a stimulus is seen (inherent in novelty responses) from whether the stimulus is familiar or not (inherent in recognition memory).

It is difficult to say with certainty whether, in human children, it is the hippocampus or parahippocampal region that subserves novelty preferences and whether novelty preferences reflect a subroutine involved in recognition memory or reflect a proxy for recognition memory per se. These are clearly questions that await further study.

Delayed Non-Match-to-Sample

What about other tasks that have been thought to reflect explicit memory, such as the DNMS task? Here a subject is presented with a sample stimulus and, following some delay (during which the stimulus cannot be observed), the sample and a novel stimuli are presented side-by-side. In the case of monkeys, the animal is rewarded for retrieving the novel stimulus; in the case of humans, some investigators implement a similar reward system and essentially adopt the animal testing model (e.g., see Overman & Bachevalier, 1993), whereas others have modified the task such that no reward is administered and looking at the novel stimulus, rather than reaching for it serves as the dependent measure (see Diamond, 1995).[3] In the classic DNMS task, it is generally reported that monkeys do not perform at adult levels until they approach 1 year of age, and performance among children does not begin to resemble adults until they are approximately 4 years of age (assuming the standard 1:4 ratio of monkey to human years, these data are remarkably consistent). Interestingly, Pascalis and Bachevalier (1999) reported that neonatal lesions of the hippocampus do *not* impair performance on the DNMS task, suggesting that the DNMS likely depends on extrahippocampal structures and of course, does *not* depend on just novelty preferences. Support for this can be found in studies reported by

---

[3] It must be acknowledged that by modifying the task in this way, the task requirements change dramatically, and thus, difficult to argue that the two tasks are the same. This makes it difficult to compare across species.

Málková, Bachevalier, Mishkin, and Saunders (2001) and Nemanic et al. (2004), in which lesions of the perirhinal cortex in adult monkeys led to impairments in visual recognition memory as inferred from the DNMS; importantly, data from the Nemanic et al. (2004) study suggests that lesions of the hippocampus and parahippocampal regions have little effect on DNMS performance. Of note is the observation that these data contradict those reported by other groups (e.g., Zola et al., 2000), where hippocampal lesions in adult monkeys *do* lead to impairments on DNMS performance. And, our group has reported hippocampal activation in human adults tested with the DNMS task (Monk et al., 2002). What is to account for these differences? First, it could be that there is a fundamental difference in structure function relations in young versus mature subjects; thus, for example, the same function could be subserved by a different structure in the developing versus the developed individual. Second, it could also mean that the demands of the DNMS task differ (or are interpreted differently) depending on developmental age (e.g., the reward value of reinforcing stimuli could differ; how the child/juvenile monkey interprets that task demands could be different from how the adult/mature monkey interprets the task demands). Third, earlier studies of hippocampal lesions in adult monkeys could have included lesions of the surrounding cortex, thus making it difficult to distinguish between impairments due to the hippocampus or perirhinal cortex.[4] Finally, in the Monk et al. (2002) neuroimaging work, it was difficult to distinguish hippocampus from adjacent cortex, and therefore, it is possible that it was the surrounding cortex that was most involved in performance on the DNMS task.

---

[4] Until approximately the late 1990s, most surgical approaches to lesioning the hippocampus involved cutting through the surrounding cortex, thereby damaging this region (e.g., entorhinal cortex) and fibers of passage. As a result, it was often difficult to ascertain whether it was lesions of the hippocampus proper that led to perturbations in performance, lesions of the surrounding cortex, or the severing of connections between the hippocampus and surrounding cortex. Recent methodological advances now employ the administration of neurotoxins directly to the targeted structure, destroying cell bodies but leaving fibers of passage intact.

Elicited Imitation

Deferred or elicited imitation is a task that has now received considerable attention by memory researchers. In the case of humans, a sequence of events is modeled, and following some delay, and without benefit of practice, the subject is then presented with the props used in the original sequence. Correct scores are given for the number of steps in the sequence that are correctly "recalled." Used extensively by Bauer and colleagues (Bauer, 2005), Hayne and colleagues (e.g., Collie & Hayne, 1999; Hayne, Boniface, & Barr, 2000), and Meltzoff and colleagues (e.g., Meltzoff, 1985, 1988, 1995), among others, the prevailing evidence is that there is a dramatic improvement in this ability starting at 6 months and continuing through at least 24 months. In this case, improvement is defined as the ability to reproduce increasingly longer sequences of objects over increasingly long delays. Indeed, as infants pass their first birthday, under certain circumstances memory for temporal order is retained over months.

Of particular relevance to this chapter is a trio of related observations. First, McDonough, Mandler, McKee, and Squire (1995) reported that human adults with bilateral damage to the medial temporal lobe (including the hippocampus) perform poorly on this task. Similarly, individuals who sustained bilateral hippocampal damage during childhood show impairments on the same task, although, interestingly, the impairments are not so severe as those observed in adults by McDonough et al. (Adlam, Vargha-Khadem, Mishkin, & de Haan, in press). Second, Eichenbaum and colleagues (e.g., Agster, Fortin, & Eichenbaum, 2002; Fortin, Agster, & Eichenbaum, 2002) reported that rodents trained to remember a sequence of odors show impairments in distinguishing one sequence from another when the hippocampus proper is lesioned. Finally, our group (e.g., de Haan, Bauer, Georgieff, & Nelson, 2000; DeBoer, Georgieff, & Nelson, in press) demonstrated impairments in elicited imitation in populations of infants presumed to have experienced pre- or perinatal damage to the hippocampus (e.g., those born very prematurely or experiencing hypoxia-ischemia prenatally). Consistent with conclusions drawn by Bauer and colleagues (e.g., Bauer, Wenner, Dropik, & Wewerka,

2000; Bauer, Wiebe, Carver, Waters, & Nelson, 2003; Carver et al., 2000; Hayne, 2004; Nelson, 1995), these data appear to support the view that performance on elicited or deferred imitation tasks depend on the integrity of the hippocampus. However, as recently discussed by Nelson and Webb (2003), like the DNMS task, the elicited imitation task is quite complex and is comprised of a collection of subtasks. For example, infants must encode not just the properties of the objects but as well, the order in which these objects are presented. Historically, it has long been known that lesions of the frontal cortex perturb the ability to reproduce a sequence of events in the correct order (for review, see Lepage & Richer, 1996). In addition to recalling the sequence in which objects are presented, the participants must also encode the physical actions performed on the objects. Here again, the frontal cortex may be involved; for example, Nishitani and Hari (2000) found that observing and imitating manual actions activated the left inferior prefrontal cortex as well as the premotor cortex and the occipital cortex. The supplementary motor area has also been implicated in motor sequencing and may encode the numerical order of components (Clower & Alexander, 1998). Collectively, although the hippocampus may underlie elements of the elicited imitation task (perhaps the recognition or recall memory of specific components, such as recognizing a familiar object or recalling a familiar sequence; see Carver et al., 2000), other components of the task may be under control of the prefrontal cortex (and presumably the basal ganglia for the coordination of the reaching and memory components). As with much of the development literature on memory, further insight into the neural correlates of elicited imitation will have to await our ability to image the brain in action.

What of the Role of Frontal Cortex in Explicit Memory?

Aside from working memory (discussed in a later section of this chapter), in the context of development virtually nothing is known about the role of the prefrontal cortex in the context of explicit memory. It is well known in the adult, however, that damage to the frontal cortex impairs performance on tasks that require strategies or organizational manipulation (for discussion, see Yancey & Phelps, 2001). Indeed, the ability to transform, manipulate, or evaluate memories appears to be a distinctly frontal lobe function (see Milner, 1995). In this context, it should not be surprising to learn that frontal lobe damage has little if any effect on recognition memory but can have a dramatic impact on recall memory, presumably because recall involves manipulating and evaluating information. Memory tasks particularly affected by damage to the frontal lobes includes *source memory* (e.g., knowing who presented the information or where the information was presented; see Janowsky, Shimamura, & Squire, 1989), *frequency memory* (e.g., which item is presented most or least often; see M. L. Smith & Milner, 1988), and consistent with our discussion of elicited imitation, *memory for temporal order* (e.g., which item was presented most recently; see Butters, Kaszniak, Glisky, Esllinger, & Schacter, 1994). What are the implications of these observations for memory development? In brief, the ability to use strategies to encode and retrieve information and the ability to perform mental operations on the contents of a person's memory are skills that develop beginning in the preschool period and continue through the immediate preadolescent period (for review of the development of prefrontal cortical functions, Luciana, 2003). Not surprisingly, this is a period of rapid development of the prefrontal cortex, including synapse elimination and myelination. Thus, the changes that have been observed in memory across the preschool and elementary school years (for review, Flavell, Miller, & Miller, 1993; Siegler, 1991) are likely not due to further maturation of medial temporal lobe structures, but rather, maturation of frontal lobe structures and importantly, increased connectivity between the medial temporal lobe and the prefrontal cortex. With the ability to employ fMRI across this age range, it would be our hope that this tool will one day be applied to test this hypothesis.

DISORDERS OF MEMORY

Recent evidence suggests that bilateral hippocampal damage sustained during childhood can lead to specific impairments in memory, a condition labeled *developmental amnesia* (Gadian et al., 2000; Vargha-Khadem et al., 1997). The neuropsychological profile of these cases appears to differ somewhat from the amnesia observed in adults following medial temporal lobe damage. One difference is that, unlike adult amnesiacs who show impairments in both recognition and recall, in at least one intensively studied case of developmental amnesia delayed recognition memory was relatively preserved whereas delayed recall was severely impaired (Baddeley, Vargha-Khadem, & Mishkin, 2001). A second difference is that, unlike adults amnesics who tend to show impairments in both episodic and semantic memory, patients with developmental amnesia tend to show severe impairments in episodic memory with semantic memory remaining fairly intact (Vargha-Khadem et al., 1997).

The reason for this difference in profile between developmental and adult-onset cases remains a matter of some debate. One possibility is that the patients with developmental amnesia generally show a milder memory impairment than adult amnesiacs because their damage is more selective. Many of the adult cases reported in the literature have widespread damage including additional areas within the temporal lobe and also extra-temporal brain regions. By contrast, at least within the medial temporal lobe, the perirhinal, entorhinal, and parahippocampal cortices of patients with developmental amnesia appear intact as measured by volumetric analysis (Schoppik et al., 2001). It is possible that these regions normally subserve recognition memory and semantic recall, and that their preservation in developmental amnesia allows for a relative preservation of these skills (Vargha-Khadem, Gadian, & Mishkin, 2001). Consistent with this view are reports that adult patients with more selective hippocampal lesions also show some preserved semantic learning (e.g., Verfaellie, Koseff, & Alexander, 2000). However, others have reported that adult patients with lesions reportedly restricted to the hippocampus do show a more general memory deficit (e.g., Manns & Squire, 1999) and that a patient with more widespread damage sustained at 6 years of age also show relatively preserved semantic learning (Brizzolara, Casalini, Montanaro, & Posteraro, 2003). These findings suggest that age of injury, rather than extent, may be critical. Understanding the separate and combined contribution of the selectivity of damage within the MTL, the degree of extra-hippocampal damage (e.g., abnormalities in the putamen, posterior thalamus, and right retrosplenial cortex are reported in developmental amnesia; Vargha-Khadem et al., 2003) and age of injury will be an important question for future studies.

For early onset injuries, the degree of hippocampal damage appears to affect the pattern of memory impairment (Isaacs et al., 2003). Compared to controls, patients with developmental amnesia (average bilateral hippocampal volume reduction of 40%, range from 27% to 56%) were impaired on tests of delayed recall while preterm children (average reduction of 8% to 9%, ranging to 23%) showed no deficit in delayed recall (but did show a deficit on prospective memory and route following). These differences cannot be accounted for by general differences in ability level as the groups were matched on IQ. However, the possibility of differences in extra-hippocampal damage, which may vary as a function of degree of hippocampal damage, is not known.

Another possible explanation for the differing profiles between child- and adult-onset cases is that early onset cases show milder impairments because the plasticity of the developing brain allows for compensation of function. In children with neonatal damage, memory impairments are not typically noted until children are school age (Gadian et al., 2000). This is surprising given that the hippocampus is believed to play a critical role in memory from birth as discussed earlier. One possible explanation is that there is a degree of compensation that allows relatively good memory skills initially but that ultimately leads to a mild form of memory impairment. A neuroimaging case study has shown that the remaining hippocampal tissue in developmental amnesia appears to be functional during memory tasks (Maguire, Vargha-Khadem, & Mishkin, 2001). However, while intact individuals showed primarily left hippocampal activation, the patient showed bilateral activation, and also showed a different pattern of connectivity of the hippocampus with other brain areas compared to controls (Maguire et al., 2001). It is thus possible that the remaining areas of functioning hippocampus organize with other brain regions to mediate the preserved memory abilities. If this is true, then we might expect that age of injury would affect the ultimate outcome, with early injury leading to better outcome than later injury due to greater plasticity. A recent report does not support this prediction, showing that delayed memory does not differ for children who sustained their injury before 1 year of age and those who sustained injury after 6 years of age (Vargha-Khadem et al., 2003). However, it is interesting to note that those with earlier lesions did perform better than those with later lesions on some tests of immediate memory, suggesting that there may be some plasticity operating.

Summary

Piecing together heterogeneous sources of information, it appears that an early form of explicit memory emerges shortly after birth (assuming a full-term delivery). This *preexplicit* memory is dependent predominantly on the hippocampus. As infants enter the second half of their 1st year of life, hippocampal maturation, coupled with development of the surrounding cortex, makes possible the emergence of *explicit* memory. A variety of tasks have been used to evaluate explicit memory, some unique to the human infant, others adopted from the monkey. Based on such tasks, we observe a gradual improvement in memory across the first few years of life, most likely due to changes in the hippocampus proper (e.g., dentate gyrus), to the surrounding cortex (e.g., parahippocampal cortex), and to increased connectivity between these areas. The changes we observe in memory from the preschool through elementary school years are likely due to changes in prefrontal cortex and connections between the prefrontal cortex and the medial temporal lobe. Such changes make possible the ability to perform mental operations on the contents of memory, such as the ability to use strategies to encode and retrieve information. Finally, changes in long-term memory are likely due to the development of the neocortical areas that are thought to store such memories, and the improved communication between the neocortex and the medial temporal lobe. It is most likely that these changes usher in the end of infantile amnesia (for elaboration, see Nelson, 1998; Nelson & Carver, 1998).

6

The Development of Nondeclarative (or Implicit) Memory

Nondeclarative or implicit forms of learning and memory functions represent an essential aspect of human cognition by which information and skills can be learned through mere exposure or practice, without requiring conscious intention or attention, eventually becoming "automatic." Although controversy exists regarding the definition of nondeclarative memory or learning, performance on most nondeclarative tasks does not appear to depend on medial temporal lobe structures. For example, patients like H. M., mentioned earlier, demonstrate severe deficits in explicit memory consistent with known insults to or disruption of medial temporal lobe memory systems. However, these patients are not impaired on classic tests of implicit memory and learning, such as perceptual priming or serial reaction time (SRT) learning (Milner, Corkin, & Teuber, 1968; Shimamura, 1986; Squire, 1986; Squire & Frambach, 1990; Squire, Knowlton, & Musen, 1993; Squire & McKee, 1993).

A multitude of tasks have emerged in the cognitive literature to assess nondeclarative cognitive functions (see Reber, 1993; Seger, 1994). Reber (1993) proposes that a distinction be made between two broad categories of nondeclarative function: implicit memory (the end-state representation of knowledge available to an individual, of which he or she is unaware) and implicit learning (the unintentional and unconscious acquisition of knowledge). Implicit learning involves learning of underlying rules and structure in the absence of any conscious awareness of those regularities. Such learning is slow and requires repeated exposure to the information to be retained. In contrast, implicit memory may occur with a single exposure to a stimulus, and results in an increased processing efficiency for subsequent presentations of that stimulus or closely related stimuli. Not only do these categories differ in their basic cognitive nature (representation versus acquisition of knowledge), but they seem to differ in their underlying neural substrates as well. In a now well-known classification of memory systems, Squire et al. (1993) identified three primary forms of implicit learning and memory: priming, procedural learning (skills and habits), and classical conditioning (associative learning), each relying on separable neural systems.

VISUAL PRIMING

Evidence for this taxonomy comes from animal and human lesion studies as well as neuroimaging methods. For example, priming, or improvements in detecting or processing a stimulus based on a recent exposure to that stimulus, appears to rely on neocortical brain regions relevant to the stimulus of interest. That is, when healthy adults are presented with a visual stimulus repeatedly, areas of extrastriate visual cortex show decreased activity, presumably reflecting diminished processing requirements when reactivating the sensory circuit (Schacter & Buckner, 1998; Squire et al., 1992). Similarly, priming in the context of an object classification task is associated with decreased activity in inferior temporal cortex and ventral prefrontal cortex (Buckner et al., 1998), regions previously linked to explicit object identification.

Although a number of studies have examined visual priming performance in infancy and early childhood (Drummey & Newcombe,

1995; Hayes & Hennessy, 1996; Parkin & Streete, 1988; Russo, Nichelli, Gibertoni, & Cornia, 1995; Webb & Nelson, 2001), few have applied brain imaging methods to examine the neural bases of this function. In general, behavioral evidence overwhelmingly suggests that young children and even infants show priming effects that are very similar to adults, supporting the idea that implicit learning and memory functions may show very little developmental change while explicit learning and memory demonstrate protracted development. Webb and Nelson (2001) used event-related potentials (ERPs) to assess visual perceptual priming in 6-month-old infants compared to adults. Although developmental differences were observed in ERP components between adults and infants, these differences were similar to differences observed during explicit memory function. However, ERP evidence of memory (an activity difference between new and repeated stimuli) was observed only for an early ERP component typically associated with attention (NC), and not at the late component typically associated with explicit memory (PSW; see Nelson, 1994; Nelson & Monk, 2001, for review of infant ERP components).

IMPLICIT SEQUENCE LEARNING

In contrast to priming, implicit learning, also called habit learning, skill learning, or procedural learning, involves the slow acquisition of a knowledge base or behavioral skill set over time. For example, in everyday life, learning to ride a bicycle involves the gradual acquisition of a skill that is very difficult or impossible to describe verbally. Although intentionally trying to learn the skill, the learner is typically unaware of what exactly is being learned. Implicit learning has most frequently been tested using sequence learning (e.g., Nissen & Bullemer, 1987) or artificial grammar learning paradigms (Reber, 1993). In the SRT task, individuals are asked to map a set of spatial or object stimuli onto an equal number of response buttons. Reaction times to match the stimulus and the button are recorded. Without the knowledge of the participant, stimuli often appear in random order, whereas at other times, the order of stimulus presentation follows a predictable and repeating sequence. Implicit learning is assumed when participants show reaction time improvements during the sequential trials compared to random trials despite no conscious awareness of the underlying regularity.

Patients with temporal lobe amnesia perform normally on sequence learning tasks. However, patients with basal ganglia damage, such as those with Parkinson's or Huntington's diseases, have been shown to be impaired on the serial reaction time task (Ferraro, Balota, & Connor, 1993; Heindel, Salmon, Shults, Walicke, & Butters, 1989; Knopman & Nissen, 1991; Pascual-Leone et al., 1993). Importantly, these patients perform normally on measures of explicit memory as well as on measures of perceptual and conceptual priming (Schwartz & Hastroudi, 1991), providing support for the separability of implicit learning and implicit memory at the neural systems level. Neuroimaging data provide supporting evidence for the role of subcortical structures in SRT learning. Common findings across a number of laboratories (Bischoff-Grethe, Martin, Mao, & Berns, 2001; Grafton, Hazeltine, & Ivry, 1995; Hazeltine, Grafton, & Ivry, 1997; Schendan, Searl, Melrose, & Stern, 2003) demonstrate differential activity in frontal-basal ganglia-thalamic circuits for sequential trials compared to random trials. Further evidence exists to suggest that connections among these frontostriatal loops and frontocerebellar loops may be an important aspect of implicit learning. Pascual-Leone et al. (1993) observed that, although adults with basal ganglia insults demonstrated significant reductions in implicit sequence learning, adults with cerebellar degeneration showed no evidence of learning on the SRT task.

Significant controversy exists regarding the developmental trajectory of implicit learning. In a study of SRT learning in 6- to 10-year-old children and adults, Meulemans, van der Linden, and Perruchet (1998) observed equivalent learning of a 10-step spatial sequence across age groups, despite overall reaction time differences with age. These data support the notion that implicit cognition may mature very early in infancy and show little variation or improvement with age (Reber, 1992). However, other measures of implicit pattern learning or contingency learning, as well as SRT data from an alternate group are less clear. Maybery, Taylor, and O'Brien-Malone (1995) report age-related improvements in covariation learning with older children showing larger learning effects than younger children. However, Lewicki (1986) found no evidence of age-related learning effects on the original version of the same task. Similarly, Thomas and Nelson (2001) found that the mean size of the implicit learning effect was similar between 4-, 7-, and 10-year-olds on an SRT task. However, some children showed no evidence of implicit learning. The number of children showing no learning was inversely related to age, with fully one-third of the youngest age group (4-year-olds) showing no evidence of learning, whereas 100% of the 10-year-olds demonstrated learning. Evidence for age-related improvements in implicit sequence learning come from an infant analogue of the SRT task: visual expectancy formation. In this task, infants are shown a repeating pattern of visual stimuli and eye movements are recorded to determine whether the infant learns to anticipate the location of the upcoming stimuli over time. Although we cannot rule out the possibility that this behavior is explicitly learned, the task have many similarities to the adult SRT paradigm. Although infants as young as 2 and 3 months of age can show reliable visual expectancy formation (Canfield, Smith, Brezsnyak, & Snow, 1997; Haith, Hazan, & Goodman, 1988) older infants are able to learn more complicated sequential relationships than younger children (Clohessy, Posner, & Rothbart, 2002; P. Smith, Loboschefski, Davidson, & Dixon, 1997).

In a recent fMRI study of the SRT task, Thomas et al. (2004) compared the neural systems subserving implicit sequence learning in 7- to 11-year-old children and adults. Overall, results from adults were consistent with previous neuroimaging studies implicating frontostriatal circuitry in visuomotor sequence learning. In particular, activity in the basal ganglia was positively correlated with the size of the implicit learning effect (greater learning was associated with increased activity in the caudate nucleus). Although children and adults showed many of the same regions of activity, relative group differences were observed overall, with children showing greater subcortical activity and adults showing greater cortical activity. Consistent with recent finding from adult SRT studies (Schendan et al., 2003), both adults and children showed activity in the hippocampus despite no explicit awareness of the sequence. This activity is unlikely to be either necessary or sufficient for implicit sequence learning given the adult literature indicating spared performance following lesions to the hippocampus. Instead, this activity may reflect a sensitivity to stimulus novelty. Children showed an inverse pattern of hippocampal activity when compared to adults (random trials elicited greater hippocampal activity than sequence trials for child participants). The SRT task used here (a variation of that used by Meulemans et al., 1998) produced significant developmental differences in the magnitude of the learning effect, with children demonstrating significantly less learning than adults. Unlike prior behavioral studies, this effect was not driven by a difference in the percentage of nonlearners in the two age groups. Rather, despite significant individual learning in both groups, adults learned to a greater extent with the same degree of exposure.

Finally, some evidence exists addressing the effects of basal ganglia insults early in development. Although early insults may lead to lasting impairments in functions subserved by the affected systems, the plastic nature of the developing brain may also allow for redistribution of function to other, unaffected regions. Structural neuroimaging studies have identified childhood attention deficit-hyperactivity disorder, as well as perinatal complications such as intraventricular hemorrhage as risk factors for disrupted basal ganglia circuitry. Castellanos et al. (2001, 2002) have reported decreases in caudate volume in children with attention deficit/hyperactivity disorder (ADHD) compared to nonaffected controls. Similarly, functional imaging studies of attentional control (see Executive Functions discussion, Chapter 10) suggest a lack of typical basal ganglia activity in ADHD (Vaidya, Gabrieli, Monti, Tinklenberg, & Yesavage, 1999). A recent paper addressing reading disabilities suggests a possible link between reduced motor sequence learning and symptoms of ADHD (Waber et al., 2003). Thomas and colleagues reported evidence of significant decrements in sequence learning for 6- to 9-year-old children diagnosed with ADHD (Thomas, Vizueta, Teylan, Eccard, & Casey, 2003). These authors also examined implicit sequence learning in children with perinatal histories of intraventricular hemorrhage (IVH; bleeding into the lateral ventricles at birth). Children whose IVH was moderate (bilateral grade II or more severe) evidenced significant decrements in the magnitude of the implicit learning effect. In contrast, children whose perinatal IVH has been relatively mild (unilateral grade II or less severe) showed no difference in learning from a full-term, age- and gender-matched control group. Together, these studies suggest a potential long-term deficit in implicit learning resulting from early insults to basal ganglia circuitry.

CONDITIONING OR ASSOCIATIVE LEARNING

In contrast to priming and implicit sequence learning, the existing knowledge regarding the neural bases of conditioning derives largely from animal studies. In conditioning paradigms, the subject learns the contingency between two previously unrelated stimuli through either association with a cue or signal (classical conditioning) or an outcome or reward (instrumental conditioning). Studies of classical eye-blink conditioning in rabbits have implicated the cerebellum and its connections to brainstem nuclei (particularly the interpositus nucleus) as a key regions necessary for normal conditioning to occur (Woodruff-Pak, Logan, & Thompson, 1990). Lesions of either of these structures can completely prevent acquisition of the conditioned response, while lesions of the cerebrum have no effect on either acquisition of the response nor maintenance of the response (Mauk & Thompson, 1987). The hippocampus is also not required for classical delay eye-blink conditioning. Patients with temporal lobe amnesia show normal performance on delay conditioning paradigms (Woodruff-Pak, 1993) whereas those with lesions to lateral cerebellum are severely impaired in acquiring the conditioned eye-blink response (Woodruff-Pak, Papka, & Ivry, 1996). In contrast, emotional fear conditioning (pairing a neutral stimulus with a shock) appears to heavily rely on the amygdala (LaBar, Gatenby, Gore, LeDoux, & Phelps, 1998; Pine et al., 2001).

Developmentally, newborn infants (10 days old) are able to acquire a conditioned eye-blink response. Therefore, like implicit sequence learning, the basic mechanism supporting conditioned responding must be present and functional at birth, although it would be misleading to suggest that its function is fully mature. Developmental improvements are observed in conditioning paradigms. For example, with age, children can handle longer and longer delays between the neutral signal and the unconditioned stimulus (Orlich & Ross, 1968). Such developmental effects might be expected given the very protracted maturational trajectory of the cerebellum (Keller et al., 2003). Much less is known regarding the development of the amygdala response in fear conditioning. Similarly, although significant behavioral research has been conducted addressing instrumental conditioning in infancy (Rovee-Collier, 1997a), relatively little is known regarding the brain systems underlying this learning (see Nelson, 1995 for speculation). Rovee-Collier (1997b) and colleagues have observed increases in the retention duration for conditioning with age. That is, older children remember the contingencies for longer periods of time than younger children do (Hartshorn et al., 1998).

7

The Development of Spatial Cognition

Spatial cognition refers to a range of abilities involved in perceiving, remembering, and mentally manipulating spatial relations and orientation at several scales including among features of a single object, between objects and their context, and of oneself in space.

MENTAL ROTATION

Mental rotation is a form of visual imagery involving "the imagined circular movement of a given object about an imagined pole in either 2 or 3 dimensional space" (Ark, 2002, p. 1). In adults, the superior parietal lobe appears to be involved in the actual act of imaginary rotation because it is not only active during mental rotation tasks but its extent of activation is related to reaction time (Richter, Ugurbil, Georgopoulos, & Kim, 1997; Richter et al., 2000). Activations in visual area MT (Cohen et al., 1996) and motor and premotor areas in the frontal cortex (Johnston, Leek, Atherton, Thacker, & Jackson, 2004; Richter et al., 2000; Windischberger, Lamm, Bauer, & Moser, 2003) have also been observed in some, but not all, studies. These activations suggest that some of the processes involved in mental rotation overlap with processes involved in actual physical rotation of a stimulus: MT activation occurs when subjects observe objects moving and premotor and motor areas are activated when subjects physically move objects. In support of this idea, one study demonstrated bilateral premotor activation during mental rotation of pairs of hands but only left premotor activation during mental rotation of tools (Vingerhoets, de Lange, Vandemaele, Deblaere, & Achten, 2002). This pattern suggests that participants were using motor imagery and imagined moving both hands in the hand condition and imagined using/moving the tools with their preferred (right) hand in the tool condition (Vingerhoets et al., 2002).

Between 8 and 12 years of age, children's mental rotation abilities become adult-like in several respects (e.g., nature of errors, relation of reaction time to degree of rotation; see Dean, Duhe, & Green, 1983; Waber, Carlson, & Mann, 1982). This is consistent with evidence that the parietal lobe begins to obtain adult-like status at about 10 to 12 years of age (Giedd et al., 1999). Indeed, neuroimaging studies comparing activation in children and adults confirm that parietal areas are activated in 8- to 12-year-old children as in adults (Booth et al., 1999, 2000; Chang, Adleman, Dienes, Menon, & Reiss, 2002; Shelton, Christoff, Burrows, Pelisari, & Gabrieli, 2001). Parietal areas are activated during mental rotation tasks regardless of individual differences in ability level (Shelton et al., 2001). However, differences between children and adults in the overall pattern of activation have been noted. For example, in one study adults and 9- to 12-year-olds were asked to mentally rotate a letter or number from one of four different rotations to its upright position and then determine whether it was forward or backward (Booth et al., 2000). Both age groups showed similar overall levels of performance and showed the typical pattern of increasing reaction time and errors with increasing degree of rotation. In spite of the similarities in behavioral performance, adults showed more activation in the superior parietal and middle frontal areas, whereas children showed more activation in the supramarginal gyrus. The authors suggest that this may reflect strategy differences, with adults engaging in more mental rotation and children engaging in more processing of the noncannonical orientations of the letters and numbers. The idea that the neural processes underlying mental rotation may differ even when performance is echoed in results of EEG studies, in which greater parietal activation was reported in 8-year-old boys than girls during 2-D mental rotation in spite of similar levels of behavioral performance (Roberts & Bell, 2002).

It is possible that some of the differences observed between children and adults are related not to developmental change in mental rotation abilities per se, but to failure to match on gender. In adults, differences in brain areas activated during mental rotation have been noted between men and women (Roberts & Bell, 2002). For example, even when performance is equated, women tend to show more bilateral activation and men more right-lateralized activation in parietal regions (Jordan, Wustenberg, Heinze, Peteres, & Jancke, 2003) and women tend to show greater activation in frontal regions (Thomsen et al., 2000; Weiss et al., 2003).

Consistent with neuroimaging results in children, which have reported bilateral parietal activation, both right and left hemisphere lesions in children appear to impair performance on mental rotation tasks (Booth et al., 2000). Adults tested in those neuroimaging studies also showed bilateral activation, although other studies have reported evidence for either left or right lateralization (Harris & Miniussi, 2003; Roberts & Bell, 2002, 2003; Zacks, Gilliam, & Ojemann, 2003). Children with unilateral lesions showed activations in similar regions as healthy children and adults but only in the intact hemisphere (Booth et al., 2000).

SPATIAL PATTERN PROCESSING

Spatial analysis involves the ability both to segment a pattern into a set of constituent parts and to integrate these parts into a coherent whole (Stiles et al., 2003b). In adults, the left inferior temporal gyrus and parts of the left fusifrom gyrus are more active than the homologous right hemisphere during pattern segmentation ("local" processing), while the homlogous areas in the right are more active than those in the left during pattern integration ("global" processing; Martinez et al., 1997). In addition, occipitoparietal regions in the area of the intraparietal sulcus, particularly on the right, are active during both types of task, with larger areas activated during pattern integration than segmentation (Martinez et al., 1997; Sasaki et al., 2001). This latter finding is consistent with the zoom-lens analogy of selective attention: attention to local features activates cortical foveal representations, whereas attention to global aspects activates peripheral areas (Sasaki et al., 2001). Studies of adult patients with brain damage have revealed parallel results, with pattern integration being linked to right hemisphere damage and pattern segmentation to left hemisphere damage (Delis, Robertson, & Efron, 1986).

Behavioral studies indicate that processing of global information develops more quickly than processing of local information, with both types reaching adult levels by 14 years of age. For example, Roe, Moses, and Stiles (1999) tested children aged 7 to 14 years using hierarchical stimuli and found that, while the left visual field advantage for global levels appeared sooner than the right visual field advantage for local levels, both present in the adult-like form by age 14 (but see Mondloch, Geldart, Maurer, & Le Grand, 2003b). There appears to be a gradual emergence of the left hemisphere bias for local levels of forms between 7 to 14 years of age.

In children, neuroimaging studies have shown that areas similar to those activated in adults are activated in typically developing 12- to 14-year-olds performing spatial processing tasks (Moses et al., 2002). Specifically, children, like adults, showed faster reaction time to global than local stimuli in the left visual field/right hemisphere but the reverse pattern of reaction time to stimuli in the right visual field/left hemisphere and they also showed the adult-like pattern of lateralized occipitotemporal activation for the two tasks. However, not all children displayed this mature pattern. A subgroup of children failed to show the expected lateral differences in the split-visual field task and also showed no task-related lateral differences during the fMRI study, only a generally greater right-hemisphere activation during both types of task (Moses et al., 2002). The authors suggest that this pattern indicates that a greater degree of brain lateralization is linked to a greater degree of skill/more mature abilities.

With respect to brain lesions, several studies of pediatric patients with right or left hemisphere damage confirm the importance of these areas for global and local processing respectively. For example, when children are shown hierarchical forms and asked to reproduce them, children with left hemisphere injury have difficulty reproducing local elements, while children with right hemisphere lesions have difficulty reproducing the global structure (adults: Delis et al., 1986; children: Stiles, Bates, Thal, Trauner, & Reilly, 1998) and these impairments persist to school age. By contrast, children as young as 4 can reproduce both levels accurately (Dukette & Stiles, 2001). On other tasks such as block construction and copying and memory for complex figures, children with either type of lesion show delays. And, even when children eventually produce relatively accurate constructions, the strategies they use to produce them are often simplified and more representative of those seen in typically developing children at a younger age.

While damage to the developing brain can produce a pattern of deficit similar to that seen in adults, these effects may be less pronounced and show more improvement with time than in adults. For example, while performance on block construction and complex pattern memory are clearly delayed, children eventually can produce accurate responses. To investigate the neural bases of this plasticity, Stiles et al. (2003a) investigated two children with frank parietal lesions and white matter loss more posterior vs. anterior regions, one with right hemisphere and one with left hemisphere involvement. During tasks requiring pattern segmentation and integration, patients showed lateralization of activity to contralesional hemisphere, suggesting that the intact hemisphere can take on some abilities normally subserved by the damaged one.

The fact that children initially seem to show bilateral activation during both global and local processing, and that pediatric patients with unilateral lesions appear to be able to use a single hemisphere to process both types of pattern, appears at odds with other findings suggesting that hemispheric biases in spatial processing are apparent very early in life. For example, 8-month-olds tend to process configural aspects more than featural aspects of faces (e.g., Schwarzer & Zauner, 2003), and by a similar age they show a right-hemisphere bias in processing faces (de Haan & Nelson, 1997, 1999; de Schonen & Mathivet, 1990) but not objects (de Haan & Nelson, 1999). More direct evidence comes from studies in which the sensitivity of the right versus the left hemisphere to featural/local compared to configural changes has been assessed by split visual-field presentation with infants. These studies also suggest that the left visual field/right hemisphere is more sensitive to global changes while the right visual field/left hemisphere is more sensitive to local changes (Deruelle & de Schonen, 1991, 1995).

The bilateral activation seen in some young children during both local and global processing may reflect less a lack of hemisphere bias and more an immature pattern in which task difficulty demands that all available resources are recruited for the task at hand. Similarly, when patients with unilateral lesions are presented with these tasks, they devote all of their limited resources to complete them. In this view, with development there is increasing specialization such that improved performance is related to recruitment of a smaller set of brain areas that are able to perform a particular task most efficiently (Johnson, 2001; Stiles et al., 2003b). In other words, there is a selective recruitment of resources rather than a recruitment of all available resources. Experience with processing the different types of stimuli is thought in part to drive this process. In support of this view, neuroimaging studies with adults have shown that perceptual learning is associated with an increasing refinement in the brain areas activated as expertise is acquired (Gauthier, Tarr, Anderson, Skudlarski, & Gore, 1999).

SPATIAL NAVIGATION

The ability to remember locations and routes in the visual environment relies on both body-centered (e.g., ocentric) and environment-centered (allocentric) spatial information. In adults, the hippocampus appears to be involved in spatial memory (Astur, Taylor, Mamelak, Philpott, & Sutherland, 2002; Nunn, Polkey, & Morris, 1998), particularly with respect to allocentric spatial memory (Abrahams, Pickering, Polkey, & Morris, 1997; Holdstock et al., 2000; Incisa della Rocchetta, 2004) and neuroimaging studies of healthy participants suggest that the hippocampus is particularly important for allocentric spatial processing. It is probably involved in the consolidation of allocentric information into long-term memory rather than the initial encoding of allocentric spatial information (Holdstock et al., 2000).

A case study of a patient with perinatal selective hippocampal damage also shows deficits in allocentric spatial processing. This patient was tested in a virtual reality town and showed a massive additional impairment when tested from the shifted viewpoint compared with a mild, list length-dependent, impairment when tested from the same viewpoint (King, Burgess, Hartley, Vargha-Khadem, & O'Keefe, 2002). The same patient was impaired on all topographical tasks on a second virtual reality study and on his recall of the context-dependent questions. In contrast, he showed normal recognition of objects from the virtual town and of "topographical" scenes (Spiers, Burgess, Hartley, Vargha-Khadem, & O'Keefe, 2001). These results suggest a relative lack of developmental plasticity following hippocampal lesions, with respect to allocentric spatial encoding.

CHAPTER

8

The Development
of Object Recognition
Face/Object Recognition

A mong the numerous visual inputs that we receive each mo-
ment, the human face is perhaps one of the most salient. The
importance of the many signals it conveys (e.g., emotion, identity,
direction of eye gaze), together with the speed and ease with which
adults typically process this information, are compelling reasons to
suppose that there may exist brain circuits specialized for processing
faces. Neuropsychological studies provided the first evidence to support this view, with reports of double dissociations of face and object
processing. That is, patients were described who showed impaired
face processing with relatively intact general vision and object
processing (with the occasional exception of color vision; reviewed
in Barton, 2003), while other patients were described who showed
the opposite pattern of deficit (e.g., Moscovitch, Winocur, &
Behrmann, 1997). These studies also hinted that damage to the
right hemisphere might be necessary for the face-processing impairments to be observed. More recently, event-related potential (ERP),
magnetoencephalography (MEG), and functional neuroimaging
methods have been used to identify the pathways involved in face
processing in the intact brain. These studies have confirmed and

extended findings from brain-injured patients, indicating that a distributed network of regions in the brain mediate face processing: Occipitotemporal regions are important for the early perceptual stages of face processing with more anterior regions, including areas of temporal and frontal cortex and the amygdala, involved in processing aspects such as identity and emotional expression (Adolphs, 2002a, 2002b; Haxby, Hoffman, & Gobbini, 2002). In this section, we focus mainly on the involvement of occipitotemporal cortex and the amygdala because these are the areas for which the most developmental data are available.

OCCIPITOTEMPORAL CORTEX

In adults, a network including the inferior occipital gyrus, the fusiform gyrus, and the superior temporal sulcus is important for the early stages of face processing (Haxby et al., 2002). In this view, the inferior occipital gyrus is primarily responsible for early perception of facial features, while the fusiform gyrus and the superior temporal sulcus are involved in more specialized processing (Haxby et al., 2002). In particular, the fusiform gyrus is thought to be involved in the processing of invariant aspects of faces (such as the perception of unique identity) while the superior temporal sulcus is involved in the processing of changeable aspects (such as perception of eye gaze, expression, and lip movement; Haxby et al., 2002; Hoffmann & Haxby, 2000).

Perhaps the most intensively studied of these regions is an area of fusiform gyrus labeled the fusiform "face area" (Kanwisher, McDermott, & Chun, 1997; Puce, Allison, Asgari, Gore, & McCarthy, 1996). This region is more activated for faces compared to a variety of other objects or body parts (Kanwisher et al., 1997; Puce et al., 1996). While some investigators have argued against the view of face-specific "patches" of cortex and have instead emphasized the distributed nature of the representation of object feature information over the ventral posterior cortex (Haxby et al., 2001), even these authors acknowledge that the response to faces appears unique in certain ways (e.g., extent of activation, modulation by attention; Ishai, Ungerleider, Martin, Haxby, 2000).

Although these studies appear to suggest that particular regions of cortex are devoted specifically to face processing, this interpretation has been questioned. In particular, it has been argued that the supposed "face-specific" cortical areas are not specific to faces per se, but instead are recruited for expert-level discrimination of complex visual patterns, whether they be faces or other classes of object (R. Diamond & Carey, 1986; Gauthier et al., 1999). In support of this view, studies have shown that the fusiform face area is also activated by nonface objects (e.g., cars) if the subjects are experts with that category (Gauthier, Skudlarski, Gore, & Anderson, 2000) and activation in the fusiform face areas increases following training of expertise with a category of visual forms (Gauthier et al., 1999).

Developmental studies can provide important information to constrain the claims of the different sides of this debate. For example, by studying when and how face-specific brain responses emerge, developmental studies can provide some hints as to whether and how much experience might be needed for these responses to emerge. Behavioral studies provide a suggestion that face-processing pathways may be functional from very early in life: newborn babies move their eyes, and sometimes their heads, longer to keep a moving facelike pattern in view than several other comparison patterns (Johnson, Dzuirwiec, Ellis, & Morton, 1991). While there is a debate as to whether this reflects a specific response to facelike configurations or a lower-level visual preference (e.g., for patterns with higher density of elements in the upper visual field; Turati, Simion, Milani, & Umilta, 2002; see also Banks & Ginsburg, 1985; Banks & Salapatek, 1981), there is some agreement among the divergent views that the ultimate result is that facelike patterns are preferred to other arrangements from the first hours to days of life (reviewed in de Haan, Johnson, & Halit, 2003).

While this might seem evidence that face-specific cortical areas are active from birth, the prevailing view is that this early preferential orienting is in fact likely to be mediated by subcortical mechanisms (e.g., superior colliculus; for a review of the evidence, see

Johnson & Morton, 1991), and that cortical mechanisms do not begin to emerge until 2 to 3 months of age. At this early age, cortical areas are thought to be relatively unspecialized (Johnson & Morton, 1991; Nelson, 2001). One possible role of the earlier developing subcortical system is to provide a "face-biased" input to the slower-developing occipitotemporal cortical system, and provide one mechanism whereby an initially more broadly tuned processing system becomes increasingly specialized to respond to faces during development (Johnson & Morton, 1991; Nelson, 2001).

The only functional neuroimaging study to investigate face processing in human infants confirms that occipitotemporal cortical pathways are involved by 2 to 3 months of age. In this study, 2-month-olds' PET activation in the inferior occipital gyrus and the fusiform gyrus, but not the superior temporal sulcus, was greater in response to a human face than to a set of three diodes (Tzourio-Mazoyer et al., 2002). These results demonstrate that areas involved in face processing in adults can also be face-activated by 2 months of age, although they do not address the question of whether these areas are specifically activated by faces rather than other visual stimuli. It is interesting that the superior temporal sulcus, suggested to be involved in the processing of information relevant to social communication, was not activated in this study. One possible explanation is that this was because the stimuli (static, neutral) were not optimal for activating processing in the superior temporal sulcus. However, the observation that activation in the superior temporal sulcus has been found in adults even in response to static, neutral faces (e.g., Kesler-West et al., 2001) argues against this interpretation. It is possible that the superior temporal sulcus plays a different role in the face-processing network in infants than in adults, since in primates, its connectivity with other visual areas is known to differ in infant compared to adult monkeys (Kennedy, Bullier, & Dehay, 1989).

ERP studies support the idea that cortical mechanisms are involved in face processing from at least 3 months of age. However, these studies also suggest that, when cortical mechanisms do become involved in infants' processing of faces, they are less "tuned in" to faces than is the mature system. For example, in two studies it has been shown that face-responsive ERP components are more specific to human faces in adults than in infants (de Haan, Pascalis, & Johnson, 2002; Halit, de Haan, & Johnson, 2003). In adults, the N170, a negative deflection over occipitotemporal electrodes that peaks approximately 170 ms after stimulus onset, is thought to reflect the initial stage of the structural encoding of the face (Bentin, Allison, Puce, Perez, & McCarthy, 1996). Although the location in the brain of the generator(s) of the N170 remains a matter of debate, it is generally believed that regions of the fusiform gyrus (Shibata et al., 2002), the posterior inferior temporal gyrus (Bentin et al., 1996; Shibata et al., 2002) lateral occipitotemporal cortex (Bentin et al., 1996) and the superior temporal sulcus (Henson et al., 2003) are involved. The N170 is typically of larger amplitude and/or has a longer latency for inverted than upright faces (Bentin et al., 1996; de Haan et al., 2002; Eimer, 2000; Itier & Taylor, 2002; Rossion et al., 2000), a pattern that parallels behavioral studies showing that adults are slower at recognizing inverted than upright faces (Carey & Diamond, 1994). In adults, the effect of inversion on the N170 is specific for human faces and does not occur for inverted compared to upright exemplars of nonface object categories (Bentin et al., 1996; Rebai Poiroux, Bernard, & Lalonde, 2001; Rossion et al., 2000), even animal (monkey) faces (de Haan et al., 2002).

Developmental studies have identified two components, the N290 and the P400, believed to be the precursors of the N170 (see Figure 8.1). Both components are maximal over posterior cortex, with the N290 peaking at about 290 ms after stimulus onset and the P400 about 100 ms later. The N290 shows an adult-like modulation of amplitude by stimulus inversion by 12 months of age: inversion increases the amplitude of the N290 for human but not monkey faces (Halit et al., 2003, Figure 5.1). The P400 has a quicker latency for faces compared to objects by 6 months of age (de Haan & Nelson, 1999) and shows an adult-like effect of stimulus inversion on peak latency by 12 months of age: It is of longer latency for inverted than upright human faces but does not differ for inverted compared to upright monkey faces (Halit et al., 2003). At 3 and 6 months, the N290 is unaffected by inversion and the P400, while modulated by inversion,

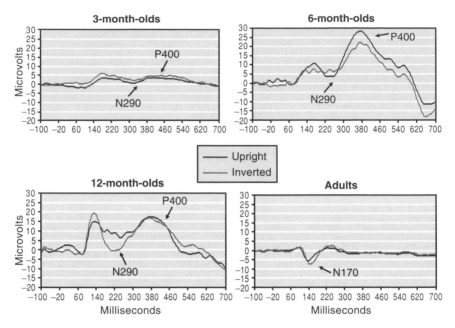

Figure 8.1   Face-specific components observed across the first year of life, and in adults, tested in the same ERP paradigm. Source: *Adapted from "Cortical Specialization for Face Processing: Face Sensitive-Event Related Potential Components in 3- and 12-Month-Old Infants," by H. Halit, M. de Haan, and M. H. Johnson, 2003,* NeuroImage, 19, *pp. 1180–1193; "Specialization of Neural Mechanisms Underlying Face Recognition in Human Infants," by M. de Haan, O. Pascalis, and M. H. Johnson, 2002,* Journal of Cognitive Neuroscience, 14(2), *pp. 199–209.*

does not show effects specific to human faces (de Haan et al., 2002; Halit et al., 2003). Overall, these findings suggest that there is a gradual emergence of face-selective responding over the first year of life (and beyond). This finding is consistent with results of a behavioral study showing a decrease in discrimination abilities for non-human faces with age: 6-month-olds can discriminate between individual humans and monkeys, while 9-month-olds and adults tested with the same procedure discriminate only between individual human faces (Pascalis, de Haan, & Nelson, 2002). The results also suggest that the structural encoding of faces may be dispersed over a longer period of time in infants rather than adults. It is possible that, as the processes become more automated, they are carried out more quickly and/or in parallel rather than serial fashion.

The spatial distribution of the N170 and P400 both change from 3 to 12 months, with maxima shifting laterally for both components (de Haan et al., 2002, 2003). In addition, the maxima of these components appear more superior than in adults, a result consistent with studies in children finding a shift from superior to inferior maximum of the N170 with age (Taylor, Edmonds, McCarthy, & Allison, 2001; Taylor, Itier, Allison, & Edmonds, 2001). This might reflect a change in the configuration of generators underlying these components with age.

Investigations with older children also support the view of a gradual specialization of face processing. ERP studies suggest that there are gradual, quantitiative improvements in face processing from 4 to 15 years of age rather than stagelike shifts (Taylor, McCarthy, Saliba, & Degiovanni, 1999). The ERP studies also provide evidence that there is a slower maturation of configural than featural processing: responses to eyes presented alone matured more slowly than responses to eyes presented in the configuration of the face (Taylor, Edmonds, et al., 2001; Taylor, Itier, et al., 2001). There have not been many functional imaging studies of face processing during childhood, but one study examining facial identity processing suggests that there are changes in the network activated in 10- to 12-year-olds compared to adults (Passarotti et al., 2003). Children showed a more distributed pattern of activation compared to adults (see Figure 8.2). In the right hemisphere, children tended to show more activation in lateral areas of the fusiform gyrus than did adults and, in the left hemisphere, children showed greater lateral than medial fusiform activation whereas adults showed no difference between the two areas. In addition, children showed twice as much activation of the middle temporal gyrus as adults. The authors interpret these results as suggesting that an increased skill is associated with a more focal pattern of activation.

Studies of children with autistic spectrum disorders support the view that atypical activation of occipitotemporal cortex is related to impairments in face processing. Autistic spectrum disorder

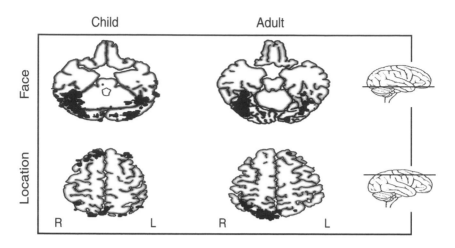

Figure 8.2   fMRI data (BOLD effect) obtained from children and adults in a face-processing task. Source: *From "Development of Face and Location Processing: An fMRI Study," by A. M. Passarotti, B. M. Paul, J. R. Bussiere, R. B. Buxton, E. C. Wong, and J. Stiles, 2003,* Developmental Science, 6, *pp. 100–117.*

is characterized by impairments in processing social information in-cluding faces. Functional imaging studies indicate that when indi-viduals with autism or Asperger syndrome view faces, they show a diminished response in the fusiform gyrus compared to controls (Huhl et al., 2003; Pierce, Muller, Ambrose, Allen, & Courchesne, 2001; Schultz et al., 2000) and show an increased activation of object-processing areas in the inferior temporal cortex (Huhl et al., 2003; Schultz et al., 2000). It is possible that this reflects a different processing strategy, in which individuals with autism focus more on featural rather than configural information in the face. In other words, individuals with autism may rely more on general purpose object-processing pathways rather than specialized face-processing pathways when viewing faces.

AMYGDALA

The amygdala is a heterogeneous collection of nuclei located in the anterior temporal lobe (Amaral, Price, Pitkanen, & Carmichael,

1992). Several studies in adults have shown that lesions to the amygdala impair emotion recognition, even when they leave other aspects of face processing intact (e.g., identity recognition; Adolphs, Tranel, Damasio, & Damasio, 1994). Lesion studies also indicate that recognition of fear is particularly vulnerable to such damage (Adolphs et al., 1994, 1999; Broks et al., 1998; Calder et al., 1996). Functional imaging studies in healthy adults and school-aged children complement these findings, with some studies showing that the amygdala responds to a variety of both positive, negative, or neutral expressions (Thomas et al., 2001a, Yang et al., 2002), and other studies suggesting that the amygdala is particularly responsive to fearful expressions (Morris et al., 1996; Whalen et al., 2001).

There is also indirect evidence that the amygdala plays a role in processing facial expressions in infants. Balaban (1995) used the eye-blink startle response (a reflex blink initiated involuntarily by sudden bursts of loud noise) to examine the psychophysiology of infants' responses to facial expressions. In adults, these reflex blinks are augmented by viewing slides of unpleasant pictures and scenes, and they are inhibited by viewing slides of pleasant or arousing pictures and scenes (Lang, Bradley, & Cuthbert, 1990, 1992). Consistent with the adult findings, Balaban found that 5-month-old infants' blinks were augmented when they viewed angry expressions and were reduced when they viewed happy expressions relative to when they viewed neutral expressions. Animal studies indicate that the fear potentiation of the startle response is mediated in part by the amygdala (Davis, 1989; Holstege, Van Ham, & Tan, 1986); these results suggest that by 5 months of age portions of the amygdala circuitry underlying the response to facial expressions may be functional.

There is evidence that early damage to the amygdala may have a more pronounced effect on recognition of facial expressions than damage sustained later in life. For example, in one study of emotion recognition in patients who had undergone a temporal lobectomy for treatment of intractable epilepsy, emotion recognition in patients with early, right mesial temporal sclerosis, but not those with left-sided damage or extra-temporal damage, showed impairments on tests of recognition of facial expressions of emotion but not on comparison tasks of face processing (Meletti et al., 2003). This deficit was most pronounced for fearful expressions, and the degree of deficit was related to the age of first seizure and epilepsy onset.

ROLE OF EXPERIENCE

The studies reviewed in this chapter suggest that the cortical system involved in face processing becomes increasingly specialized for faces throughout the course of development. Several developmental theories propose that experience is necessary for this process of specialization to occur (e.g., Nelson, 2001). Only a few studies have directly examined the role of experience in development of face processing. In one series of studies, the face-processing abilities of patients with congenital cataracts who were deprived of patterned visual input for the first months of life where tested years after this period of deprivation. These patients show normal processing of featural information (e.g., subtle differences in the shape of the eyes and mouth), but show impairments in processing configural information (i.e., the spacing of features within the face; Le Grand et al., 2001; Geldart, Mondloch, Maurer, deSchonen, & Brent, 2002). This pattern was specific to faces in that both featural and configural aspects of geometric patterns were processed normally (Le Grand et al., 2001). Moreover, when patients were examined whose visual input had been restricted mainly to one hemisphere during infancy, it was found that visual input to the right hemisphere, but not the left hemisphere, was critical for expert level of face processing to develop (Le Grand, Mondloch, Maurer, & Brent, 2003). These studies suggest that visual input during early infancy is necessary for the normal development of at least some aspects of face processing.

Another way in which the role of experience has been investigated is by studying children who experience atypical early emotional environments. For example, Pollak and colleagues have found that perception of the facial expression of anger, but not other expressions, is altered in children who are abused by their parents. Specifically, they report that, compared to nonabused children, abused children show a response bias for anger (Pollak, Cicchetti, Hornung, & Reed, 2000), identify anger based on less perceptual input (Pollak & Sinha, 2002), and show altered category boundaries for anger (Pollak & Kistler, 2002). Similarly, Parker, Nelson, and colleagues (2005) have shown that early components of the ERP among children abandoned at birth and living in institutions in Bucharest, Romania, differ from those of noninstitutionalized children. These results suggest that atypical frequency and content of their emotional interactions with their caregivers results in a change in the basic perception of emotional expressions in abused children.

IS THERE A VISUOSPATIAL MODULE?

There are different perspectives regarding whether visuospatial processing is mediated by a specific module in the brain. According to the innate modularity view, the cognitive modules observed in adults are genetically specified and are already present from the beginnings of development. This view predicts that, even early in development, one or more modules can be impaired without affecting other modules. Williams syndrome, together with another developmental disorder called Specific Language Impairment (SLI), provides support for this view. In Williams syndrome, language is a strength in spite of lowered intellect; in SLI, language is impaired in spite of normal intellect. The double dissociation of language and general intellect across the two developmental disorders is taken by some to support the view that there is a language module that can be selectively spared or impaired. Also consistent with this view is the finding that LIMK1 hemizygosity in Williams syndrome is related to impaired visuospatial constructive cognition (Frangiskakis et al., 1996).

An opposing view is that the brain is not initially organized into distinct modules and only becomes so during development as an emergent property of both biological maturation and experience in the environment. One piece of evidence in support of this view is that the cognitive profile of Williams syndrome is not constant over development. For example, while adults and older children with Williams syndrome show a strength in verbal skills and weakness in number skills, infants show the opposite pattern (Paterson, Brown, Gsodl, Johnson, & Karmiloff-Smith, 1999). This finding is incompatible with the innate modularity view that certain modules are impaired or intact from the start, since it shows that early abilities do not necessarily predict later ones.

Advocates of the innate modularity view might argue that there could still be innate modules, because face processing has been noted as a strength even from early in life in children with Williams syndrome. Moreover, adults with Williams syndrome can achieve near normal performance on standardized tests of face recognition. Could this be an intact innate module? Proponents of the interactive specialization view point out that, if so, face recognition should be accomplished by the same cognitive mechanisms as in typically developing individuals. However, several studies show this is not the case. For example, individuals with Williams syndrome appear to rely less than typically developing children on cues from the configuration of features in the face to recognize identity (Deruelle, Mancini, Livet, Casse-Perrot, & de Schonen, 1999). In addition their ERPs show atypical patterns within the first several hundred milliseconds of processing (Grice et al., 2001). Together, these results argue against the view that the cognitive strengths in Williams syndrome reflect the operation of intact, specific modules.

9

The Development of Social Cognition

Successful navigation of the social world requires numerous skills that typical adults smoothly coordinate on a daily basis. Recently, there has been an increased interest in understanding the neural bases of these social cognitive skills, both with respect to their normal development and their failure when the brain is damaged. This chapter focuses on two related areas of social cognition: (1) processing social information in the face, and (2) theory of mind.

PROCESSING SOCIAL INFORMATION IN THE FACE

The ability to accurately decode information in the face such as identity, emotion, and direction of gaze is an important part of our social interactions in the everyday world (face detection was discussed in Chapter 8). This information is one piece of immediately observable information that we can use to decode others' intention, part of the process of "mentalizing" (see next section). Neuroimaging studies with adults and investigations of adults with brain lesions suggest that a widespread network in the brain contributes to process of the social information conveyed by the face including occipitotemporal cortex, superior temporal sulcus, amygdala, and areas of frontal cortex and somatosensory cortex (reviewed in Adolphs, 2002a; Haxby et al., 2002). In the following sections, we briefly review the development of infants' abilities to process facial information and then turn in more detail to the underlying neural bases.

Neural theories of the early development of face processing have focused primarily on the question of how infants recognize "facedness" (i.e., identify a visual pattern as a face versus something else) and facial identity. A prominent theory is the Conspec/Conlern theory, which argues that a subcortical system involving the superior colliculus functions from birth to orient infants' visual attention to faces (Johnson & Morton, 1991). According to this view, additional cortical systems emerge by 2 months of age that lead to more sophisticated face-processing abilities. For example, at 3 months of age, but not before, infants are able to form an average face prototype from the faces they see (de Haan, Johnson, Maurer, & Perrett, 2001). This is an important development because it provides them with the potential to use their experience of prior faces to guide how they encode new faces.

While there is an ongoing debate as to whether this early apparent bias really reflects orienting to faces or can be accounted for by a lower-level perceptual bias (e.g., Casia, Turati, & Simion, 2004), the resulting tendency to orient to faces, together with other factors that operate to orient babies toward faces (e.g., preferential orienting to familiar voices), may result in the baby receiving a face-biased visual input that helps him or her to quickly learn about faces. Although studies of processing of facial identity suggest that young babies may initially focus on the external features of the face rather than the internal ones that denote expression or direction of gaze (Pascalis, de Schonen, Morton, Deruelle, & Fabre-Grent, 1995), studies looking directly at the latter abilities indicate that even very young infants can detect/discriminate some aspects of social signals communicated by the internal facial features (Farroni, Csibra, Simion, & Johnson, 2004; Field, Cohen, Garcia, & Collins, 1983; Field, Woodson, Greenberg, & Cohen, 1982). Thus, infants' bias for orienting to faces could also promote their sensitivity to aspects of facial information in addition to facial identity.

FACIAL EXPRESSIONS OF EMOTION

Recognition of emotional expressions in the face involves linking the specific perceptual representation of that expression with one of several types of knowledge. In adults, a variety of sources of information are potentially available to contribute to recognition of the meaning of an expression (Adolphs, 2002a, 2002b): (a) knowledge of the verbal label for the expression, (b) conceptual knowledge about the emotion the expression conveys, (c) perceiving the emotional response in oneself that is triggered by seeing an expression, and (d) knowledge about the motor representations required to produce the expression. Infants clearly have fewer sources of information about the meaning of expressions since, for example, they cannot verbally label them. However, young infants do have available some ways of perceiving the social message of facial expressions. Two ways in which young infants might signal at least some level of understanding of the social message conveyed by facial expressions are: (1) the expression may trigger a specific response in the infant, such as facial expressions of his or her own and/or vocalizations and body movements that are consistently related to particular expressions; and (2) the infant may use the facial expressions to regulate his or her behavior (see Soken & Pick, 1999; for further discussion, see de Haan & Groen, 2006).

With respect to the former, two studies have reported that newborns, including those born prematurely, are able to imitate facial expressions of emotion (Field et al., 1982, 1983): Adults viewing videotapes of infants seeing happiness, sadness, or surprise were able to guess at a level above chance which expression the infant was viewing on the basis of the infant's face alone. This could represent an early form of a mechanism that also contributes to adults' recognition of emotion. In adults, the *simulation theory* of expression recognition argues that viewing facial expressions of emotion triggers an emotion response in the perceiver that mirrors the emotion being viewed. In one formulation of this view, seeing an expression triggers an imitation of the expression in the viewer's face, which then would trigger the related emotional state in the viewer and thereby contribute to understanding of the other person's emotional state. Evidence to support this view comes from a variety of sources in adults (reviewed in Adolphs, 2002a, 2002b) including studies showing that: (a) viewing facial expressions results in expressions in one's own face that mimic the expression shown (these may not be readily visible but are detectable in recordings of facial muscle activity; Dimberg, 1982; Hess & Blairy, 2001; Jaencke, 1994), and (b) production of emotional expressions can lead to changes in emotional experience (e.g., Adelman & Zajonc, 1989). Seen in the light of simulation theory, the ability of newborns to imitate facial expressions might reflect the beginnings of one pathway for understanding emotional meaning.

This view is consistent with reports that infants couple their own expressive behaviors to the mother's expression (Trevarthen, 1979), and that during face-to-face interactions mothers complement what the infant is expressing (Legerstee & Varghese, 2001). Alternatively, it has been argued that, at least in very young infants, imitation of facial gestures may not represent imitation of emotion per se, as they are also known to "imitate" very nonspecific actions, such as imitating the looming of a pencil with a tongue protrusion. Some facial gestures that newborns imitate may be a more general reaction to an interesting stimulus rather than an imitation of a specific action or emotional state per se (Jones, 1996).

There is evidence to support the possibility that infants have at least some ability to recognize the social importance of faces and the emotional information they convey even in the first months of life. However, this understanding is based primarily on particular attentional and motoric reactions triggered by the faces and, in this way, their understanding still appears immature. By the second year of life, infants appear to have a more advanced understanding, whereby they can seek out the face as a source of emotional cues and guide their behavior based on the cues perceived (social referencing). This has been assessed in tasks where infants are placed in an ambiguous situation (e.g., a stranger approaching, a novel or unusual toy), and the mother or other adult poses a positive, negative, or neutral expression. The experimenter then observes whether the infant attends to the mother, and whether the mother's posed expression modulates the baby's behavioral or emotional response to the novel stimulus. These types of studies have shown that infants as young as 9 to 12 months are guided by the parents' reactions. However, at this age, the infant's response may be based more on the voice than the face, since infants of the same age show behavioral regulation in response to a voice alone (Mumme, Fernald, & Herrera, 1996) and when they attend to the parent they do not look more at the face than at other parts of the body (Walden & Ogan, 1988). However, during the second year of life, infants begin to show a preference to look directly at the parent's face during these ambiguous situations (Walden & Ogan, 1988) and to guide their behavioral reactions based on their parents' expressions (Walden & Baxter, 1989; Walden & Ogan, 1988). The extent to which infants' understanding of facial expressions in this type of paradigm involves mainly a positive-negative differentiation or involves more specific understanding of different types of positive or negative expressions is not entirely clear.

The ability to recognize facial expressions of emotion continues to develop beyond infancy. Generally, studies of preschool and school-aged children indicated that recognition of a happy expression is most consistent while recognition of a negative expression develops more slowly. However, there have been relatively few studies that have examined children over a wide age span using the same procedure to document precisely the developmental trajectory of this ability throughout childhood.

EYE GAZE

In addition to emotion, another important social cue in the face is direction of eye gaze: For example, "Is someone looking at me? Are they looking at something in the environment that I should take notice of?" Infants are able to notice the difference between direct and averted gaze from the first days of life. In one study, 2- to 5-day-old infants' looking was measured as they viewed a face with averted gaze alongside the face of the same person with direct gaze (Farroni et al., 2002). Of the 17 infants tested, all oriented more times toward the face with direct gaze and 15 looked longer at this face. While these results show that infants are sensitive to direction of gaze from early in life, the ability continues to develop through childhood. For example, one study found that when children were asked to match direction of gaze while ignoring differences in identity and which way the head was facing, performance was not adult-like until 10 years of age (Mondloch, Geldart, Maurer, & de Schonen, 2003a).

There is interest in the development of the ability to perceive direction of gaze in part because use of this cue to share attention with others or direct their attention is considered an important part of social-communicative competence and early language learning. The precise age at which infants first follows another's direction of gaze remains to be determined, but occurs sometime between 6 to 18 months of age (Butterworth & Cochran, 1980; Corkum & Moore, 1995; Scaife & Bruner, 1975). Initially infants will follow another's gaze but not necessarily direct their attention to the object of the other person's attention, but by about 1 year of age they are able accomplish this feat (Carpenter, Nagell, & Tomasello, 1998; but see Slaughter & McConnell, 2003).

NEURAL BASES

As mentioned earlier, in adults the brain network involved in processing social cues in the face includes the occipitotemporal cortex, superior temporal sulcus, amygdala, and areas of frontal cortex and somatosensory cortex (reviewed in Adolphs, 2002a; Haxby et al., 2002). Next we focus on each of these areas in turn, first briefly reviewing the role they play in face processing in adults and then considering how they are integrated into this network during development.

OCCIPITOTEMPORAL REGIONS

Adults

There is a large body of evidence documenting the importance of occipitotemporal regions in face processing (reviewed in Hoffman & Haxby, 2000). These regions appear to be primarily concerned with processing of the stimulus as a face and extracting information relevant to facial identity, rather than specifically processing information related to emotion or direction of gaze. These regions are believed to provide the initial structural representation of the faces that is fed forward to the regions described next to extract these social cues. As is also described in more detail later (see Amygdala section), occipitotemporal regions do likely also receive input from these emotion-related brain areas that modulates their perceptual processing.

Infants and Children

A small number of studies using fMRI or event-related potentials suggest that occipitotemporal cortical pathways are involved in infant face processing by 2 to 3 months of age. The event-related potential studies (ERPs), focusing in the face-sensitive N170 component, provide indirect evidence on this point and are discussed in more detail in Chapter 8. The single fMRI study to examine this in infants, 2-month-olds' activation in the inferior occipital gyrus and the fusiform gyrus, but not the superior temporal sulcus, was greater in response to a human face than to a set of three diodes (Tzourio-Mazoyer et al., 2002). This study demonstrated that areas involved in face processing in adults can also be activated by faces by 2 months of age, although it did not address the question of whether these areas are specifically activated by faces rather than other visual stimuli. Moreover, because this study did not employ neutral faces and did not manipulate direction of gaze, it is not clear what additional activations may have been seen of emotion or direction of gaze had been altered. It is interesting that the superior temporal sulcus, suggested to be involved in the processing of information relevant to social communication, was not activated in this study. One possible explanation is that this was because the stimuli (static, neutral) were not optimal for activating processing in the superior temporal sulcus. It is possible that the superior temporal sulcus plays a different role in the face-processing network in infants than in adults. In primates, for example, its connectivity with other visual areas is known to differ in infant compared to adult monkeys (Kennedy et al., 1989).

SUPERIOR TEMPORAL SULCUS

Adults

In adults, several neuroimaging studies have shown that superior temporal sulcus seems to be involved in processing the direction of eye gaze in a face (Hoffman & Haxby, 2000; Hooker et al., 2003). One study also demonstrated parametrically that increasing proportion of direct gaze related to increased activation of the superior and medial temporal gyri (Calder et al., 2002). Another study confirmed that the superior temporal sulcus is not preferentially activated by moving eyes and mouths rather than moving nonface patterns (Puce, Allison, Bentin, Gore, & McCarthy, 1998; see also Klingstone, Tipper, Ristic, & Ngan, 2004 for results confirming this area responds specifically to direction of eyes rather than directional information generally). Disrupting the function of the superior temporal sulcus using transcranial magnetic stimulation also disrupts detection of eye gaze (but not emotion) in the face (Pourtois et al., 2004).

Individuals with autism, who show difficulties in use of eye gaze to interpret another person's intentions, show atypical modulation of the superior temporal sulcus in that its activation is not influenced by the intentions conveyed by observed shifts of gaze (Pelphrey, Morris, & McCarthy, 2005).

Infants and Children

Relatively little is known regarding the role of the superior temporal regions in infants' and children's processing of facial expressions of emotion or eye gaze. Imaging studies that have investigated the amygdala's response to emotional expressions, for example, have not analyzed these regions. Findings from infant ERP studies examining the infant N170 component have indicated that this component's amplitude is enhanced by direct compared to averted gaze in upright, but not inverted, faces (Farroni, Johnson, & Csibra, 2004; Farroni et al., 2002). By contrast, the N170 in children and adults is not consistently affected by direction of gaze (Taylor, Itier, Allison, & Edmonds, 2001). While some propose that the N170 may be generated by the superior temporal sulcus, others propose regions outside this area (Bentin et al., 1996; Shibata et al., 2002), thus the meaning of these findings with respect to the role of the superior temporal sulcus in the development of processing social cues in the face remains unclear.

AMYGDALA

The amygdala is a heterogeneous collection of nuclei located in the anterior temporal lobe (Amaral, Price, Pitkanen, & Carmichael, 1992). Substantial input to the amygdala comes from the more advanced areas along the ventral "what" visual stream in the temporal cortex, but not from earlier levels in the hierarchy of visual processing. Conversely, projections from the amygdala back to the visual cortex terminate not only in the higher-order visual areas but also in primary visual cortex (Amaral, 2002). In addition to this cortical

127

route, the amygdala also receives projections from a subcortical visual route via the superior colliculus and pulvinar. The subcortical pathway may be involved in rapid, coarse processing of facial expression information that in turn can modulate the cortical pathway that is involved in slower, more detailed analysis (Adolphs, 2002a, 2002b). However, evidence for existence of this pathway comes primarily from studies in the auditory modality. Electrophysiological data provide less support for the involvement of such a pathway in the visual domain. For example, in one study using intracranial electrodes to investigate activity elicited by facial expression in adults, differential activity related to fear began only 200 ms after stimulus onset in the amygdala (Krolak-Salmon, Henaff, Vighetto, Bertand, & Mauguiere, 2004). This late timing is inconsistent with activation of a direct thalamo-amygdalar pathway. This conclusion is echoed in that drawn from studies of scalp-recorded ERPs in response to emotional expressions (Blair, 2003).

Adults

The amygdala has been associated with processing of emotion and social behavior in a variety of tasks in both animals (Amaral, 2002; Bachevalier, 1994; Daenen, Wolterink, Gerrits, & Van Ree, 2002) and human adults (Adolphs, 2002a, 2002b). With respect to humans, several studies have shown that lesions to the amygdala impair recognition of facial expressions of emotion, even when they leave other aspects of face processing intact (e.g., identity recognition; Adolphs, Tranel, Damasio, & Damasio, 1994). Functional imaging studies in healthy adults complement these findings, confirming that the amygdala responds to facial expressions of emotion (Thomas et al., 2001b; Yang et al., 2002). These results might indicate that the amygdala responds generally to emotions, such as sadness, happiness, and fear, all of which serve as primary reinforcers (Blair, 2003). Alternatively, some studies have indicated that recognition of fear seems to be particularly, though not necessarily exclusively, affected following amygdala damage (Adolphs et al., 1994, 1999; Broks et al., 1998; Calder et al., 1996). Some functional imaging studies in healthy adults has shown a similar pattern of circumstances (Morris et al., 1996; Whalen et al., 2001). Whether the amygdala is disproportionately activated by fear compared to other expressions may depend in part on the nature of the task. The results of some studies have suggested that the greater activation to fearful faces may occur only during tasks involving passive or implicit processing of fear (Hariri, Bookheimer, and Mazziotta, 2000), and that when adults are instead required to explicitly label emotions, there is actually a deactivation of the amygdala to fearful faces (Critchley et al., 2000).

The amygdala is also responsive to direct gaze, although it may not play a role in detecting direction of gaze per se. For example, in one study, participants were tested under a condition in which they had to detect directional information from eye gaze and in a separate condition when they had to detect if the eyes in the face were looking directly at them (Hooker et al., 2003). The results showed that the amygdala did not show differential activation in the directional task, but did show greater activation during periods when direct gaze did not occur than during periods when it did occur. This pattern of findings was interpreted as indicating that increases in neural processing in the amygdala facilitate the analysis of gaze cues when a person is actively monitoring for emotional gaze events. These findings are consistent with others suggesting that the amygdala is sensitive to direct eye contact (Kawashima et al., 1999). This sensitivity to the eyes may relate to the amygdala's responsivity to wide-eyed expressions such as fear. A recent study has found that the whites of fearful eyes alone, even when they are presented without other facial information and are subsequently masked and thus not consciously perceived, are sufficient to activate the ventral amygdala (Whalen et al., 2004).

A variety of roles for the amygdala in processing of social information by adults have been proposed, including: (a) providing top-down feedback to early stages of face processing via connections to extrastriate cortex; (b) retrieving conceptual knowledge about the viewed expression via projections to other regions of cortex and medial temporal lobe; and/or (c) triggering emotional responses via connections to motor structures, the hypothalamus, and brain stem nuclei (reviewed in Adolphs, 2002a, 2002b).

The timing of the amygdala's response to emotional stimuli suggests that it might be part of a route for top-down influence on early perceptual processing in the occipitotemporal cortex. For example, using fMRI, George, Driver, and Dolan (2001) found that the correlation between activity in the amygdala and the fusiform gyrus increased when faces with direct gaze were shown. As discussed earlier, direct gaze is thought to be a particular important signal for social interaction, thus these findings show a link between brain regions processing a face as a visual object and those extracting the affective significance of the face. ERP studies in adults have also reported that affective judgments of faces (Pizzagelli et al., 2002) and facial expressions of emotion (Sato, Kochiyama, Yoshikawa, & Matsumura, 2001) might modulate early activity in the occipitotemporal cortex. Thus, one role of the amygdala could be to modulate perceptual representations via feedback. This might contribute to fine-tuning the categorization of facial expression and allocation of attention to certain expression or features within expressions.

Infants and Children

There is suggestive evidence that the amygdala also plays a role in processing facial expressions in infants and children. One line of evidence comes from a study of emotional modulation of the eye-blink startle response in infants. The eye-blink startle response is a reflex blink initiated involuntarily by sudden bursts of loud noise. In adults, these reflex blinks are augmented by viewing slides of unpleasant pictures and scenes, and they are inhibited by viewing slides of pleasant or arousing pictures and scenes (Lang, Bradley, & Cuthbert, 1990, 1992). Based on work in animals, it has been argued that fear-potentiation of the startle response is mediated by the central nucleus of the amygdala, which in turn directly projects to the brainstem center that mediates the startle and efferent blink reflex activity (Davis, 1989; Holstege, Van Ham, & Tan, 1986). Balaban (1995) used a procedure very similar to that used with adults to examine the psychophysiology of infants' responses to facial expressions. Five-month-old infants watched slides depicting eight different adults posing happy, neutral, and angry expressions. Each slide was presented for 6 seconds, followed 3 seconds later by an acoustic startle probe. Consistent with the adult literature, infants' blinks were augmented when they viewed angry expressions and were reduced when they viewed happy expressions, relative to when they viewed neutral expressions. These results suggest that by 5 months of age, at least portions of the amygdala circuitry underlying the response to facial expressions is functional.

Neuroimaging studies of children ranging in age from 8 to 16 years indicate that, unlike adults, typically developing children do not show increased activation of the amygdala to fearful compared to neutral faces (although they do show increased activation relative to fixation; Thomas, Drevets, Dahl, et al., 2001a; Thomas, Drevets, Whalen, et al., 2001b). Children with emotional disorders show atypical patterns: children with anxiety disorders do show an increased response in the right amygdala for fearful versus neutral expressions, while children with depression show a decreased response to fearful faces versus fixation in the left amygdala (Thomas et al., 2001b).

Studies of children with developmental disorders involving deficits in face processing provide converging evidence for the amygdala's role in young children's abilities to recognize facial expressions. For example, autism, a disorder characterized by deficits in language, the presence of stereotypic or repetitive behaviors and social impairments, is associated with impairments in face recognition and anatomical abnormalities in the amygdala (reviewed in Sweeten, Posey, Shekhar, & McDougle, 2002). Individuals with autism are often able to discriminate between faces differing in identity (Hauck, Fein, Maltby, Waterhouse, & Feinstein, 1998), but their performance is impaired on more demanding tasks, or when elements of emotion are included (Davies, Bishop, Manstead, & Tantam, 1994; Tantum, Monaghan, Nicholson, & Stirling, 1989; for review, see Marcus & Nelson, 2001). In addition, individuals with autism seem to use a different, more feature-based, strategy to process faces and facial expressions, suggesting that at least part of their difficulty is in perceptual processing of faces (but see, e.g., Blair, 2003 for a different view). Their processing of faces is associated with atypical neural correlates: The brain regions typically activated in response to faces and facial expressions (e.g., the amygdala, as well as the occipitotemporal cortical regions described earlier) are not activated in individuals with autism when they are viewing these stimuli (Critchley et al., 2000; Pierce, Muller, Ambrose, Allen, & Courchesne, 2001; Schultz et al., 2000). Instead, faces maximally activate aberrant and individual-specific neural sites (e.g., frontal cortex, primary visual cortex, or even inferior temporal gyri that are typically involved in nonface object recognition; Critchley et al., 2000; Pierce et al., 2001). Moreover, individuals with autism pay particular attention to the mouth instead of the eye region of faces (Klin, Jones, Schultz, Volkmar, & Cohen, 2002). Similarly, Baron-Cohen et al. observed that, when required to infer mental state from expression of the eyes alone, individuals with autism showed impaired performance and the typical activation of the amygdala was not observed (Baron-Cohen et al., 1999).

Converging evidence for the role of the amygdala in processing of facial information also comes from Turner syndrome. Individuals with this syndrome have been found to be impaired at face recognition, identification of facial expressions of emotion (especially fear), and processing of displays of the eye region affording social and affective information (Lawrence, Campbell, et al., 2003; Lawrence, Kuntsi, Campbell, Coleman, & Skuse, 2003). As in autism, preliminary structural imaging evidence suggests anatomical abnormalities in the amygdala in these people (Good et al., 2001).

There is evidence that early damage to the amygdala may have a more pronounced effect on recognition of facial expression than damage sustained later in life. For example, in one study of emotion recognition in patients who had undergone temporal lobectomy as treatment for intractable epilepsy, emotion recognition in patients with early, right mesial temporal sclerosis, but not those with left-sided damage or extratemporal damage, showed impairments on tests of recognition of facial expressions of emotion but not on comparison tasks of face processing (Meletti et al., 2003). This deficit was most pronounced for fearful expressions, and the degree of deficit was related to the age of first seizure and epilepsy onset. These results suggest that early damage to the amygdala may have a more severe impact on emotion recognition than late damage.

In summary, evidence from a variety of sources converges to suggest an important role for the amygdala in processing facial expressions of emotion, particularly fearful expressions, at least in adults. Although there is little information regarding the neuroanatomical development of the amgydala in human infants, there is some evidence from studies using the eye-blink startle response and studies examining children with early lesions or developmental disorders to suggest that the amygdala may also play a role in processing facial expression early in life. One possible role the amygdala may play is to provide top-down input into the occipitotemporal areas involved in processing perceptual information in the face. In this way, the amygdala may provide a signal to these regions that mark faces (possibly especially those with direct gaze) and facial expressions as emotionally salient and may play a role in shaping perceptual representations of these categories (Grelotti, Gauthier, & Schultz, 2002). Whether and when the amygdala also begins to play a role in other aspects of emotion processing, such as providing inputs to brain areas storing conceptual knowledge or involved in motor responses, remains unclear.

FRONTAL CORTEX

Adults

Specific regions of the frontal cortex appear to play a role in adults' recognition of facial expressions of emotion. For example, damage to the orbitofrontal cortex (OFC), especially the right, can impair recognition of emotion from the face and voice (Hornak, Rolls, & Wade, 1996), and electrophysiological recordings in patients have shown selectivity for faces over objects (Marinkovic,

Trebon, Chauvel, & Halgren, 2000) and discrimination between happy and fearful facial expressions (Kawasaki et al., 2001) in the right prefrontal cortex. Furthermore, several imaging studies in healthy adults have implicated the prefrontal cortex in emotion recognition, especially when the task requires explicit identification of emotions (Nakamura et al., 1999; Narumoto et al., 2000). It has been proposed that the orbitofrontal cortex is particularly involved in the processing of angry expressions, and that it plays a role in modulation of behavioral responding that is necessary for appropriate reaction to angry faces (Blair, 2003). The orbitofrontal cortex, like the amygdala, may provide top-down influences on early perceptual processing, and links to conceptual knowledge and motor responses (Adolphs, 2002a, 2002b).

Infants and Children

With respect to infants, there are no studies that directly relate orbitofrontal or prefrontal cortex activity to expression recognition, but there is some indirect evidence from EEG studies that could indicate involvement of frontal cortex in emotion recognition early in life. Laterality of EEG recorded over the frontal lobes has been associated with a broad set of emotion-processing situations in adults, children, and infants. In general, activation (as reflected by a decrease in alpha activity) of the left and right frontal regions is associated with positive and negative emotion, respectively. These frontal asymmetries have been interpreted as reflecting a fundamental dichotomy between the two hemispheres in the control of two basic circuits each mediating different forms of motivation and emotion. In one view, the left frontal region is associated with an approach system that facilitates appetitive behavior and generates certain types of positive affect, while the right frontal region is associated with a withdrawal system that facilitates the withdrawal of an individual from sources of aversive stimulation and generates certain forms of negative affect (e.g., fear, disgust; Davidson, 1994, 2000; in Fox, 1994; Gray, 1994; see Dawson, 1994, for a somewhat different formulation of the lateral differences in terms of emotion regulation). Studies with infants suggest that they may show a similar pattern of laterality of frontal activation under a variety of emotion-eliciting circumstances. With regard to the processing of facial expressions, one study (Davidson & Fox, 1982) found that infants of 10 months of age show greater relative left frontal activation in response to happy facial expressions in comparison to sad facial expressions. This result provides some preliminary evidence that at 10 months of age the frontal circuits involved in emotion processing are at least partially active. However, these results are not conclusive because it cannot be firmly concluded that activity recorded over frontal scalp actually originates in the frontal cortex.

OTHER BRAIN AREAS

Two other brain areas that have been implicated in emotion recognition in adults are the basal ganglia and the somatosensory cortex. With respect to the basal ganglia, neuropsychological and neuroimaging studies provide evidence that they are involved in recognition of expressions, particularly for the expression disgust (Adolphs, 2002a, 2002b; Phillips et al., 1997). There is no evidence regarding whether the basal ganglia are also involved in emotion recognition in infants, or indeed whether infants can discriminate or categorize disgust expressions.

With regard to the somatosensory cortex, emotion recognition has been found to be impaired in patients with lesions in the right ventral primary and secondary somatosensory areas, and to a lesser extent in the insula and anterior supramarginal gyrus (Adolphs, Damasio, Tranel, Cooper, & Damasio, 2000). Transcranial magnetic stimulation over the right somatosensory cortex also disrupts emotion (but not gaze) detection (Pourtois et al., 2004). These findings provide some support for the simulation theory discussed earlier. The fact that infants imitate facial expressions of emotion could indicate that this component of the neural system is, at least partly, online at an early age. However, the neural bases of infants' imitative behavior have yet to be determined. Otherwise, there is relatively little information about the role of these regions in infants' processing of social information in the face.

ROLE OF EXPERIENCE

There has been an increased recognition that experience plays a role in the development of processing social information in the face, at least with respect to emotional expressions. If the experience plays an important role in normative development of expression recognition, than infants who experience atypical early emotional environments should show an atypical pattern of abilities. This has been demonstrated by Pollak and colleagues, who have found that perception of the facial expression of anger, but not other expressions, is altered in children who experienced the culturally atypical environment of parental abuse. Specifically, they report that, compared to nonabused children, abused children show a response bias for anger (Pollak, Cicchetti, Hornung, & Reed, 2000), they identify anger based on less perceptual input (Pollak & Sinha, 2002), and they show altered category boundaries for anger (Pollak & Kistler, 2002). These results suggest that atypical frequency and content of their emotional interactions with their caregivers results in a change in the basic perception of emotional expressions in abused children. On this basis, we might predict that exposure to this type of environment during infancy would lead to a different (possibly enhanced) pattern of response to anger in habituation studies.

Another recent study investigated ERPs to fearful, angry, happy, and sad expressions in children aged 7 to 32 months who were receiving institutionalized care and compared them with children of the same age range who had never been institutionalized (Parker, Nelson, et al., 2005a). It was hypothesized that institutionalization during the first months and years of life may deprive the developing brain of normal social experiences that are important for normal development. The results indicated that all components elicited were reduced in amplitude for the institutionalized compared to comparison children, and that the pattern of ERP response elicited by the various emotional expressions (early latency components like the N100 and P250 in particular) differed for the two groups. Although more subtle differences may have been obscured by the wide age range grouped together (ERPs change rapidly during the first years of life), the results reported could indicate an effect of institutionalization on the early perceptual processing of faces.

Another study indicates that variations in social experience could also have an impact on development of emotion recognition in typically developing children (de Haan, Belsky, Reid, Volein, & Johnson, 2004). This study investigated the potential role of experience indirectly by investigating the relationship between the emotional environment provided by the mothers (as indexed by measures of their emotional personality) and 7-month-olds' processing of happy and fearful expressions ERP and looking time responses to faces. The results showed that infants with highly positive mothers looked longer at fearful than happy expressions, and a subset of these infants who themselves also scored highly on positive temperament, showed a larger negative central (Nc) component in the ERP to fearful than happy faces. No relations were found for maternal negativity, although this may have been due to the sample studied which tend to score low on this dimension.

SUMMARY

Research with adults suggest that a brain network involving occipitotemporal cortex, superior temporal regions, amygdala, frontal cortex, and somatosensory cortex is involved in processing social information, in particular emotions and direction of eye gaze, from the face. Infants show sensitivity to this social information from very early in life, although mature processing seems to emerge only after a more protracted developmental course. Although there is some evidence that at least parts of the adult "social brain" are functioning early in life, this evidence is still limited and it is not clear whether during development these regions function in the same way as in the mature system.

THEORY OF MIND

Theory of mind, or *mentalizing,* refers to the ability to detect others' mental states (beliefs, desires, intentions) and use them to predict or explain their actions. Theory of mind is often broken down into a set of subabilities, such as processing belief contents or decoding mental states versus reasoning about goals and actions (Sabbagh, 2004; Saxe, Carey, & Kanwisher, 2004; Tager-Flusberg, 2001), or as a representational system for representing beliefs and desires versus an inhibitory selection process that enables successful reasoning (Leslie, Friedman, & German, 2004). The ability to attribute mental states is typically thought to emerge before the ability to reason about goals and actions (Sabbagh, 2004; Saxe et al., 2004). Some also note a "true-belief default" (Leslie et al., 2004) whereby usually the best guess about someone else's belief is that they are the same as one's own. Other argue that this bias is like the "curse of knowledge" phenomenon observed in adults, and that children's difficulties with theory of mind tasks are a manifestation of this same cognitive bias (Birch & Bloom, 2004).

The strongest evidence that one understands another person's thoughts or beliefs and how they would influence behavior is the ability to predict another's actions/thoughts when they differ from one's own. This ability is often assessed using "false-belief" tasks. In the typical false-belief task (Wimmer, & Perner, 1983), Max has some chocolate, puts it away in a blue cupboard and leaves. Then his mother comes in and moves it to a green cupboard. Max comes back to get his chocolate. The question is, "Where will Max look for the candy?" or "Where does Max think the candy is?" The correct answer is that Max will look in the blue cupboard because he believes the chocolate still to be there. However, children younger than 3 to 4 years typically answer that Max will look in the green cupboard. The explanation is that, since these children know where the candy is, they incorrectly attribute to Max the same knowledge.

This basic phenomenon has been well replicated; however, the major question often debated in the field is, what underlies this developmental change? Is it the acquisition of a new specific ability to

mentally represent other's beliefs (Perner, 1993), or is it a consequence of development of other more general skills that allow this
ability to be expressed such as improvements in language (e.g., de
Villiers & Pyers, 2002) or executive function (e.g., Flynn, O'Malley,
& Wood, 2004)? For example, it might be that children older than 3
to 4 pass the task not because they have acquired a new representational ability, but because improvements in inhibitory control allow
them more successfully to inhibit the tendency to focus on a salient
fact (their knowledge of where the candy really is) and focus on the
less salient but correct answer.

Neural Bases

There is an increasing appreciation that a cognitive neuroscience
approach can provide important data relevant to these debates
(Saxe et al., 2004). Neuroimaging data can provide information as
to whether theory of mind is dependent on a domain-specific au-
tonomous core system by examining whether it is mediated by dis-
tinctive neuronal circuitry. In the following sections, four aspects
of the neuronal circuitry believed to be involved in theory of mind
are considered: superior temporal sulcus, medial frontal cortex,
amygdala, and mirror neurons, followed by a discussion of their
development.

Superior Temporal Sulcus

The superior temporal sulcus appears to be involved in processing
information related to eye gaze and facial movement as well as other
stimuli involving biological motion (see earlier discussion, and reviewed in more detail in Puce & Perrett, 2003; although the region
can be activated by static stimuli, too). It is also believed to be an
important part of the neural circuit underlying mentalizing (reviewed in Frith & Frith, 2003) and could be involved in decoding
mental states and/or detection of agency. Generally speaking, the
region seems to be activated when there are sudden changes in complex behavior patterns, a characteristic more likely to be observed in

living things than mechanical ones (Frith & Frith, 2003). There is some disagreement as to whether the areas of the superior temporal sulcus involved in perceiving biological motion are the same as or different from those involved in mentalizing. Some have emphasized the seeming overlap of these two regions (e.g., Calder et al., 2002; Frith & Firth, 2003). However, one study that compared activations to the two types of tasks within the same experiment found that the two regions are distinct: the temporoparietal junction showed activation during false belief stories while the posterior superior temporal sulcus showed activation during viewing of walking actions (Saxe, Xiao, Kovacs, Perrett, & Kanwisher, cited in Saxe et al., 2004).

Medial Frontal Cortex. The medial prefrontal cortex has direct connections with the superior temporal sulcus, and has been found to be activated in many neuroimaging studies of mentalizing (reviewed in Frith & Frith, 2003; Saxe et al., 2004). Damage to this region, particularly on the right, can cause impairments in theory of mind tasks (Shamay-Tsoory, Tomer, Berger, Goldsher, & Aharon-Peretz, 2005).

This region is believed to be involved in reasoning about mental states. However, another possible explanation of this region's activation during tasks involving mentalizing is that it reflects response inhibition, as frontal areas are known to be involved in this skill. One piece of evidence against this view is the lack of relationship between performance of patients with frontal lesions on theory of mind reasoning tasks and measure of inhibition as well as other aspects of executive function (Rowe, Bullock, Polkey, & Morris, 2001; see also Fine, Lumsden, & Blair, 2001; but see Channon & Crawford, 2002, for a link between the two abilities in patients with anterior frontal damage). Similarly, a recent review of the neuroimaging literature concluded that the regions are likely separate (Saxe et al., 2004).

Amygdala. The exact role of the amygdala in theory of mind remains debated. Some argue that it is important both for normal development of theory of mind as well as for normal online mentalizing in adults (e.g., Baron-Cohen et al., 2000), whereas others argue it is mainly important for the former (e.g., Frith & Frith, 2003). One study examined mentalizing abilities in individuals who had lesions of the amygdala arising congenitally or in early childhood with those who had acquired damage in adulthood (Shaw et al., 2004). Participants with early lesions had impairments in higher level mentalizing abilities (e.g., detecting ironic comments) whereas participants with late lesions showed no impairments relative to either healthy or clinically matched control groups.

Mirror Neurons. Mirror neurons are neurons in the monkey ventral premotor cortex that discharge during the execution of goal-directed movements and also when the monkey observes similar actions (Rizzolatti, Fadiga, Matelli, et al., 1996). Neuroimaging studies indicating that the inferior frontal gyrus, among other regions, is also activated by both observed and executed actions, provides evidence that a similar mechanism may operate in humans (Rizzolatti, Fadiga, Fogassi, & Gallese, 2002; Rizzolatti et al., 1996). These data have contributed to the simulation theory of mentalizing, which argues that we understand other peoples' behavior by mentally simulating it.

This aspect of theory of mind may be part of an early developing process. For instance, the neural resonance between observed and executed actions may underlie imitation of facial gestures that has been observed in human neonates. In this view, mirror neurons may provide an early system for beginning to understand that others are like me and may thus underlie development of mentalizing (Meltzoff & Decety, 2002).

Neural Bases in Development

There are few neuroimaging studies of mentalizing in developing populations, however one recent fMRI examined brain activation while 7- to 13-year-old children viewed animations of triangles moving in an intentional versus random manner (Onishi et al., 2004). The results showed activation in the fusiform gyri, superior temporal sulcus, medial frontal cortex, temporal pole, and inferior parietal cortex. Although the study did not test adults and thus did not allow a direct comparison, the findings indicate that at least aspects of the network activated during adults are also observed in school-aged children.

Other developmental data relevant to this question come from investigations of autism. As mentioned earlier, autism is a developmental disorder that is often apparent early in life and involves a failure to develop normal social interactions, impaired communications and rigidity in behavior. This pattern of symptoms might be accounted for by a fundamental deficit in theory of mind reasoning (Baron-Cohen, Leslie, & Frith, 1985). Indeed, many individuals with autism spectrum disorders have been reported to fail theory of mind tasks (reviewed in Baron-Cohen, 2001) and their performance is not improved by modifications that can make the tasks easier for typically developing children (Surian & Leslie, 1999). Neuroanatomical investigations have not presented a uniform pattern of neuropathology (which perhaps is to be expected given the heterogeneity of the disorder), but abnormalities of the amygdala (Abell et al., 1999; Happe et al., 1996) and medial prefrontal cortex have been reported in several studies (Carper & Courchesne, 2000; Howard et al., 2000). Thus, abnormalities in this circuit during development could underlie the impairments in theory of mind observed in individuals with autism.

CONCLUSIONS

Networks in the brain involving lateral temporal, medial temporal, and ventromedial frontal cortex are involved in processing various aspects of social information. There is some evidence to indicate that some aspects of this network function early in life; however, how the development of this network unfolds and influences, and is in turn influenced by, children's behavior remains to be explicated. In addition, the degree to which these areas are diverse in function and mediate various aspects of information processing and the degree to which there are more fine functional subdivisions that mediate only specific aspects of processing remains a matter of debate.

10

The Development of Higher Cognitive (Executive) Functions

M ost high-level cognitive functions involve executive processes, or cognitive control functions, such as attention, planning, problem solving, and decision making. These processes are largely voluntary (as opposed to automatic) and are highly effortful. Such functions, including selective and executive attention, inhibition, and working memory, are hypothesized to improve with age and/or practice, and to vary with individual differences in motivation or intelligence. These cognitive control processes have been described as providing a "supervisory attention system" (Shallice, 1988)—a system for inhibiting or overriding routine or reflexive behaviors in favor of more controlled or situationally appropriate or adaptive behaviors. Desimone and Duncan (1995) describe this system as an attentional bias that provides a mechanism for attending to relevant information by simultaneously inhibiting irrelevant information (Casey, Durston, & Fossella, 2001). The ability to override a dominant response or ignore irrelevant information is critical in everyday life, as evidenced by the functional impairments associated with chronic inattention, behavioral impulsivity, or poor planning and decision making.

143

Classic lesion cases, such as the famous case of Phineas Gage, indicate that injury to the prefrontal cortex can result in difficulties in behavioral regulation, such as impulsivity and socially inappropriate behavior (Fuster, 1997), as well as disruptions in planning, working memory, and focused attention. Students of cognitive development will recognize these same functions as showing relatively protracted behavioral maturation, often not reaching adult levels of performance until late adolescence (Anderson, Anderson, Northam, Jacobs, & Catroppa, 2001). It may not be surprising therefore that prefrontal cortex shows one of the longest periods of development of any brain region (Diamond, 2002; Luciana, 2003, for reviews). In fact, the relation between prefrontal cortex development and the development of executive functions is probably one of the clearest relations in the developmental cognitive neuroscience literature. However, this does not imply that we fully understand the instantiation of attention, working memory, or inhibition in the brain. Instead, we have significant evidence from lesion and neuroimaging methods to relate subregions of prefrontal cortex to specific aspects of cognitive control in adulthood, as well as a growing body of literature addressing the normative and atypical function of these regions, and their connected networks of structures, in the development of cognitive control. Due to space limitations, only illustrative examples from normative behavioral development, animal models, adult and pediatric neuroimaging studies, and atypical developmental populations are provided here (Casey, Durston, et al., 2001; Diamond, 2002; Luciana, 2003).

DOMAINS OF EXECUTIVE FUNCTION

Many researchers have identified working memory and behavioral inhibition as the primary functions of prefrontal cortex, and by extension, the basic components of executive function (e.g., Diamond, 2001). Working memory has typically been associated with dorsolateral prefrontal cortex (DLPFC; Cohen et al., 1994; Fuster, 1997; Levy & Goldman-Rakic, 2000), while more ventral regions have been implicated in inhibition of a prepotent behavioral response (Casey et al., 1997a; Kawashima et al., 1996; Konishi et al., 1999). Other investigators have parsed their definition of executive functions somewhat differently in an effort to include the voluntary and effortful aspects of attentional control as well as response inhibition. Whatever scheme is used, it is apparent that the classic executive function tasks involve more than one of these aspects of voluntary control or regulation. In the following sections, we provide examples of behavioral tasks thought to tap various aspects of executive function across development, as well as provide select examples as evidence of the role of specific regions of prefrontal cortex in supporting cognitive control. Prefrontal cortex does not act in isolation. Other brain regions are assumed to be integral to the executive function system, providing input and feedback, as well as receiving inputs from prefrontal cortex. Developmental improvements in executive function may arise as much from the development of such functional integration as from the architectural and physiological development of prefrontal cortex (Anderson et al., 2001, Anderson, Levin, & Jacobs, 2002).

VISUOSPATIAL WORKING MEMORY

Working memory is generally thought of as the ability to monitor, process, and then maintain information on a second-by-second basis. It "allows humans . . . to maintain a limited amount of information in an active state for a brief period of time and to manipulate that information" (E. Smith & Jonides, 1998 p. 12061). For adults, the number of items is estimated at 1 to 10 over 0 to 60 seconds (E. Smith & Jonides, 1998).

Working memory is often divided into three components: the central executive that controls and regulates the working memory system and two domain-specific slave systems responsible for processing information in the phonological (phonological loop) or visuospatial (visuospatial sketchpad) form (Baddeley, 1986; Baddeley & Hitch, 1974).

It is clear that visuospatial working memory improves with age into adolescence (e.g., Luciana & Nelson, 2000). One important question is what drives these changes? One factor known to be related to improvements in visuospatial working memory is *phonological encoding*. From about 8 years of age, children increasingly use verbal strategies during visual memory tasks (e.g., object memory), and that improvements in phonological encoding facilitate use of this strategy (Pickering, 2001a, 2001b). However, this cannot completely account for developmental changes in visuospatial working memory because there are also developmental changes on tasks that are more purely visuospatial (e.g., Corsi Blocks; Isaacs & Vargha-Khadem, 1989). These changes may be due to: (a) changes in knowledge base, (b) changes in strategy, (c) changes in processing speed, and (d) changes in attentional focus (reviewed in Pickering, 2001a).

With respect to neural substrates, studies with adults show that a frontoparietal network plays an important role in visuospatial working memory (possibly especially on the right and possibly with a dorsal-ventral distinction in frontal areas for visual versus spatial; Ruchkin et al., 1997; Sala, Rama, & Courtney, 2003). This has been studied mainly for visuospatial but there is some evidence for activation of similar pathways during audiospatial working memory tasks (Martinkauppi, Rama, Aronen, Korvenoja, & Carlson, 2000) though single-cell studies suggest different but parallel populations of neurons are involved (Kikuchi-Yorioka & Sawaguchi, 2000). The visual superior posterior parietal and premotor areas may be involved in rehearsal (that can reactivate rapidly decaying contents of the storage component), while inferior posterior parietal and anterior occipital regions may mediate storage (whose contents decay rapidly; E. Smith & Jonides, 1999). A frontoparietal network also appears to be involved in children (Casey et al., 1995; Kwon, Reiss, & Menon, 2002; Nelson et al., 2000; Thomas et al., 1999; Zago & Tzourio-Mazoyer, 2002). However, there are also changes that occur with development. For example, older children show greater activation in the superior frontal and intraparietal cortex than younger children. Moreover, working memory capacity is significantly correlated with brain ac-

146

tivity in the same regions (Klingberg, Forssberg, & Westerberg, 2002; Kwon et al., 2002). Regions thought to underlie the phonological loop are activated during spatial tasks (Kwon et al., 2002).

These studies thus suggest that increases in working memory are associated with increases in activation in the frontoparietal network. Interestingly, studies with adults also show increase activity in these areas with improvements in working memory following training (Olesen, Westerberg, & Klingberg, 2004). In children, diffusion tensor imaging studies suggest that developmental increases in grey matter activation in frontal and parietal cortex could be due to maturation of white matter connections (Olesen, Nagy, Westerberg, & Klingberg, 2003). Thus, there is evidence of increased activation of the working memory network with increases in age/working memory abilities.

The developmental increases in working memory coincide with the time of several neurodevelopmental processes including a decrease in synaptic density (Bourgeois & Rakic, 1993), axonal elimination (LaMantia & Rakic, 1990), changes in global cerebral metabolism (Chugani & Phelps, 1986), myelination (Paus et al., 1999), and changes in catecholamine receptor structure and density (Lambe, Krimer, & Goldman-Rakic, 2000). The inferior parietal cortex is one of the last areas to myelinate, a change that would increase transmission locally within parietal cortex and also its communication with frontal cortex. This could result in more stable frontoparietal activity during working memory delays and cue periods, and thus less resistance to interference (Klingberg et al., 2002). Synaptic pruning and axonal pruning could also result in less competition with input from other areas leaving the frontoparietal network more stable.

Several developmental disorders also implicate a frontoparietal network in visuospatial working memory. With respect to lesions, right frontal cortex damage at 7 years is related to visuospatial impairments in working memory (Eslinger & Biddle, 2000). Turner's syndrome is associated with deficits in visuospatial working memory (Cornoldi, Marconi, & Vecchi, 2001; Haberecht et al., 2001). In Turner's syndrome, imaging studies show decreased activation in the supramarginal gyrus, dorsolateral prefrontal cortex, and the caudate, with a suggestion that these abnormalities in frontoparietal and frontostriatal circuits are related to poor working memory performance (Haberecht et al., 2001). Individuals with fragile X syndrome are also known to have impairments in visuospatial working memory, and appear to be unable to modulate activation in the prefrontal and parietal cortex in response to an increasing working memory load. These deficits are related to a lower level of fMRP expression in individuals with fragile X syndrome compared to typical subjects (Kwon et al., 2001).

VISUOSPATIAL RECOGNITION AND RECALL MEMORY

In addition to the frontoparietal network implicated in spatial processing and working memory, medial temporal lobe structures, particularly in the right hemisphere, have been implicated in visuospatial memory. The question of whether a similar hemispheric bias exists in children has been investigated in studies of children with unilateral temporal lobe epilepsy. In one study, children who had either early (0 to 5 years) or later (5 to 10 years) onset of seizures were tested with visual and verbal tasks; children with early onset performed generally poorly, while children with later onset showed a material specific pattern of deficit (Lespinet, Bresson, N'Kaoua, Rougier, & Claverie, 2002). Two other studies investigating children following surgical removal of the epilotogenic tissue noted that visuospatial deficits were most pronounced and persistent (Hepworth & Smith, 2002; Mabbott & Smith, 2003).

WORKING MEMORY REDOUX

Perhaps the task most clearly associated with both child development and prefrontal cortex is the classic A-not-B task. In this paradigm (or its close cousin, the delayed response task), an infant or animal watches an object being hidden at one of two identical locations, and after some delay is rewarded for retrieving the object. This task requires both holding information in mind across a delay and, on subsequent trials when the hiding location changes, inhibiting a prepotent tendency to return to a previously correct response location (Diamond, 1985). Animal lesion studies support the importance of DLPFC in successful performance on the A-not-B and delayed response tasks (Diamond & Goldman-Rakic, 1989; Fuster & Alexander, 1970; Goldman & Rosvold, 1970). In addition, electrophysiological studies indicate that cells in this region actively respond during the delay interval, suggesting that DLPFC is involved in the maintenance of information in working memory (Fuster & Alexander, 1971; Funahashi, Bruce, & Goldman-Rakic, 1989). Further investigation demonstrates that lesions to this region impair performance only under delay conditions and not during immediate object retrieval (Diamond & Goldman-Rakic, 1989). Functional imaging studies suggest that developmental differences in working memory function, at least in middle childhood, may be reflected in less efficient or less focal activation of DLPFC. That is, developmental fMRI studies have demonstrated that children activate similar regions of DLPFC compared to adults during both verbal and spatial working memory tasks, but also may activate additional areas of prefrontal cortex, including ventral lateral regions (VLPFC) (Casey et al., 1995; Nelson et al., 2000; Thomas et al., 1999).

INHIBITORY CONTROL

Although working memory has been associated with dorsolateral regions of the prefrontal cortex, the ability to inhibit inappropriate behaviors has typically been associated with ventral medial or orbital frontal cortex (Casey et al., 1997b; Konishi et al., 1999). In adults, lesions to ventral prefrontal cortex lead to impulsive and/or socially inappropriate behavior (Barrash, Tranel, & Anderson, 1994; Damasio, Grabowski, Frank, Galaburda, & Damasio, 1994).

One common developmental test of response inhibition is the go/no-go paradigm. In this task, children are asked to respond to every stimulus *except* one (e.g., all letters except X). The task is designed such that the majority of trials are "go" trials, building up a compelling behavioral response tendency. The child's ability to refrain from making the response at the occurrence of the "no-go" stimulus is used as a measure of inhibitory control. Such behaviors have been shown to increase across the preschool and school-age years (e.g., Ridderinkhof, van der Molen, Band, & Bashore, 1997). Neuroimaging studies using the go/no-go paradigm have demonstrated signal increases in ventral PFC during periods high in inhibitory demand (Casey et al., 1997b; Casey, Forman, et al., 2001), with correspondingly lower levels of activity during periods of low inhibitory demand. Konishi et al. (1999) observed increased ventral PFC activation during no-go trials in an event-related fMRI paradigm. Recent developmental neuroimaging studies have demonstrated both developmental differences in activation of ventral prefrontal cortex (Bunge, Dudukovic, Thomason, Vaidya, & Gabrieli, 2002), with children showing reduced signal compared to adults, and increasing activation of ventral lateral PFC with increasing inhibitory load (Durston, Thomas, & Yang, 2002). Durston and colleagues (2002) showed that behavioral performance on the go/no-go task was significantly correlated with activity in inferior frontal cortex, as well as other prefrontal regions, including the anterior cingulate gyrus (ACC).

Importantly, these same studies highlight the importance of regions beyond the prefrontal cortex. In particular, basal ganglia structures have also been shown to be involved in response inhibition (e.g., Luna et al., 2001), perhaps particularly so for children (Bunge et al., 2002; Casey et al., 1997a; Durston et al., 2002). Children with attention deficit hyperactivity disorder (ADHD) show significantly lower activity in basal ganglia regions during performance of a go/no-go task than typically developing children (Durston et al., 2003; Vaidya et al., 1998) and show high rates of false alarms on the task. Children with ADHD showed additional recruitment of dorsolateral PFC not observed for the control group who performed at a high rate of accuracy (Durston et al., 2003). Interestingly, when taking medication to treat their inattention and impulsivity, children with ADHD show basal ganglia activity equivalent to the typically developing group along with parallel improvements in behavioral performance (Vaidya et al., 1998). Other developmental disorders, such as Tourette syndrome, obsessive-compulsive disorder, and childhood-onset schizophrenia also have been associated with disruption of frontal-striatal circuitry (connections between basal ganglia and frontal cortex) and impaired performance on tasks involving attentional control (see following discussion).

ATTENTIONAL CONTROL

Beyond the general processes of working memory or inhibition, many real-world and experimental tasks require selectively focusing attention on relevant task information while simultaneously suppressing interference from salient but irrelevant or misleading information (Casey, Durston, et al., 2001). Perhaps the most studied adult task of this type is the color-word Stroop paradigm, in which participants are asked to identify the color of ink in which a word is written but, in the case of a color word, have to inhibit a natural tendency to read the word instead (e.g., the word "BLUE" presented in red ink). Neuroimaging data from the Stroop paradigm identify medial prefrontal cortex, specifically the anterior cingulate cortex, as particularly important in detecting (e.g., Botvinick, Braver, Barch, Carter, & Cohen, 2001; Bush, Luu, & Posner, 2000; Bush et al., 1999; Duncan & Owen, 2000; Fan, Flombaum, McCandliss, Thomas, & Posner, 2003; MacDonald, Cohen, Stenger, & Carter, 2000; Posner & Petersen, 1990) and perhaps even resolving this type of attentional conflict.

DLPFC and other regions of prefrontal cortex may also be activated during cognitive conflict depending on demands of the specific task. For instance, in the Simon task, a spatial conflict is created between the location of a stimulus (left or right side of the screen) and the required response (left or right button) (Gerardi-Caulton, 2000). In a study by Fan et al. (2003), this conflict was associated with activation of superior frontal gyrus as well as anterior cingulate cortex while conflict in the Stroop task was associated with activity in ventral lateral prefrontal cortex. When the same adult participants performed the Eriksen flanker task, which requires focusing attention on a central stimulus and actively ignoring competing flanking stimuli, these authors observed attention related activity in premotor cortex. Despite these task-related differences, a conjunction analysis demonstrated overlapping regions of activity in the anterior cingulate gyrus and the left prefrontal cortex across all three tasks, suggesting some common activity related to cognitive control or managing cognitive conflict (Fan et al., 2003). Other neuroimaging studies of the Eriksen flanker task, have indicated that prefrontal cortex is differentially activated based on the degree of cognitive conflict within the same task (Casey et al., 2000; Durston et al., 2003). Durston and colleagues (2003) found that parametric manipulations of conflict on the flanker task were associated with monotonic increases in both DLPFC and ACC. Additional brain regions are activated beyond prefrontal cortex, such as superior parietal cortex, perhaps related to the spatial nature of the task. That is, applying the concept of a "spotlight of attention" (Posner & Raichle, 1997), the flanker task requires narrowing the spatial distribution of attentional focus to reduce interference or conflict from the irrelevant flanking stimuli.

A related aspect of cognitive control arises when the individual is required not only to ignore irrelevant information, but to shift among multiple rules for responding. The classic adult task of this type is the Wisconsin Card Sorting Task (WCST) in which participants must discover the sorting rule simply from positive and negative feedback on their card sorting behavior. Healthy adults show rapid acquisition of the initial sorting rule and quickly alter their behavior when the rule is changed. Lesions to left DLPFC but not other regions of prefrontal cortex impair performance on switching tasks (Keele & Rafal, 2000; Owen et al., 1993; Shallice & Burgess, 1991). Such switching problems are not observed when adults are asked to shift sets within the same dimension, and DLPFC is not increased for such within-dimension shifts. Perhaps not surprisingly, adults with frontal lobe lesions perform very similarly to typically developing 3-year-olds.

Behaviorally, the cognitive control tasks just described show significant developmental changes across early and middle childhood, and in some cases, even into adolescence. Casey, Durston, and Fossella (2001) provide developmental data demonstrating that, for tasks such as the Eriksen flanker and Stroop, adult-like performance is not achieved until early adolescence. In addition, Diamond (2002) highlights the developmental trajectories of other control tasks, including pediatric variants of task switching (dimensional card sort) and the Simon effect. Neuroimaging studies of task switching implicate DLPFC and basal ganglia circuits in task switching and reversal learning (Cools, Clark, Owen, & Robbins, 2002; Cools, Clark, & Robbins, 2004).

To date, few published studies have used neuroimaging techniques to assess developmental changes in the recruitment and efficiency of prefrontal cortex in such cognitive conflict tasks. Therefore, it remains to be seen whether normal functional brain activation in children maps on to the same circuits known to be disrupted in adult lesion populations.

CHAPTER

11

The Development of Attention

The concepts of attentional control and cognitive conflict discussed in Chapter 11 are difficult to apply to the earliest periods of development. Although infant tasks such as the A-not-B or delayed response fall under the broad rubric of executive functions, the majority of infant research on attention involves more basic processes, such as maintaining an alert state and orienting to stimuli in the environment. Though these functions can involve voluntary or controlled processes (Posner & Raichle, 1997), often they reflect automatic or obligatory responses.

ALERTING, VIGILANCE, OR AROUSAL

One major function of the attentional system is to maintain alertness or vigilance (also called arousal). Vigilance processes allow the brain to prepare for upcoming stimuli that may require decision making and/or a behavioral response. Alertness or arousal is associated with improved behavioral performance in a nonspecific or unfocused way (Posner & Raichle, 1997). Although researchers have proposed various neural mechanisms subserving arousal, one common view of arousal is Posner's alerting model, identifying regions of right frontal and parietal cortices and the norepinephrine system as critical players in vigilance (Lewin et al., 1996). In this model, alertness leads to quieting of other activity in the brain via the release of norepinephrine (NE) from the locus coeruleus. The presence of NE is hypothesized to bring on the state of alertness by enhancing the signal-to-noise ratio in regions where it is acting. As alerting-related activity in right frontal cortex increases, activity in the anterior cingulate cortex (ACC), a region associated with target detect, decreases. Posner suggests that this decrease in activity is important for the brain to reduce potential sources of interference during the waiting period prior to the appearance of a target stimulus (Posner & Raichle, 1997). Arousal or sustained attention is associated with decreases in heart rate, both in adults and in infants, reflecting activity of cardioinhibitory centers in the brain, particularly in orbitofrontal cortex (Richards, 2001). Using heart rate measures as an index of the brain's arousal system, Richards and colleagues have demonstrated developmental changes in sustained attention in the first 6 months of life (Casey & Richards, 1988; Richards, 1994). Likewise, certain components of the scalp-recorded event-related potential (ERP) in infancy are thought to reflect automatic alerting responses, particularly in response to novel stimuli (Courchesne, 1978). Richards and colleagues have examined the role of the arousal system in modulating selective attention effects across infancy. For instance, selective attention effects are enhanced during periods of sustained attention (as measured by heart rate deceleration) compared to periods of arousal termination (Richards, 1998). Specifically, eye-blink startle responses are enhanced during periods of both alerting and selective attention. The effects of sustained attention on selective attention show developmental increases from 8 to 26 weeks of age. ERP studies of the response to familiar and novel events in 6-month-olds show that the early negative component (Nc) typically elicited by stimulus novelty is enhanced during periods of sustained attention (as indexed by heart rate deceleration) compared to periods of attention termination (Richards, 1998). However, during sustained attention, the Nc

155

component did not differentiate among familiar and novel stimuli. Instead, during sustained attention, a later component, the positive slow wave (PSW) was enhanced to familiar but infrequently occurring stimuli (Richards, 1998).

ORIENTING

Posner describes both overt and covert forms of orienting, or attentional shifting, in adults (Posner & Raichle, 1997; Posner, Walker, Friedrich, & Rafal, 1984). When a cue stimulus flashes in the periphery, adults tend to automatically shift eye gaze to the periphery (overt attention shift). In contrast, a centrally presented stimulus can cue the individual to orient either overtly (by shifting eye gaze to fixate) or covertly (by shifting attention without shifting eye gaze). Therefore, in adults, centrally presented cues allow the individual to choose to orient in a controlled manner, whereas peripheral cues tend to elicit automatic orienting responses. An extensive neuropsychological literature implicates parietal cortex in the ability to orient attention (e.g., Posner et al., 1984). Specifically, adults with parietal lesions show a deficit in the ability to disengage attention from one stimulus in order to shift attention elsewhere. Single-cell recordings in animals suggest that cells in the thalamus and parietal cortex show increased activity during covert shifts of attention (Robinson, Bowman, & Kertzman, 1995). Lesions in other brain regions can mimic the unilateral behavioral neglect observed with parietal lesions, but do not appear to disrupt covert orienting (Posner et al., 1984). Functional imaging studies of covert orienting in adults show activity in superior parietal cortices, particularly contralateral to the direction of attention (Corbetta, Kincade, Olinger, McAvoy, & Shulman, 2000). In contrast to the inability to disengage attention observed with parietal lesions, damage to the midbrain visual system (superior colliculus) involved in saccadic eye movements leads to difficulty in moving between stimuli, a separate step in visual orienting (Rafal, Posner, Friedman, Inhoff, & Bernstein, 1988). Finally, damage to the pulvinar (part of the thalamus) yields difficulties in reengaging attention or amplifying the target location once a movement has been made (Danziger, Ward, Owen, & Rafal, 2001).

Several major developments occur in visual orienting behavior that is assumed to reflect development of the brain systems supporting orienting in adults. For example, around 1 month of age, when infants are able to fixate voluntarily on a stimulus, infants experience a period of obligatory looking, during which they stare fixedly at objects, and they may have difficulty disengaging their fixation. This obligatory looking can be distressing when a baby becomes fixated on certain strong visual stimuli, like checkerboard patterns, but is very adaptive for forming social bonds when the baby is fixated on the caregiver's face. Obligatory looking disappears around 4 months of age when infants develop more voluntary control of their orienting (Posner & Raichle, 1997). Developments in orienting have been examined using the inhibition of return paradigm. Inhibition of return refers to the tendency to avoid returning attention to a location just previously attended, even if the actual movement is never made. Studies of infants 3, 4, 6, 12, and 18 months of age showed that, although 6- to 18-month-olds showed inhibition of return equivalent to adults, 3- and 4-month-olds showed no evidence of inhibition of return (Clohessy, Posner, Rothbart, & Vecera, 1991; Johnson, Posner, & Rothbart, 1994). This age coincides with behavioral evidence of the development of saccadic eye movements, as well as PET evidence of the age at which parietal metabolism reaches adult levels (Chugani, Phelps, & Mazziotta, 1987). When a cue is too short in duration to elicit an eye movement, 4-month-olds show improved performance for targets presented at the cued location (evidence of covert orienting in infancy; Hood, Atkinson, & Braddick, 1998). The importance of the development of the abilities to disengage, shift, and reengage attention are evident in work addressing infants' abilities to regulate their level of distress. Parents report that around 3 months of age, methods of distracting the child with novel stimuli, which would not be effective without an ability to orient attention, can reduce the infant's distress level. However, as interest and attention wane, the distress returns back to its original level (Harman, Rothbart, & Posner, 1997), suggesting that the reduction of distress is simply a temporary shift of attention.

CONCLUSION

Work in infancy has clearly articulated the origins of the ability to engage and disengage attention. Unfortunately, little is known about these functions between the ages of roughly 18 months and middle childhood; clearly the focus of future research should be on the full elaboration of attentional control from early infancy through adolescence.

CHAPTER

12

———— ❦ ————

The Future of Developmental Cognitive Neuroscience

We now know a considerable amount about the neural bases of a variety of cognitive abilities, although our knowledge base is uneven both between and within developmental periods. For example, we know more about the neural bases of memory in infancy than we do in childhood, and we know more about some executive functions than others (e.g., working memory versus planning).

What does the future have in store for those interested in this area? For starters, as our knowledge of brain development improves, our ability to ground behavior in the brain should similarly improve. This, in turn, should permit more biologically plausible models of behavioral development to be established (connectionist models should in particular benefit from this advance). Second, as our knowledge of neural plasticity and molecular biology increases, we will do a better job of designing studies that shed light on which behaviors are derived from experience-dependent versus experience-independent processes. This, in turn, should lead us away from strongly held nativist beliefs, at least in the context of higher-level cognitive functions. Third, we anticipate a judicious increase in the study of clinical populations because such study has the potential to provide converging information on typical development. Fourth, given increased interest in using neuroimaging tools to study affective development, we anticipate increased interest in linking cognitive and emotional development in the context of brain development. Fifth, increased attention will be paid to the co-registration of imaging modalities, particularly ERPs and fMRI. Sixth, as investigators gain more experience in conducting fMRI studies with children, and as physicists and engineers improve MR scanning parameters, the field should experience a downward shift in the age at which such studies can be performed. In addition, the length of time required to conduct a scan will also decrease. Scanning infants will always prove difficult, but with these changes scanning preschool-age children may prove less challenging.

These are just a few of the areas of growth we anticipate in the coming decade—others will surface as the field evolves. We remain optimistic that interest in linking brain with behavior in the context of development is now firmly entrenched in developmental psychology.

References

Abell, F., Krams, M., Ashburner, J., Passingham, R., Friston, K., Frackowiak, R., et al. (1999). Neuroanatomy of autism: A voxel-based whole brain analysis of structural scans. *NeuroReport, 10*, 1647–1651.

Abrahams, S., Pickering, A., Polkey, C. E., & Morris, R. G. (1997). Spatial memory deficits in patients with unilateral damage to the right hippocampal formation. *Neuropsychologia, 35*, 11–24.

Adelman, P. K., & Zajonc, R. (1989). Facial efference and the experience of emotion. *Annual Review of Psychology, 40*, 249–280.

Adlam, A., Vargha-Khadem, F., Mishkin, M., & de Haan, M. (in press). Deferred imitation in developmental amnesia. *Journal of Cognitive Neuroscience*.

Adolphs, R. (2002a). Neural systems for recognizing emotion. *Current Opinion in Neurobiology, 12*, 169–177.

Adolphs, R. (2002b). Recognizing emotion from facial expressions: Psychological and neurological mechanisms. *Behavioural and Cognitive Neuroscience Reviews, 1*, 21–61.

Adolphs, R., Damasio, H., Tranel, D., Cooper, G., & Damasio, A. R. (2000). A role for somatosensory cortices in the visual recognition of emotion as revealed by three-dimensional lesion mapping. *Journal of Neuroscience, 20*, 2683–2690.

Adolphs, R., Tranel, D., Damasio, H., & Damasio, A. (1994). Impaired recognition of emotion in facial expressions following bilateral damage to the human amygdala. *Nature, 372*, 669–672.

Adolphs, R., Tranel, D., Hamann, S., Young, A. W., Calder, A. J., Phelps, E. A., et al. (1999). Recognition of facial emotion in nine individuals with bilateral amygdala damage. *Neuropsychologia, 37*, 1111–1117.

Agster, K. L., Fortin, N. J., & Eichenbaum, H. (2002). Hippocampus and disambiguation of overlapping sequences. *Journal of Neuroscience, 22,* 5760–5768.

Ahmad, S., Martin, P. E., & Evans, W. H. (2001). Assembly of gap junction channels: Mechanism, effects of calmodulin antagonists and identification of connexin oligomerization determinants. *European Journal of Biochemistry, 268*(16), 4544–4552.

Aizawa, H., Hu, S.-C., Bobb, K., Balakrishnan, K., Ince, G., Gurevich, I., et al. (2004). Dendrite development regulated by CREST, a calcium-regulated transcriptional activator. *Science, 303,* 197–202.

Alvarado, M. C., Wright, A. A., & Bachevalier, J. (2002). Object and spatial relational memory in adult rhesus monkeys is impaired by neonatal lesions of the hippocampal formation but not the amygdaloid complex. *Hippocampus, 12,* 421–433.

Amaral, D. G. (2002). Primate amygdala and the neurobiology of social behavior: Implications for understanding social anxiety. *Biological Psychiatry, 51,* 11–17.

Amaral, D. G., Price, J. L., Pitkanen, A., & Carmichael, T. (1992). Anatomical organization of the primate amygdaloid complex. In J. Aggleton (Ed.), *Amygdala: Neurobiological aspects of emotion, memory, and mental dysfunction* (pp. 1–66). New York: Wiley-Liss.

Anderson, V., Anderson, P., Northam, E., Jacobs, R., & Catroppa, C. (2001). Development of executive functions through late childhood and adolescence in an Australian sample. *Developmental Neuropsychology, 20*(1), 385–406.

Anderson, V., Levin, H., & Jacobs, R. (2002). Executive functions after frontal lobe injury: A developmental perspective. In D. Stuss & R. Knight (Eds.), *Principles of frontal lobe function* (pp. 504–527). New York: Oxford University Press.

Andreassi, J. (1989). *Psychophysiology: Human behavior and physiological response* (2nd ed.). Hillsdale, NJ: Erlbaum.

Ark, W. S. (2002, January). *Neuroimaging studies give new insight to mental rotation.* Proceedings of the 35th Hawaii International Conference on System Sciences.

Astur, R. S., Taylor, L. B., Mamelak, A. N., Philpott, L., & Sutherland, R. J. (2002). Humans with hippocampus damage display severe spatial memory impairments in a virtual Morris water task. *Behavioral Brain Research, 132,* 77–84.

Bachevalier, J. (1994). Medial temporal lobe structures and autism: A review of clinical and experimental findings. *Neuropsychologia, 32*(6), 627–648.

Baddeley, A. (1986). *Working memory.* Oxford, England: Clarendon.

Baddeley, A., & Hitch, G. J. (1974). Working memory. In G. A. Bower (Ed.), *Recent advances in learning and motivation* (Vol. 7, pp. 47–90). New York: Academic Press.

Baddeley, A., Vargha-Khadem, F., & Mishkin, M. (2001). Preserved recognition in a case of developmental amnesia: Implications for the acquisition of semantic memory? *Journal of Cognitive Neuroscience, 13*(3), 357–369.

Baillargeon, R. (1987). Object permanence in 3.5- and 4.5-month-old infants. *Developmental Psychology, 23,* 655–664.

Baillargeon, R., Spelke, E., & Wasserman, S. (1985). Object permanence in 5-month-old infants. *Cognition, 20,* 191–208.

Baird, A. A., Kagan, J., Gaudatte, T., Walz, T. A., Hershlag, N., & Boas, D. A. (2002). Frontal lobe activation during object permanence: Data from functional near infrared spectroscopy. *Neuroimage, 16,* 1120–1125.

Balaban, M. T. (1995). Affective influences on startle in 5-month-old infants: Reactions to facial expressions of emotion. *Child Development, 66,* 28–36.

Banks, M. S., & Ginsburg, A. P. (1985). Infant visual preferences: A review and new theoretical treatment. *Advances in Child Development and Behavior, 19,* 207–246.

Banks, M. S., & Salapatek, P. (1981). Infant pattern vision: A new approach based on the contrast sensitivity function. *Journal of Experimental Child Psychology, 31,* 1–45.

Barinaga, M. (2003). Newborn neurons search for meaning. *Science, 299,* 32–34.

Baron-Cohen, S. (2001). Theory of mind and autism: A review. In L. M. Glidden (Ed.), *International review of research in mental retardation: Autism* (pp. 169–184). San Diego, CA: Academic Press.

Baron-Cohen, S., Leslie, A. M., & Frith, U. (1985). Does the autistic child have a theory of mind? *Cognition, 21,* 37–46.

Baron-Cohen, S., Ring, H. A., Bullmore, E. T., Wheelwright, S., Ashwin, C., & Williams, S. C. (2000). Amydala theory of autism. *Neuroscience and Biobehavioral Reviews, 24,* 355–364.

Baron-Cohen, S., Ring, H. A., Wheelwright, S., Bullmore, E. T., Brammer, M. J., Simmons, A., et al. (1999). Social intelligence in the normal and autistic brain: An fMRI study. *European Journal of Neuroscience, 11,* 1891–1898.

Barrash, J., Tranel, D., & Anderson, S. (1994). Assessment of dramatic personality changes after ventromedial frontal lesions. *Journal of Clinical and Experimental Neuropsychology, 18,* 355–381.

Barton, J. J. (2003). Disorders of face perception and recognition. *Neurologic Clinics, 21*(2), 521–548.

Bates, E., Reilly, J., Wulfeck, B., Dronkers, N., Opie, M., Fenson, J., et al. (2001). Differential effects of unilateral lesions on language production in children and adults. *Brain and Language, 79,* 223–265.

Bates, E., & Roe, K. (2001). Language development in children with unilateral brain injury. In C. A. Nelson & M. Luciana (Eds.), *Handbook of developmental cognitive neuroscience* (pp. 281–307). Cambridge, MA: MIT Press.

Bauer, P. J. (2005). Event memory. In W. Damon, R. Lerner, D. Kuhn, & R. Siegler (Eds.), *Handbook of child psychology: Vol. 2. Cognitive, perception and language* (6th ed.). Hoboken, NJ: Wiley.

Bauer, P. J., Wenner, J. A., Dropik, P. L., & Wewerka, S. S. (2000). Parameters of remembering and forgetting in the transition from infancy to early childhood. *Monographs of the Society for Research in Child Development, 65,* 1–204.

Bauer, P. J., Wiebe, S. A., Carver, L. J., Waters, J. M., & Nelson, C. A. (2003). Electrophysiological indices of long-term recognition predict infants' long-term recall. *Psychological Science, 14,* 629–635.

Benes, F. M. (2001). Development of prefrontal cortex: Maturation of neurotransmitter systems and their interactions. In C. A. Nelson & M. Luciana (Eds.), *Handbook of developmental cognitive neuroscience* (pp. 79–92). Cambridge, MA: MIT Press.

Bentin, S., Allison, T., Puce, A., Perez, E., & McCarthy, G. (1996). Electrophysiological studies of face perception in humans. *Journal of Cognitive Neuroscience, 8*(6), 551–565.

Bernier, P. J., Bédard, A., Vinet, J., Lévesque, M., & Parent, A. (2002). Newly generated neurons in the amygdala and adjoining cortex of adult primates. *Proceedings of the National Academy of Sciences, USA, 99,* 11464–11469.

Birch, S. A. H., & Bloom, P. (2004). Understanding children's and adults' limitations in mental state reasoning. *Trends in Cognitive Sciences, 8,* 255–260.

Bischoff-Grethe, A., Martin, M., Mao, H., & Berns, G. (2001). Context of uncertainty modulates the subcortical response to predictability. *Journal of Cognitive Neuroscience, 13*(7), 986–993.

Bixby, J. L., & Harris, W. A. (1991). Molecular mechanisms of axon growth and guidance. *Annual Review of Cell Biology, 7,* 117–159.

Black, J. E., Jones, T. A., Nelson, C. A., & Greenough, W. T. (1998). Neuronal plasticity and the developing brain. In N. E. Alessi, J. T. Coyle, S. I. Harrison, & S. Eth (Eds.), *Handbook of child and adolescent psychiatry: Vol. 6. Basic psychiatric science and treatment* (pp. 31–53). New York: Wiley.

Blair, R. J. R. (2003). Facial expressions, their communicatory functions and neuro-cognitive substrates. *Philosophical Transactions of the Royal Society of London—Series B: Biological Sciences, 358,* 561–572.

Bloch, F. (1946). Nuclear induction. *Physiological Reviews, 70,* 460–474.

Bloom, F. E., Nelson, C. A., & Lazerson, A. (2001). *Brain, mind, and behavior* (3rd ed.). New York: Worth.

Blum, T., Bauer, R., Arabin, B., Reckel, S., & Saling, E. (1987). Prenatally recorded auditory evoked neuromagnetic field of the human fetus. In C. Barber & T. Blum (Eds.), *Evoked potentials* (pp. 136–142). Boston: Butterworth.

Blum, T., Saling, E., & Bauer, R. (1984). Fetal magnetoencephalography: Pt. 1. 1st prenatal registration of auditory evoked neuromagnetic fields [German]. *Zelektroenzephalogr. Elektromyogry. Ver. Geb.*, *15*, 34–37.

Blum, T., Saling, E., & Bauer, R. (1985). Fetal magnetoencephalographic recordings of the brain activity of a human fetus. *British Journal of Obstetrics and Gynecology*, *92*, 1224–1249.

Booth, J. R., Macwhinney, B., Thulborn, K. R., Sacco, K., Voyvodic, J., & Feldman, H. M. (1999). Functional organization of activation patterns in children: Whole brain fMRI imaging during thee different cognitive tasks. *Progress in Neuro-Psychopharmacology and Biological Psychiatry*, *23*, 669–682.

Booth, J. R., Macwhinney, B., Thulborn, K. R., Sacco, K., Voyvodic, J., & Feldman, H. M. (2000). Developmental and lesion effects in brain activation during sentence comprehension and mental rotation. *Developmental Neuropsychology*, *18*, 139–169.

Botvinick, M., Braver, T., Barch, D., Carter, C., & Cohen, J. (2001). Conflict monitoring and cognitive control. *Psychological Review*, *108*(3), 624–652.

Bourgeois, J.-P., & Rakic, P. (1993). Changes of synaptic density in the primary visual cortex of the macaque monkey from fetal to adult stage. *Journal of Neuroscience*, *13*, 2801–2820.

Bourgeois, J.-P., Reboff, P. J., & Rakic, P. (1989). Synaptogenesis in visual cortex of normal and preterm monkeys: Evidence from intrinsic regulation of synaptic overproduction. *Proceedings of the National Academy of Sciences, USA*, *86*, 4297–4301.

Braver, T., Cohen, J., Nystrom, L., Jonides, J., Smith, E., & Noll, D. (1997). A parametric study of prefrontal cortex involvement in human working memory. *NeuroImage*, *5*, 49–62.

Brizzolara, D., Casalini, C., Montanaro, D., & Posteraro, F. (2003). A case of amnesia at an early age. *Cortex*, *39*(4/5), 605–625.

Broks, P., Young, A. W., Maratos, E. J., Coffey, P. J., Calder, A. J., Isaac, C. L., et al. (1998). Face processing impairments after encephalitis: Amygdala damage and recognition of fear. *Neuropsychologia*, *36*(1), 59–70.

Bronner-Fraser, M., & Hatten, M. B. (2003). Neurogenesis and migration. In L. R. Squire, F. E. Bloom, S. K. McConnell, J. L. Roberts, N. C. Spitzer, & M. J. Zigmond (Eds.), *Fundamental neuroscience* (2nd ed., pp. 391–416). New York: Academic Press.

Brown, M., Keynes, R., & Lumsden, A. (2001). *The developing brain*. Oxford, England: Oxford University Press.

Brown, S. A., Warburton, D., Brown, L. Y., Yu, C. Y., Roeder, E. R., Stengel-Rutkowski, S., et al. (1998). Hologrosencephaly due to mutations in ZIC2, a homologue of Drosophila odd-paired. *Nature Genetics*, *20*, 180–193.

Buckner, R., Goodman, J., Burock, M., Rotte, M., Koutstaal, W., Schacter, D., et al. (1998). Functional-anatomic correlates of object priming in humans revealed by rapid event-related fMRI. *Neuron, 20,* 285–296.

Bunge, S., Dudukovic, N., Thomason, M., Vaidya, C., & Gabrieli, J. (2002). Immature frontal lobe contributions to cognitive control in children: Evidence from fMRI. *Neuron, 33*(2), 301–311.

Burrone, J., O'Byrne, M., & Murthy, V. N. (2002). Multiple forms of synaptic plasticity triggered by selective suppression of activity in individual neurons. *Nature, 420,* 414–418.

Bush, G., Frazier, J., Rauch, S., Seidman, L., Whalen, P., Jenike, M., et al. (1999). Anterior cingulate cortex dysfunction in attention-deficit/ hyperactivity disorder revealed by fMRI and the Counting Stroop. *Biological Psychiatry, 45*(12), 1542–1552.

Bush, G., Luu, P., & Posner, M. (2000). Cognitive and emotional influences in anterior cingulate cortex. *Trends in Cognitive Sciences, 4,* 215–222.

Butters, M. A., Kaszniak, A. W., Glisky, E. L., Esllinger, P. J., & Schacter, D. L. (1994). Recency discrimination deficits in frontal lobe patients. *Neuropsychologia, 8,* 343–353.

Butterworth, G., & Cochran, E. (1980). Towards a mechanism of joint visual attention in human infancy. *International Journal of Behavioral Development, 3,* 253–272.

Calder, A. J., Lawrence, A. D., Keane, J., Scott, S. K., Owen, A. M., Christoffels, I., et al. (2002). Reading the mind from eye gaze. *Neuropsychologia, 40,* 1129–1138.

Calder, A. J., Young, A. W., Rowland, D., Perett, D. I., Hodges, J. R., & Etcoff, N. L. (1996). Facial emotion recognition after bilateral amygdala damage: Differentially severe impairment of fear. *Cognitive Neuropsychology, 13,* 699–745.

Canfield, R., Smith, E., Brezsnyak, M., & Snow, K. (1997). Information processing through the first year of life: A longitudinal study using the visual expectancy paradigm. *Monographs of the Society for Research in Child Development, 62*(2).

Carey, S., & Diamond, R. (1994). Are faces perceived as configurations more by adults than children? *Visual Cognition, 1,* 253–274.

Carleton, A., Petreanu, L. T., Lansford, R., Alvarez-Buylla, A., & Lledo, P.-M. (2003). Become a new neuron in the adult olfactory bulb. *Nature Neuroscience, 6,* 507–518.

Carpenter, M., Nagell, K., & Tomasello, M. (1998). Social cognition, joint attention and communicative competence from 9 to 15 months of age. *Monographs of the Society for Research in Child Development, 63,* 1–143.

Carper, R. A., & Courchesne, E. (2000). Inverse correlation between frontal lobe and cerebellum sizes in children with autism. *Brain, 123,* 836–844.

Carver, L. J., Bauer, P. J., & Nelson, C. A. (2000). Associations between infant brain activity and recall memory. *Developmental Science, 3,* 234–246.

Casey, B., Cohen, J., Jezzard, P., Turner, R., Noll, D., Trainor, R., et al. (1995). Activation of prefrontal cortex in children during a nonspatial working memory task with functional MRI. *NeuroImage, 2,* 221–229.

Casey, B., Durston, S., & Fossella, J. (2001). Evidence for a mechanistic model of cognitive control. *Clinical Neuroscience Research, 1,* 267–282.

Casey, B., Forman, S., Franzen, P., Berkowitz, A., Braver, T., Nystrom, L., et al. (2001). Sensitivity of prefrontal cortex to changes in target probability: A functional MRI study. *Human Brain Mapping, 13,* 26–33.

Casey, B., & Richards, J. (1988). Sustained visual attention in young infants measured by with an adapted version of the visual preference paradigm. *Child Development, 59,* 1515–1521.

Casey, B., Thomas, K., Welsh, T., Badgaiyan, R., Eccard, C., Jennings, J., et al. (2000). Dissociation of response conflict, attentional control, and expectancy with functional magnetic resonance imaging (fMRI). *Proceedings of the National Academy of Sciences, USA, 97*(15), 8728–8733.

Casey, B., Trainor, R., Giedd, J., Vauss, Y., Vaituzis, C., Hamburger, S., et al. (1997a). Role of the anterior cingulate in automatic and controlled processes: A developmental neuroanatomical study. *Developmental Psychobiology, 30,* 61–69.

Casey, B., Trainor, R., Orendi, J., Schubert, A., Nystrom, L., Cohen, J., et al. (1997b). A pediatric functional MRI study of prefrontal activation during performance of a go-no-go task. *Journal of Cognitive Neuroscience, 9,* 835–847.

Casia, V. M., Turati, C., & Simion, F. (2004). Can a non-specific bias toward top-heavy patterns explain newborns' face preference? *Psychological Science, 15,* 379–383.

Castellanos, F., Giedd, J., Berquin, P., Walter, J., Sharp, W., Tran, T., et al. (2001). Quantitative brain magnetic resonance imaging in girls with attention-deficit/hyperactivity disorder. *Archives of General Psychiatry, 58,* 289–295.

Castellanos, F., Lee, P., Sharp, W., Jeffries, N., Greenstein, D., Clasen, L., et al. (2002). Developmental trajectories of brain volume abnormalities in children and adolescents with Attention-Deficit/Hyperactivity Disorder. *Journal of the American Medical Association, 288,* 1740–1748.

Chang, K. D., Adleman, N., Dienes, K., Menon, V., & Reiss, A. (2002, October). *fMRI of visuospatial working memory in boys with bipolar disorder.* Poster session presented at the 49th annual meeting of the American Academy of Child and Adolescent Psychiatry, San Francisco, CA.

Changeux, J., & Danchin, A. (1976). Selective stabilization of developing synapses as a mechanism for the specification of neuronal networks. *Nature, 64*(5588), 705–712.

Channon, S., & Crawford, S. (2002). Effects of anterior lesions on performance on a story comprehension test: Left anterior impairment on a theory of mind-type task. *Neuropsychologia, 38*, 1006–1017.

Chechik, G., Meilijson, I., & Ruppin, E. (1999). Neuronal regulation: A mechanism for synaptic pruning during brain maturation. *Neural Computation, 11*(8), 2061–2080.

Cheng, E. F., & Merzenich, M. M. (2003). Environmental noise retards auditory cortical development. *Science, 300*, 498–502.

Chenn, A., & McConnell, S. K. (1995). Cleavage orientation and the asymmetric inheritance of Notch1 immunoreactivity in mammalian neurogenesis. *Cell, 82*, 631–641.

Cheour, M., Ceponiene, R., Lehtokoski, A., Kuuk, A., Allik, J., Alho, K., et al. (1998). Development of language-specific phoneme representations in the infant brain. *Nature Neuroscience, 1*, 351–353.

Cheour, M., Imada, T., Taulu, S., Ahonen, A., Salonen, J., & Kuhl, P. (2004). Magnetoencephalography is feasible for infant assessment of auditory discrimination. *Experimental Neurology, 190*(Suppl. 1), S44–S51.

Cheour, M., Shestakova, A., Alku, P., Ceponiene, R., & Näätänen, R. (2002). Mismatch negativity shows that 3- to 6-year-old children can learn to discriminate non-native speech sounds within two months. *Neuroscience Letters, 325*, 187–190.

Cheour-Luhtanen, M., Alho, K., Sainio, K., Rinne, T., Reinkainen, K., Pohjavuori, M., et al. (1996). Ontogenetically earliest discriminative response of the human brain. *Psychophysiology, 33*, 478–481.

Chugani, H. T., & Phelps, M. E. (1986). Maturational changes in cerebral function in infants determined by 18FDG positron emission tomography. *Science, 231*, 840–843.

Chugani, H., Phelps, M., & Mazziotta, J. (1987). Positron emission tomography study of human brain functional development. *Annals of Neurology, 22*(4), 487–497.

Churchill, J. D., Beckel-Mitchener, A., Weiler, I. J., & Greenough, W. T. (2002). Effects of fragile X syndrome and an FMR1 knockout mouse model on forebrain neuronal cell biology. *Microscopy Research and Technique, 57*, 156–158.

Churchill, J. D., Galvez, R., Colcombe, S., Swain, R. A., Kramer, A. F., & Greenough, W. T. (2002). Exercise, experience and the aging brain. *Neurobiology of Aging, 23*, 941–955.

Cline, H. (2003). Sperry and Hebb: Oil and vinegar? *Trends in Neuroscience, 26*, 655–661.

Clohessy, A., Posner, M., & Rothbart, M. (2002). Development of the functional visual field. *Acta Psychologia, 106*(1/2), 51–68.

Clohessy, A., Posner, M., Rothbart, M., & Vecera, S. (1991). Development of inhibition of return in early infancy. *Journal of Cognitive Neuroscience, 3*(4), 345–350.

Clower, W. T., & Alexander, G. E. (1998). Movement sequence-related activity reflecting numerical order of components in supplementary and presupplementary motor areas. *Journal of Neurophysiology, 80*, 1562–1566.

Cohen, J., Forman, S., Braver, T., Casey, B., Servan-Schreiber, D., & Noll, D. (1994). Activation of prefrontal cortex in a non-spatial working memory task with functional MRI. *Human Brain Mapping, 1*, 293–304.

Cohen, M. S., Kosslyn, S. M., Breiter, H. C., DiGirolamo, G. J., Thompson, W. L., Anderson, A. K., et al. (1996). Changes in cortical activity during mental rotation: A mapping study using functional MRI. *Brain, 119*, 89–100.

Colcombe, S. J., Kramer, A. F., Erikson, K. I., Scalf, P., McAuley, E., Cohen, N. J., et al. (2004). Cardiovascular fitness, cortical plasticity, and aging. *Proceedings of the National Academy of Sciences, USA, 101*, 3316–3321.

Cole, M., & Cole, S. R. (1996) *The Development of Children* (3rd ed.). New York: W.H. Freeman and Company.

Collie, R., & Hayne, H. (1999). Deferred imitation by 6- and 9-month-old infants: More evidence for declarative memory. *Developmental Psychobiology, 35*, 83–90.

Condron, B. (2002). Gene expression is required for correct axon guidance. *Current Biology, 12*, 1665–1669.

Cools, R., Clark, L., Owen, A., & Robbins, T. (2002). Defining the neural mechanisms of probabilistic reversal learning using event-related functional magnetic resonance imaging. *Journal of Neuroscience, 22*(11), 4563–4567.

Cools, R., Clark, L., & Robbins, T. (2004). Differential responses in human striatum and prefrontal cortex to changes in object and rule relevance. *Journal of Neuroscience, 24*(5), 1129–1135.

Corbetta, M., Kincade, J., Ollinger, J., McAvoy, M., & Shulman, G. (2000). Voluntary orienting is dissociated from target detection in human posterior parietal cortex. *Nature Neuroscience, 3*(3), 292–297.

Corkin, S. (2002). What's new with amnesic patient H. M.? *Nature Reviews Neuroscience, 3*, 153–160.

Corkum, V., & Moore, C. (1995). Development of joint attention in infants. In C. Moore & P. J. Dunham (Eds.), *Joint attention: Its origins and role in development* (pp. 61–83). Hillsdale, NJ: Erlbaum.

Cornoldi, C., Marconi, F., & Vecchi, T. (2001). Visuospatial working memory in Turner's syndrome. *Brain and Cognition, 46*, 90–94.

Courchesne, E. (1978). Neurophysiological correlates of cognitive development: Changes in long-latency event-related potentials from childhood to adulthood. *Electroencephalography and Clinical Neurophysiology, 45*, 468–482.

Critchley, H. D., Daly, E., Phillips, M., Brammer, M., Bullmore, E., Williams, S., et al. (2000). Explicit and implicit neural mechanisms for processing of social information from facial expressions: A functional magnetic imaging study. *Human Brain Mapping, 9,* 93–105.

Cycowicz, Y. M. (2000). Memory development and event-related brain potentials in children. *Biological Psychology, 54,* 145–174.

Daenen, E. W. P. M., Wolterink, G., Gerrits, M. A. F. M., & Van Ree, J. M. (2002). Effects of neonatal lesions in the amygdala or ventral hippocampus on social behavior later in life. *Behavioral Brain Research, 136,* 571–582.

Damasio, H., Grabowski, T., Frank, R., Galaburda, A., & Damasio, A. (1994). The return of Phineas Gage: Clues about the brain from the skull of a famous patient. *Science, 264,* 1102–1105.

Danziger, S., Ward, R., Owen, V., & Rafal, R. (2001). Effects of unilateral pulvinar damage in humans on reflexive orienting and filtering of irrelevant information. *Behavioral Neurology, 13*(3/4), 95–104.

Davidson, R. J. (1994). Asymmetric brain function, affective style, and psychopathology: Role of early experience and plasticity. *Development and Psychopathology, 6,* 741–758.

Davidson, R. J. (2000). Neuroscience of affective style. In M. Gazzaniga (Ed.), *New cognitive neurosciences* (2nd ed., pp. 1149–1159). Cambridge, MA: MIT Press.

Davidson, R. J., & Fox, N. A. (1982). Asymmetrical brain activity discriminates between positive versus negative affect in human infants. *Science, 218,* 1235–1237.

Davies, S., Bishop, D., Manstead, A. S. R., & Tantam, D. (1994). Face perception in children with autism and Asperger's syndrome. *Journal of Child Psychology and Psychiatry and Allied Disciplines, 35*(6), 1033–1057.

Davis, M. (1989). Role of the amygdala and its efferent projections in fear and anxiety. In P. Tyrer (Ed.), *Psychopharmacology of anxiety* (pp. 52–79). Oxford, England: Oxford University Press.

Dawson, G. (1994). Development of emotional expression and emotion regulation in infancy: Contributions of the frontal lobe. In G. Dawson & K. Fisher (Eds.), *Human behavior and the developing brain* (pp. 346–379). New York: Guilford Press.

Dean, A. L., Duhe, D. A., & Green, D. A. (1983). Development of children's mental tracking strategies on a rotation task. *Journal of Experimental Child Psychology, 36,* 226–240.

DeBoer, T., Georgieff, M. K., & Nelson, C. A. (in press). Elicited imitation: A tool to investigate the impact of abnormal prenatal environments on memory development. In P. Bauer (Ed.), *Varieties of early experience: Influences on declarative memory development.* Hillsdale, NJ: Erlbaum.

DeBoer, T., Scott, L., & Nelson, C. (2004). Event-related potentials in developmental populations. In T. Handy (Ed.), *Event-related potentials: A methods handbook*. Cambridge, MA: MIT Press.

de Castro, F. (2003). Chemotropic molecules: Guides for axonal pathfinding and cell migration during CNS development. *News Physiological Sciences, 18*, 130–136.

de Haan, M., Bauer, P. J., Georgieff, M. K., & Nelson, C. A. (2000). Explicit memory in low-risk infants aged 19 months born between 27 and 42 weeks of gestation. *Developmental Medicine and Child Neurology, 42*, 304–312.

de Haan, M., Belsky, J., Reid, V., Volein, A., & Johnson, M. H. (2004). Maternal personality and infants' neural and visual responsivity to facial expression of emotion. *Journal of Child Psychology and Psychiatry, 45*, 1209–1218.

de Haan, M., & Groen, M. (in press). Neural bases of infants' processing of social information in faces. In N. Fox & P. Marshal (Eds.), *Development of social engagement: Neurobiological perspectives* Oxford, England: Oxford University Press.

de Haan, M., & Johnson, M. H. (2003). *Cognitive neuroscience of development*. London: Psychology Press.

de Haan, M., Johnson, M. H., & Halit, H. (2003). Development of face-sensitive event-related potentials during infancy: A review. *International Journal of Psychophysiology, 51*, 45–58.

de Haan, M., Johnson, M. H., Maurer, D., & Perrett, D. (2001). Recognition of individual faces and average face prototypes by 1- and 3-month-old infants. *Cognitive Development, 16*, 659–678.

de Haan, M., & Nelson, C. A. (1997). Recognition of the mother's face by 6-month-old infants: A neurobehavioral study. *Child Development, 68*, 187–210.

de Haan, M., & Nelson, C. A. (1999). Brain activity differentiates face and object processing in 6-month-old infants. *Developmental Psychology, 35*, 1113–1121.

de Haan, M., Pascalis, O., & Johnson, M. H. (2002). Specialization of neural mechanisms underlying face recognition in human infants. *Journal of Cognitive Neuroscience, 14*(2), 199–209.

Dehaene, S., Dupoux, E., Mehler, J., Cohen, L., Paulesu, E., Perani, D., et al. (1997). Anatomical variability in the cortical representation of first and second language. *NeuroReport, 8*, 3809–3815.

Dehaene-Lambertz, G., Dehaene, S., & Hertz-Pannier, L. (2002). Functional neuroimaging of speech perception in infants. *Science, 298*, 2013–2015.

Dehaene-Lambertz, G., & Gliga, T. (2004). Common neural basis for phoneme processing in infants and adults. *Journal of Cognitive Neuroscience, 16*, 1375–1387.

Delis, D. C., Roberston, L. C., & Efron, R. (1986). Hemispheric specialization of memory for visual hierarchical stimuli. *Neuropsychologia, 24,* 205–214.

Deruelle, C., & de Schonen, S. (1991). Hemispheric asymmetries in visual pattern processing in infancy. *Brain and Cognition, 16,* 151–179.

Deruelle, C., & de Schonen, S. (1995). Pattern processing in infancy: Hemispheric differences in the processing of shape and location visual components. *Infant Behavior and Development, 18,* 123–132.

Deruelle, C., Mancini, J., Livet, M. O., Casse-Perrot, C., & de Schonen, S. (1999). Configural and local processing of faces in children with Williams syndrome. *Brain and Cognition, 41,* 276–298.

de Schonen, S., & Mathivet, E. (1990). Hemispheric asymmetry in a face discrimination task in infants. *Child Development, 61,* 1192–1205.

Desimone, R., & Duncan, J. (1995). Neural mechanisms of selective visual attention. *Annual Review of Neuroscience, 18,* 193–222.

de Villiers, J., & Pyers, J. E. (2002). Complements to cognition: A longitudinal study of the relationship between complex syntax and false-belief-understanding. *Cognitive Development, 17,* 1037–1060.

Diamond, A. (1985). Development of the ability to use recall to guide action, as indicated by infants' performance on A-not-B. *Child Development, 56,* 868–883.

Diamond, A. (1995). Evidence of robust recognition memory early in life even when assessed by reaching behavior. *Journal of Experimental Child Psychology, 59,* 419–456.

Diamond, A. (2001). A model system for studying the role of dopamine in the prefrontal cortex during early development in humans: Early and continuously treated phenylketonuria. In C. Nelson & M. Luciana (Eds.), *Handbook of developmental cognitive neuroscience* (pp. 433–472). Cambridge, MA: MIT Press.

Diamond, A. (2002). Normal development of prefrontal cortex from birth to young adulthood: Cognitive functions, anatomy, and biochemistry. In D. Stuss & R. Knight (Eds.), *Principles of frontal lobe function* (pp. 466–503). New York: Oxford University Press.

Diamond, A., & Goldman-Rakic, P. (1989). Comparison of human infants and rhesus monkeys on Piaget's A-not-B task: Evidence for dependence on dorsolateral prefrontal cortex. *Experimental Brain Research, 74,* 24–40.

Diamond, R., & Carey, S. (1986). Why faces are and are not special: An effect of expertise. *Journal of Experimental Psychology: General, 115,* 107–117.

Dimberg, U. (1982). Facial reactions to facial expressions. *Psychophysiology, 19*(6), 643–647.

Draganski, B., Gaser, C., Busch, V., Schuierer, G., Bogdahn, U., & May, A. (2004). Changes in grey matter induced by training. *Nature, 427,* 311–312.

Drummey, A., & Newcombe, N. (1995). Remembering versus knowing the past: Children's explicit and implicit memories for pictures. *Journal of Experimental Child Psychology, 59,* 549–565.

Dukette, D., & Stiles, J. (2001). The effects of stimulus density on children's analysis of hierarchical patterns. *Developmental Science, 4*(2), 233–251.

Duncan, J., & Owen, A. (2000). Common regions of the human frontal lobe recruited by diverse cognitive demands. *Trends in Neurosciences, 23,* 475–483.

Durston, S., Hulshoff Pol, H. E., Casey, B. J., Giedd, J. N., Buitelaar, J. K., & van Engeland, H. (2001). Anatomical MRI of the developing human brain: What have we learned? *Journal of the American Academy of Child and Adolescent Psychiatry, 40,* 1012–1020.

Durston, S., Thomas, K., & Yang, Y. (2002). Development of neural systems involved in overriding behavioral responses: An event-related fMRI study. *Developmental Science, 5,* 9–16.

Durston, S., Tottenham, N., Thomas, K., Davidson, M., Eigsti, I., Yang, Y., et al. (2003). Differential patterns of striatal activation in young children with and without ADHD. *Biological Psychiatry, 53*(10), 871–878.

Dworetzky, J. P. (1996). *Introduction to child development* (6th ed.). St. Paul, MN: West Company.

Eichenbaum, H. (2002). *Cognitive neuroscience of memory.* Oxford, England: Oxford University Press.

Eichenbaum, H. (2003). Learning and memory: Brain systems. In L. R. Squire, F. E. Bloom, S. K. McConnell, J. L. Roberts, N. C. Spitzer, & M. J. Zigmond (Eds.), *Fundamental neuroscience* (2nd ed., pp. 1299–1327). New York: Academic Press.

Eichenbaum, H. B., Cahill, L. F., Gluck, M. A., Hasselmo, M. E., Keil, F. C., Martin, A. J., et al. (1999). Learning and memory: Systems analysis. In M. J. Zigmond, F. E. Bloom, S. C. Landis, J. L. Roberts, & L. R. Squire (Eds.), *Fundamental neuroscience* (pp. 1455–1486). New York: Academic Press.

Eimas, P. D. (1975). Auditory and phonetic coding of the cues for speech discrimination of the/r-l/distinction by young infants. *Perception and Psychophysics, 18,* 341–347.

Eimas, P. D., Siqueland, E. R., Jsczk, P., & Vigorito, J. (1971). Speech perception in infants. *Science, 171,* 303–306.

Eimer, M. (2000). Face-specific N170 component reflects late stages in the structural encoding of faces. *NeuroReport, 11,* 2319–2324.

Ekdahl, C. T., Claasen, J.-H., Bonde, S., Kokaia, Z., & Lindvall, O. (2003). Inflammation is detrimental for neurogenesis in adult brain. *Proceedings of the National Academy of Sciences, USA, 100,* 13622–13637.

Elbert, T., Pantev, C., Wienbruch, C., Rockstroh, B., & Taub, E. (1995). Increased cortical representation of the fingers of the left hand in string players. *Science, 270,* 305–307.

Elman, J. L., Bates, E., Johnson, M., Karmiloff-Smith, A., Parisi, D., & Plunkett, K. (1996). *Rethinking innateness: A connectionist perspective on development.* Cambridge, MA: MIT Press/Bradford Books.

Elvevåg, B., & Weinberger, D. R. (2001). Neuropsychology of schizophrenia and its relationship to the neurodevelopmental model. In C. A. Nelson & M. Luciana (Eds.), *Handbook of developmental cognitive neuroscience* (pp. 577–595). Cambridge, MA: MIT Press.

Erickson, C. A., Jagadeesh, B., & Desimone, R. (2000). Clustering of perirhinal neurons with similar properties following visual experience in adult monkeys. *Nature Neuroscience, 3,* 1066–1068.

Eslinger, P. J., & Biddle, K. R. (2000). Adolescent neuropsychological development after early right prefrontal cortex damage. *Developmental Neuropsychology, 18,* 297–329.

Eswaran, H., Preissl, H., Wilson, J. D., Murphy, P., Robinson, S. E., Rose, D. F., et al. (2002a). Short-term serial magnetoencephalography recordings of fetal auditory evoked responses. *Neuroscience Letters, 331,* 128–132.

Eswaran, H., Wilson, J. D., Preissl, H., Robinson, S. E., Vrba, J., Murphy, P., et al. (2002b). Magnetoencephalographic recordings of visual evoked brain activity in the human fetus. *Lancet, 360,* 779–780.

Fan, J., Flombaum, J., McCandliss, B., Thomas, K., & Posner, M. (2003). Cognitive and brain consequences of conflict. *NeuroImage, 18*(1), 42–57.

Farah, M. J., Rabinowitz, C., Quinn, G. E., & Liu, G. T. (2000). Early commitment of neural substrates for face recognition. *Cognitive Neuropsychology, 17,* 117–124.

Farroni, T., Csibra, G., Simion, F., & Johnson, M. H. (2002). Eye contact detection in humans from birth. *Proceedings of the National Academy of Sciences, USA, 99,* 9602–9605.

Farroni, T., Johnson, M. H., & Csibra, G. (2004). Mechanisms of eye gaze perception during infancy. *Journal of Cognitive Neuroscience, 16,* 1320–1326.

Ferguson, J. N., Aldag, J. M., Insel, T. R., & Young, L. J. (2001). Oxytocin in the medial amygdala is essential for social recognition in the mouse. *Journal of Neuroscience, 21,* 8278–8285.

Ferguson, J. N., Young, L. J., Hearn, E. F., Matzuk, M. M., Insel, T. R., & Winslow, J. T. (2000). Social amnesia in mice lacking the oxytocin gene. *Nature Genetics, 25,* 284–288.

Ferraro, F., Balota, D., & Connor, L. (1993). Implicit memory and the formation of new associations in nondemented Parkinson's disease individuals and individuals with senile dementia of the Alzheimer type: A serial reaction time (SRT) investigation. *Brain and Cognition, 21,* 163–180.

Field, T. M., Cohen, D., Garcia, R., & Collins, R. (1983). Discrimination and imitation of facial expressions by term and preterm neonates. *Infant Behavior and Development, 6,* 485–489.

Field, T. M., Woodson, R., Greenberg, R., & Cohen, D. (1982). Discrimination and imitation of facial expressions by neonates. *Science, 218,* 179–181.

Fine, C., Lumsden, J., & Blair, R. J. G. (2001). Dissociation between "theory of mind" and executive functions in a patient with early left amygdala damage. *Brain, 124,* 287–298.

Finney, E. M., Fine, I., & Dobkins, K. R. (2001). Visual stimuli activate auditory cortex in the deaf. *Nature Neuroscience, 4,* 1171–1173.

Flavell, J. H., Miller, P. H., & Miller, S. A. (1993). *Cognitive development* (3rd ed.). Englewood Cliffs, NJ: Prentice-Hall.

Flynn, E., O'Malley, C., & Wood, D. (2004). A longitudinal, microgenetic study of the emergence of false belief understanding and inhibition skills. *Developmental Science, 7,* 103–115.

Fortin, N. J., Agster, K. L., & Eichenbaum, H. B. (2002). Critical role of the hippocampus in memory for sequences of events. *Nature Neuroscience, 5,* 458–462.

Fox, N. A. (1994). Dynamic cerebral processes underlying emotion regulation. *Monographs of the Society for Research in Child Development, 59*(2/3), 152–166.

Francis, D. D., Szegda, K., Campbell, G., Martin, W. D., & Insel, T. R. (2003). Epigenetic sources of behavioral differences in mice. *Nature Neuroscience, 6,* 445–446.

Frith, U., & Frith, C. D. (2003). Development and neurophysiology of mentalizing. *Philosophical Transactions of the Royal Society of London—Series B: Biological Sciences, 358,* 459–473.

Funahashi, S., Bruce, C., & Goldman-Rakic, P. (1989). Mnemonic coding of visual space in the monkey's dorsolateral prefrontal cortex. *Journal of Neurophysiology, 61,* 1–19.

Fuster, J. (1997). *Prefrontal cortex: Anatomy, physiology, and neuropsychology of the frontal lobe* (3rd ed.). Philadelphia: Lippencott-Raven Press.

Fuster, J., & Alexander, G. (1970). Delayed response deficit by cryogenic depression of frontal cortex. *Brain Research, 61,* 79–91.

Fuster, J., & Alexander, G. (1971). Neuron activity related to short-term memory. *Science, 173,* 652–654.

Gadian, D. G., Aicardi, J., Watkins, K. E., Porter, D. A., Mishkin, M., & Vargha-Khadem, F. (2000). Developmental amnesia associated with early hypoxic-ischaemic injury. *Brain, 123*(3), 499–507.

Gage, F. H. (2000). Mammalian neural stem cells. *Science, 287,* 14333–14338.

Gauthier, I., Skudlarski, P., Gore, J. C., & Anderson, A. W. (2000). Expertise for cars and birds recruits brain areas involved in face recognition. *Nature Neuroscience, 3,* 191–197.

Gauthier, I., Tarr, M. J., Anderson, A. W., Skudlarski, P., & Gore, J. C. (1999). Activation of the middle fusiform "face area" increases with expertise in recognizing novel objects. *Nature Neuroscience, 2,* 568–573.

Geldart, S., Mondloch, C. J., Maurer, D., de Schonen, S., & Brent, H. P. (2002). Effect of early visual deprivation on the development of face processing. *Developmental Science, 5*(4), 490–501.

George, N., Driver, J., & Dolan, R. J. (2001). Seen gaze-direction modulates fusiform activity and its coupling with other brain areas during face processing. *NeuroImage, 13,* 1102–1112.

Geraldi-Caulton, G. (2000). Sensitivity to spatial conflict and the development of self-regulation in children 24 to 30 months of age. *Developmental Science, 3,* 397–404.

Giedd, J. N., Blumenthal, J., Jeffries, N. O., Castellanos, F. X., Liu, H., Zijdenbos, A., et al. (1999). Brain development during childhood and adolescence: A longitudinal MRI study. *Nature Neuroscience, 2,* 861–863.

Giedd, J. N., Snell, J. W., Lange, N., Rajapakse, J. C., Casey, B. J., Kozuch, P. L., et al. (1996). Quantitative magnetic resonance imaging of human brain development: Ages 4 to 18. *Cerebral Cortex, 6,* 551–560.

Giedd, J. N., Vatuzis, A. C., Hamburger, S. D., Lange, N., Rajapakse, J. C., Kaysen, D., et al. (1996). Quantitative MRI of the temporal lobe, amygdala, and hippocampus in normal human development: Ages 4 to 18 years. *Journal of Comparative Neurology, 366,* 223–230.

Goldman, P., & Rosvold, H. (1970). Localization of function within the dorsolateral prefrontal cortex of the rhesus monkey. *Experimental Neurology, 29,* 291–304.

Goldman-Rakic, P. S. (1987). Development of cortical circuitry and cognitive function. *Child Development, 58,* 601–622.

Good, C., Elgar, K., Kuntsi, J., Akers, R., Price, C., Ashburner, J., et al. (2001). Gene deletion mapping of the X-chromosome: Human brain mapping. *NeuroImage, 13,* S793.

Gould, E. (2003, July). *Neurogenesis in the adult brain.* Paper presented at the Merck Summer Institute on Developmental Disabilities, Princeton University, Princeton, NJ.

Gould, E., Beylin, A., Tanapat, P., Reeves, A., & Shors, T. J. (1999). Learning enhances adult neurogenesis in the hippocampal formation. *Nature Neuroscience, 2,* 260–265.

Gould, E., & Gross, C. G. (2002). Neurogenesis in adult mammals: Some progress and problems. *Journal of Neuroscience, 22,* 619–623.

Gould, E., Vail, N., Wagers, M., & Gross, C. G. (2001). Adult-generated hippocampal and neocortical neurons in macaques have a transient existence. *Proceedings of the National Academy of Sciences, USA, 98,* 10910–10917.

Grafton, S., Hazeltine, E., & Ivry, R. (1995). Functional mapping of sequence learning in normal humans. *Journal of Cognitive Neuroscience, 7*(4), 497–510.

Gray, J. A. (1994). Three fundamental emotion systems. In P. Ekman & R. J. Davidson (Eds.), *Nature of emotion: Fundamental questions* (pp. 243–247). New York: Oxford University Press.

Greenough, W. T., Juraska, J. M., & Volkmar, F. R. (1979). Maze training effects on dendritic branching in occipital cortex of adult rats. *Behavioral and Neural Biology, 26,* 287–297.

Greenough, W. T., Madden, T. C., & Fleischmann, T. B. (1972). Effects of isolation, daily handling, and enriched rearing on maze learning. *Psychonomic Science, 27,* 279–280.

Grelotti, D. J., Gauthier, I., & Schultz, R. T. (2002). Social interest and the development of cortical face specialization: What autism teaches us about face processing. *Developmental Psychobiology, 40,* 213–225.

Grice, S. J., Spratling, M. W., Karmiloff-Smith, A., Halit, H., Csibra, G., de Haan, M., et al. (2001). Disordered visual processing and oscillatory brain activity in autism and Williams syndrome. *NeuroReport, 12,* 2697–2700.

Grossman, A. W., Churchill, J. D., Bates, K. E., Kleim, J., & Greenough, W. T. (2002). A brain adaptation view of plasticity: Is synaptic plasticity an overly limited concept. In M. A. Hofman, G. J. Boer, A. J. G. D. Holtmaat, E. J. W. Van Someren, J. Verhaagen, & D. F. Swaab (Eds.), *Progress in brain research* (Vol. 138, pp. 91–108). New York: Elsevier.

Haberecht, M. F., Menon, V., Warsofsky, I. S., White, C. D., Dyer-Friedman, J., Glover, G. H., et al. (2001). Functional neuroanatomy of visuo-spatial working memory in Turner syndrome. *Human Brain Mapping, 14,* 96–107.

Hahn, E. (1950). Spin echoes. *Physiological Reviews, 80,* 580–594.

Haith, M., Hazan, C., & Goodman, G. (1988). Expectation and anticipation of dynamic visual events by 3.5-month-old babies. *Child Development, 59,* 467–479.

Halit, H., de Haan, M., & Johnson, M. H. (2003). Cortical specialization for face processing: Face sensitive-event related potential components in 3- and 12-month-old infants. *NeuroImage, 19,* 1180–1193.

Hamilton, R., Keenan, J. P., Catala, M., & Pascual-Leone, A. (2000). Alexia for Braille following a bilateral occipital stroke in an early blind woman. *NeuroReport, 11,* 237–240.

Hanashima, C., Li, S. C., Shen, L., Lai, E., & Fishell, G. (2004). *Foxg1* suppresses early cortical cell fate. *Science, 303,* 56–59.

Happe, F., Ehlers, S., Fletcher, P., Frith, U., Johansson, M., Gillberg, C., et al. (1996). "Theory of mind" in the brain: Evidence from a PET scan study of Asperger syndrome. *NeuroReport, 8,* 197–201.

Hariri, A. R., Bookheimer, S. Y., & Mazziotta, J. C. (2000). Modulating emotional responses: Effects of a neocortical network on the limbic system. *NeuroReport, 11,* 43–48.

Harman, C., Rothbart, M., & Posner, M. (1997). Distress and attention interactions in early infancy. *Motivation and Emotion*, *21*(1), 27–43.

Harris, I. M., & Miniussi, C. (2003). Parietal lobe contribution to mental rotation demonstrated with rTMS. *Journal of Cognitive Neuroscience*, *15*, 315–323.

Hartshorn, K., Rovee-Collier, C., Gerhardstein, P., Bhatt, R., Klein, P., & Aaron, F. (1998). Developmental changes in the specificity of memory over the first year of life. *Developmental Psychobiology*, *33*, 61–78.

Hatten, M. E. (2002). New directions in neuronal migration. *Science*, *297*, 1660–1663.

Hauck, M., Fein, D., Maltby, N., Waterhouse, L., & Feinstein, C. (1998). Memory for faces in children with autism. *Child Neuropsychology*, *4*, 187–198.

Haxby, J. V., Gobbini, M. I., Furey, M. L., Ishai, A., Schouten, J. L., & Pietrini, P. (2001). Distributed and overlapping representations of faces and objects in ventral temporal cortex. *Science*, *293*, 2425–2430.

Haxby, J. V., Hoffman, E. A., & Gobbini, I. M. (2000). Distributed human neural system for face perception. *Trends in Cognitive Sciences*, *4*, 223–233.

Haxby, J. V., Hoffman, E. A., & Gobbini, M. I. (2002). Human neural systems for face recognition and social communication. *Biological Psychiatry*, *51*, 59–67.

Hayes, B., & Hennessy, R. (1996). Nature and development of nonverbal implicit memory. *Journal of Experimental Child Psychology*, *63*, 22–43.

Hayne, H. (2004). Infant memory development: Implications for childhood amnesia. *Developmental Review*, *24*, 33–73.

Hayne, H., Boniface, J., & Barr, R. (2000). Development of declarative memory in human infants: Age-related changes in deferred imitation. *Behavioral Neuroscience*, *114*, 77–83.

Hazeltine, E., Grafton, S., & Ivry, R. (1997). Attention and stimulus characteristics determined the locus of motor sequence encoding: A PET study. *Brain*, *120*, 123–140.

Heindel, W., Salmon, D., Shults, C., Walicke, P., & Butters, N. (1989). Neuropsychological evidence for multiple implicit memory systems: A comparison of Alzheimer's, Huntington's, and Parkinson's disease patients. *Journal of Neuroscience*, *9*(2), 582–587.

Henson, R. N., Goshen-Gottstein, Y., Ganel, T., Otten, L. J., Quayle, A., & Rugg, M. D. (2003). Electrophysiological and haemodynamic correlates of face perception, recognition and priming. *Cerebral Cortex*, *13*, 795–805.

Hepworth, S., & Smith, M. (2002). Learning and recall of story content and spatial location after unilateral temporal-lobe excision in children and adolescents. *Neuropsychology, Development, and Cognition, Section C, Child Neuropsychology*, *8*, 16–26.

Hess, U., & Blairy, S. (2001). Facial mimicry and emotional contagion to dynamic emotional facial expressions and their influence on decoding accuracy. *International Journal of Psychophysiology, 40*(2), 129–141.

Hof, F. A., Geurds, M. P., Chatkupt, S., Shugart, Y. Y., Balling, R., Schrander-Stumpel, C. T., et al. (1996). PAX genes and human neural tube defects: An amino acide substitution in PAS1 in a patient with spina bifida. *Journal of Medical Genetics, 33,* 655–660.

Hoffman, E., & Haxby, J. V. (2000). Distinct representations of eye gaze and identity in the distributed human neural system for face perception. *Nature Neuroscience, 3,* 80–84.

Holdstock, J. S., Mayes, A. R., Cezayirli, E., Isaac, C. L., Aggleton, J. P., & Roberts, N. (2000). A comparison of egocentric and allocentric spatial memory in a patient with selective hippocampal damage. *Neuropsychologia, 38,* 410–425.

Holstege, G., Van Ham, J. J., & Tan, J. (1986). Afferent projections to the orbicularis oculi motoneural cell group: An autoradiographical tracing study in the cat. *Brain Research, 374,* 306–320.

Hood, B., Atkinson, J., & Braddick, O. (1998). Selection-for-action and the development of orienting and visual attention. In J. Richards (Ed.), *Cognitive neuroscience of attention: A developmental perspective* (pp. 219–250). Mahwah, NJ: Erlbaum.

Hooker, C. I., Paller, A., Gitelman, D. R., Parrish, T. B., Mesulam, M.-M., & Reber, P. J. (2003). Brain networks for analyzing eye gaze. *Cognitive Brain Research, 17,* 406–418.

Hornak, J., Rolls, E. T., & Wade, D. (1996). Face and voice expression identification in patients with emotional and behavioral changes following ventral frontal lobe damage. *Neuropsychologia, 34,* 247–261.

Howard, M. A., Cowell, P. E., Boucher, J., Broks, P., Mayes, A., Farrant, A., et al. (2000). Convergent neuroanatomical and behavioral evidence of an amygdala hypothesis of autism. *NeuroReport, 11,* 2981–2985.

Huang, E. J., & Reichardt, L. F. (2001). Neurotrophins: Roles in neuronal development and function. *Annual Review of Neuroscience, 24,* 677–736.

Hubel, D. (n.d.). *Eye, brain, and vision.* Retrieved June 6, 2005, from http://neuro.med.harvard.edu/site/dh/b24.htm.

Huhl, D., Bolte, S., Feineis-Matthews, S., Lanfermann, H., Federspiel, A., Strik, W., et al. (2003). Functional imbalance of visual pathways indicates alternative face processing strategies in autism. *Neurology, 61,* 1232–1237.

Huotilainen, M., Kujala, A., Hotakainen, M., Shestakova, A., Kushnerenko, E., Parkkonen, L., et al. (2003). Auditory magnetic responses of healthy newborns. *NeuroReport, 14,* 1871–1875.

Huttenlocher, P. R. (1994). Synaptogenesis, synapse elimination and neural plasticity in human cerebral cortex. In C. A. Nelson (Ed.), *Minnesota*

Symposia on Child Psychology: Vol. 27. Threats to optimal development—Integrating biological, psychological and social risk factors (pp. 35–54). Hillsdale, NJ: Erlbaum.

Huttenlocher, P. R. (2002). *Neural plasticity: Effects of environment on the development of the cerebral cortex.* Cambridge, MA: Harvard University Press.

Huttenlocher, P. R., & Dabholkar, A. S. (1997). Regional differences in synaptogenesis in human cerebral cortex. *Journal of Comparative Neurology, 387*(2), 167–178.

Huttenlocher, P. R., & de Courten, C. (1987). Development of synapses in striat cortex of man. *Human Neurobiology, 6,* 1–9.

Hynes, R. O., & Lander, A. D. (1992). Contact and adhesive specificities in the associations, migrations, and targeting of cells and axons. *Cell, 68*(2), 303–322.

Incisa della Rocchetta, A., Samson, S., Ehrle, N., Denos, M., Hasboun, D., & Baulac, M. (2004). Memory for visuospatial location following selective hippocampal sclerosis: Use of different coordinate systems. *Neuropsychology, 18,* 15–28.

Isaacs, E., & Vargha-Khadem, F. (1989). Differential course of development of spatial and verbal memory span: A normative study. *British Journal of Developmental Psychology, 7,* 377–380.

Isaacs, E. B., Vargha-Khadem, F., Watkins, K. E., Lucas, A., Mishkin, M., & Gadian, D. G. (2003). Developmental amnesia and its relationship to degree of hippocampal atrophy. *Proceedings of the National Academy of Sciences, USA, 100*(22), 13060–13063.

Ishai, A., Ungerleider, L. G., Martin, A., & Haxby, J. V. (2000). Representation of objects in the human occipital and temporal cortex. *Journal of Cognitive Neuroscience, 12*(Suppl. 2), 35–51.

Itier, R. J., & Taylor, M. J. (2002). Inversion and contrast polarity reversal affect both encoding and recognition processes of unfamiliar faces: A repetition study using ERPs. *NeuroImage, 15*(2), 353–372.

Jaencke, L. (1994). An EMG investigation of the coactivation of facial muscles during the presentation of affect-laden stimuli. *Journal of Psychophysiology, 8*(1), 1–10.

Janowsky, J. S., Shimamura, A. P., & Squire, L. R. (1989). Source memory impairment in patients with frontal lobe lesions. *Neuropsychologia, 8,* 1043–1056.

Jernigan, T. L., Trauner, D. A., Hesselink, J. R., & Tallal, P. A. (1991). Maturation of human cerebrum observed in vivo during adolescence. *Brain, 114,* 2037–2049.

Jessell, T. M., & Sanes, J. R. (2000). Induction and patterning of the nervous system. In E. R. Kandel, J. H. Schwartz, & T. M. Jessell (Eds.), *Principles of neuroscience* (4th ed., pp. 1020–1021). New York: McGraw-Hill.

Johnson, M. H. (1998). Neural basis of cognitive development. In W. Damon, D. Kuhn, & R. S. Siegler (Series Eds.) & D. Kuhn & R. S. Siegler (Vol. Eds.), *Handbook of child psychology: Vol. 2. Cognition, perception and language* (5th ed., pp. 1–49). New York: Wiley.

Johnson, M. H. (2001). Functional brain development in humans. *Nature Reviews Neuroscience, 2,* 475–483.

Johnson, M., de Haan, M., Oliver, A., Smith, W., Hatzakis, H., Tucker, L., et al. (2001). Recording and analyzing high-density event-related potentials with infants: Using the Geodesic sensor net. *Developmental Neuropsychology, 19*(3), 295–323.

Johnson, M. H., Dziurawiec, S., Ellis, H., & Morton, J. (1991). Newborns' preferential tracking of face-like stimuli and its subsequent decline. *Cognition, 40,* 1–19.

Johnson, M. H., & Morton, J. (1991). *Biology and cognitive development: Case of face recognition.* Oxford, England: Blackwell.

Johnson, M., Posner, M., & Rothbart, M. (1994). Facilitation of saccades toward a covertly attended location in early infancy. *Psychological Science, 5*(2), 90–93.

Johnston, S., Leek, E. C., Atherton, C., Thacker, N., & Jackson, A. (2004). Functional contribution of medial premotor cortex to visuo-spatial transformation in humans. *Neuroscience Letters, 355,* 209–212.

Jones, S. S. (1996). Imitation or exploration? Young infants' matching of adults' oral gestures. *Child Development, 67,* 1952–1969.

Jordan, K., Wustenberg, T., Heinze, H. J., Peteres, M., & Jancke, L. (2003). Women and men exhibit different cortical activation patterns during mental rotation tasks. *Neuropsychologia, 40,* 2397–2408.

Kanwisher, N., McDermott, J., & Chun, M. M. (1997). Fusiform face area: A module in human extrastriate cortex specialized for face perception. *Journal of Neuroscience, 17,* 4302–4311.

Kawasaki, H., Adophs, R., Kaufman, O., Damasio, H., Damasio, A. R., Granner, M., et al. (2001). Single-unit responses to emotional visual stimuli recorded in human ventral prefrontal cortex. *Nature Neuroscience, 4,* 15–16.

Kawashima, R., Satoh, K., Itoh, H., Ono, S., Furumoto, S., Grotoh, R., et al. (1996). Functional anatomy of GO/NO-GO discrimination and response selection: A PET study in man. *Brain Research, 728,* 79–89.

Kawashima, R., Sugiura, M., Kato, T., Nakamura, A., Hatano, K., Ito, K., et al. (1999). The human amygdala plays an important role in gaze monitoring. *Brain, 122,* 779–783.

Keele, S., & Rafal, R. (2000). Deficits of task set in patients with left prefrontal cortex lesions. In S. Monsell & J. Driver (Eds.), *Control of cognitive processes, attention and performance* (Vol. 18). Cambridge, MA: MIT Press.

Keith, A. (1948). *Human embryology and morphology*. London: Edward Arnold & Company.

Keller, A., Castellanos, F. X., Vaituzis, A. C., Jeffries, N. O., Giedd, J. N., & Rapoport, J. L. (2003). Progressive loss of cerebellar volume in childhood-onset schizophrenia. *American Journal of Psychiatry, 160*(1), 128–133.

Kennedy, H., Bullier, J., & Dehay, C. (1989). Transient projection from the superior temporal sulcus to area 17 in the newborn macaque monkey. *Proceedings of the National Academy of Sciences, USA, 86,* 8093–8097.

Kesler-West, M. L., Andersen, A. H., Smith, C. D., Avison, M. J., Davis, C. E., Kryscio, R. J., et al. (2001). Neural substrates of facial emotion processing using fMRI. *Brain Research: Cognitive Brain Research, 11,* 213–226.

Kikuchi-Yorioka, Y., & Sawaguchi, T. (2000). Parallel visuospatial and audiospatial working memory processes in the monkey dorsolateral prefrontal cortex. *Nature Neuroscience, 3,* 1075–1076.

King, J. A., Burgess, N., Hartley, T., Vargha-Khadem, F., & O'Keefe, J. (2002). Human hippocampus and viewpoint dependence in spatial memory. *Hippocampus, 12,* 811–820.

Kinsley, C. H., Madonia, L., Gifford, G. W., Tureski, K., Griffin, G. R., Lowry, C., et al. (1999). Motherhood improves learning and memory. *Nature, 402,* 137–138.

Klin, A., Jones, W., Schultz, R., Volkmar, F., & Cohen, D. (2002). Visual fixation patterns during viewing of naturalistic social situations as predictors of social competence in individuals with autism. *Archives of General Psychiatry, 59*(9), 809–816.

Klingberg, T., Forssberg, H., & Westerberg, H. (2002). Increased brain activity in frontal and parietal cortex underlies the development of visuospatial working memory capacity during childhood. *Journal of Cognitive Neuroscience, 14*(1), 1–10.

Klingstone, A., Tipper, C., Ristic, J., & Ngan, E. (2004). The eyes have it! An fMRI investigation. *Brain and Cognition, 55,* 269–271.

Knopman, D., & Nissen, M. (1991). Procedural learning is impaired in Huntington's disease: Evidence from the serial reaction time task. *Neuropsychologia, 29*(3), 245–254.

Knudsen, E. I. (2003a). *Annual report: MacArthur Foundation research network on early experience and brain development.*

Knudsen, E. I. (2003b). Early experience and critical periods. In L. R. Squire, F. E. Bloom, S. K. McConnell, J. L. Roberts, N. C. Spitzer, & M. J. Zigmond (Eds.), *Fundamental neuroscience* (2nd ed., pp. 555–573). New York: Academic Press.

Knudsen, E. I. (2004). Sensitive periods in the development of the brain and behavior. *Journal of Cognitive Neuroscience, 16,* 1412–1425.

Kolb, B., Gibb, R., & Robinson, T. E. (2003). Brain plasticity and behavior. *Current Directions in Psychological Science, 12,* 1–5.

Kolb, B., & Whishaw, I. Q. (1998). Brain plasticity and behavior. *Annual Review of Psychology, 49,* 43–64.

Konishi, S., Nakajima, K., Uchida, I., Kikyo, H., Kameyama, M., & Miyashita, Y. (1999). Common inhibitory mechanism in human inferior prefrontal cortex revealed by event-related functional MRI. *Brain, 122,* 981–999.

Kornack, D. R., & Rakic, P. (1999). Continuation of neurogenesis in the hippocampus of the adult macaque monkey. *Proceedings of the National Academy of Sciences, USA, 98,* 5768–5773.

Kostovic, I. (1990). Structural and histochemical reorganization of the human prefrontal cortex during perinatal and postnatal life. *Progress in Brain Research, 85,* 223–239.

Kozlowski, P. B., Brudkowska, J., Kraszpulski, M., Sersen, E. A., Wrzolek, M. A., Anzil, A. P., et al. (1997). Microencephaly in children congenitally infected with human immunodeficiency virus: A gross-anatomical morphometric study. *Acta Neuropathologica, 93*(2), 136–145.

Kriegstein, A. R., & Götz, M. (2003). Radial glia diversity: A matter of cell fate. *Glia, 43,* 37–43.

Krolak-Salmon, P., Henaff, M.-A., Vighetto, A., Bertand, O., & Mauguiere, F. (2004). Early amygdala reaction to fear spreading in occipital, temporal and frontal cortex: A depth electrode ERP study in human. *Neuron, 42,* 666–676.

Kuhl, P. K. (2004). Early language acquisition: Cracking the speech code. *Nature Reviews Neuroscience, 5,* 831–843.

Kuhl, P. K., Tsao, F. M., & Liu, H. M. (2003). Foreign-language experience in infancy: Effects of short-term exposure and social interaction on phonetic learning. *Proceedings of the National Academy of Sciences, USA, 100,* 9096–9101.

Kujala, A., Huotilainen, M., Hotakainen, M., Lennes, M., Parkkonen, L., Fellman, V., et al. (2004). Speech-sound discrimination in neonates as measured with MEG. *NeuroReport, 15,* 2089–2092.

Kwon, H., Menon, V., Eliez, S., Warsofsky, I. S., White, C. D., Dyer-Friedman, J., et al. (2001). Functional neuroanatomy of visuospatial working memory in fragile X syndrome: Relation to behavioral and molecular measures. *American Journal of Psychiatry, 158,* 1040–1051.

Kwon, H., Reiss, A. L., & Menon, V. (2002). Neural basis of protracted developmental changes in visuo-spatial working memory. *Proceedings of the National Academy of Sciences, USA, 99,* 13336–13341.

Kwong, K., Belliveau, J., Chesler, D., Goldberg, I., Weisskoff, R., Poncelet, B., et al. (1992). Dynamic magnetic resonance imaging of human brain activity during primary sensory stimulation. *Proceedings of the National Academy of Sciences, USA, 89,* 5675.

LaBar, K., Gatenby, J., Gore, J., LeDoux, J., & Phelps, E. (1998). Human amygdala activation during conditioned fear acquisition and extinction: A mixed-trial fMRI study. *Neuron, 20,* 937–945.

LaMantia, A. S., & Rakic, P. (1990). Axon overproduction and elimination in the corpus callosum of the developing rhesus monkey. *Journal of Neuroscience, 10,* 2156–2175.

Lambe, E. K., Krimer, L. S., & Goldman-Rakic, P. S. (2000). Differential postnatal development of catecholamine and serotonin inputs to identified neurons in prefrontal cortex of rhesus monkey. *Journal of Neuroscience, 20,* 8780–8787.

Lang, P. J., Bradley, M. M., & Cuthbert, B. N. (1990). Emotion, attention, and the startle reflex. *Psychological Review, 97,* 377–395.

Lang, P. J., Bradley, M. M., & Cuthbert, B. N. (1992). A motivational analysis of emotion: Reflex-cortex connections. *Psychological Science, 3,* 44–49.

Lanzenberger, R., Uhl, F., Windischberger, C., Gartus, A., Streibl, B., Edward, V., et al. (2001). Cross-modal plasticity in congenitally blind subjects. *International Society for Magnetic Resonance Medicine, 9,* 670.

Lawrence, K., Campbell, R., Swettenham, J., Terstegge, J., Akers, R., Coleman, M., et al. (2003). Interpreting gaze in Turner syndrome: Impaired sensitivity to intention and emotion, but preservation of social cueing. *Neuropsychologia, 41,* 894–905.

Lawrence, K., Kuntsi, J., Campbell, R., Coleman, M., & Skuse, D. (2003). Face and emotion recognition deficits in Turner syndrome: A possible role for X-linked genes in amygdala development. *Neuropsychology, 17,* 39–49.

Legerstee, M., & Varghese, J. (2001). Role of maternal affect mirroring on social expectancies of 3-month-old infants. *Child Development, 72,* 1301–1313.

Le Grand, R., Mondloch, C. J., Maurer, D., & Brent, H. P. (2001). Early visual experience and face processing. *Nature, 410,* 890.

Le Grand, R., Mondloch, C. J., Maurer, D., & Brent, H. P. (2003). Expert face processing requires input to the right hemisphere during infancy. *Nature Neuroscience, 6,* 1108–1112.

Lepage, M., & Richer, F. (1996). Inter-response interference contributes to the sequencing deficit in frontal lobe lesions. *Brain, 119,* 1289–1295.

Leslie, A. M., Friedman, O., & German, T. P. (2004). Core mechanisms in theory of mind. *Trends in Cognitive Sciences, 8,* 528–533.

Lespinet, V., Bresson, C., N'Kaoua, B., Rougier, A., & Claverie, B. (2002). Effect of age of onset of temporal lobe epilepsy on the severity and the nature of preoperative memory deficits. *Neuropsychologia, 40,* 1591–1600.

Levitt, P. (2003). Structural and functional maturation of the developing primate brain. *Journal of Pediatrics, 143*(Suppl. 4), S35–S45.

Levy, R., & Goldman-Rakic, P. (2000). Segregation of working memory functions within the dorsolateral prefrontal cortex. *Experimental Brain Research, 133*(1), 23–32.

Lewicki, P. (1986). Processing information about covariations that cannot be articulated. *Journal of Experimental Psychology: Learning, Memory and Cognition, 12*, 135–146.

Lewin, J., Friedman, L., Wu, D., Miller, D., Thompson, L., Klein, S., et al. (1996). Cortical localization of human sustained attention: Detection with functional MRI using a vigilance paradigm. *Journal of Computer Assisted Tomography, 20*(5), 695–701.

Lie, D. C., Song, H., Colamarino, S. A., Ming, G.-I., & Gage, F. H. (2004). Neurogenesis in the adult brain: New strategies for central nervous system diseases. *Annual Review of Pharmacology and Toxicology, 44*, 399–421.

Luciana, M. (2003). Neural and functional development of human prefrontal cortex. In M. de Haan & M. H. Johnson (Eds.), *Cognitive neuroscience of development* (pp. 157–179). London: Psychology Press.

Luciana, M., & Nelson, C. A. (2000). Neurodevelopmental assessment of cognitive function using the Cambridge Neuropsychological Testing Automated Battery (CANTAB): Validation and future goals. In M. Ernst & J. Rumsey (Eds.), *Functional neuroimaging in child psychiatry* (pp. 379–397). Cambridge, England: Cambridge University Press.

Lumsden, A., & Kintner, C. (2003). Neural induction and pattern formation. In L. R. Squire, F. E. Bloom, S. K. McConnell, J. L. Roberts, N. C. Spitzer, & M. J. Zigmond (Eds.), *Fundamental neuroscience* (2nd ed., pp. 363–390). New York: Academic Press.

Luna, B., Thulborn, K., Munoz, D., Merriam, E., Garver, K., Minshew, N., et al. (2001). Maturation of widely distributed brain function subserves cognitive development. *NeuroImage, 13*, 786–793.

Mabbott, D. J., & Smith, M. L. (2003). Memory in children with temporal or extra-temporal excisions. *Neuropsychologia, 41*, 995–1007.

MacDonald, A., Cohen, J., Stenger, V., & Carter, C. (2000). Dissociating the role of the dorsolateral prefrontal and anterior cingulate cortex in cognitive control. *Science, 288*(5472), 1835–1838.

Maguire, E. A., Gadian, D. G., Johnsrude, I. S., Good, C. D., Ashburner, J., Frackowiak, R. S. J., et al. (2000). Navigation-related structural change in the hippocampi of taxi drivers. *Proceedings of the National Academy of Sciences, USA, 97*, 4398–4403.

Maguire, E. A., Vargha-Khadem, F., & Mishkin, M. (2001). Effects of bilateral hippocampal damage on fMRI regional activations and interactions during memory retrieval. *Brain, 124*(Pt. 6), 1156–1170.

Málková, L., Bachevalier, J., Mishkin, M., & Saunders, C. (2001). Neurotoxic lesions of perirhinal cortex impair visual recognition memory in rhesus monkeys. *NeuroReport, 12*, 1913–1917.

Manns, J. R., & Squire, L. R. (1999). Impaired recognition memory on the Doors and People Test after damage limited to the hippocampal region. *Hippocampus, 9*(5), 495–499.

Manns, J. R., Stark, C. E., & Squire, L. R. (2000). Visual paired-comparison task as a measure of declarative memory. *Proceedings of the National Academy of Sciences, 97,* 12375–12379.

Marcus, D., & Nelson, C. A. (2001). Neural bases and development of face recognition in autism. *CNS Spectrums, 6,* 36–59.

Marinkovic, K., Trebon, P., Chauvel, P., & Halgren, E. (2000). Localized face processing by the human prefrontal cortex: Face-selective intracerebral potential and post-lesion deficits. *Cognitive Neuropsychology, 17,* 187–199.

Marin-Padilla, M. (1978). Dual origin of the mammalian neocortex and evolution of the cortical plate. *Anatomical Embryology, 152,* 109–126.

Martinez, A., Moses, P., Frank, L., Buxton, R., Wong, E., & Stiles, J. (1997). Hemispheric asymmetries in global and local processing: Evidence from fMRI. *NeuroReport, 8,* 1685–1689.

Martinkauppi, S., Rama, P., Aronen, H. J., Korvenoja, A., & Carlson, S. (2000). Working memory of auditory localization. *Cerebral Cortex, 10,* 889–898.

Mauk, M., & Thompson, R. (1987). Retention of classically conditioned eyelid responses following acute decerebration. *Brain Research, 403,* 89–95.

Maybery, M., Taylor, M., & O'Brien-Malone, A. (1995). Implicit learning: Sensitive to age but not to IQ. *Australian Journal of Psychology, 47,* 8–17.

Mayberry, R. I., Lock, E., & Kazmi, H. (2002). Linguistic ability and early language exposure. *Nature, 417,* 38.

McDonough, L., Mandler, J. M., McKee, R. D., & Squire, L. R. (1995). Deferred imitation task as a nonverbal measure of declarative memory. *Proceedings of the National Academy of Sciences, USA, 92,* 7580–7584.

McKee, R. D., & Squire, L. R. (1993). On the development of declarative memory. *Journal of Experimental Psychology: Learning, Memory, and Cognition, 19,* 397–404.

Meek, J. (2002). Basic principles of optical imaging and application to the study of infant development. *Developmental Science, 5,* 371–380.

Meletti, S., Benuzzi, F., Rubboli, G., Cantalupo, G., Stanzani Maserati, M., Nichelli, P., et al. (2003). Impaired facial emotion recognition in early-onset right mesial temporal epilepsy. *Neurology, 60,* 426–431.

Meltzoff, A. N. (1985). Immediate and deferred imitation in 14-month and 24-month-old infants. *Child Development, 56,* 62–72.

Meltzoff, A. N. (1988). Infant imitation and memory: Nine-month-olds in immediate and deferred tests. *Child Development, 59,* 217–225.

Meltzoff, A. N. (1995). What infant memory tells us about infantile amnesia: Long-term recall and deferred imitation. *Journal of Experimental Child Psychology, 59,* 497–515.

Meltzoff, A. N., & Decety, J. (2002). What imitation tells us about social cognition: A rapprochement between developmental psychology and cognitive neuroscience. *Philosophical Transactions of the Royal Society of London—Series B: Biological Sciences, 358,* 491–500.

Mettke-Hofmann, C., & Gwinner, E. (2003). Long-term memory for a life on the move. *Proceedings of the National Academy of Sciences, USA, 100,* 5863–5866.

Meulemans, T., van der Linden, M., & Perruchet, P. (1998). Implicit sequence learning in children. *Journal of Experimental Child Psychology, 69,* 199–221.

Millhouse, O. E., & Stensaas, S. (n.d.). *Central nervous system.* Retrieved June 6, 2005, from http://www-medlib.med.utah.edu/kw/sol/sss/subj2.html.

Mills, D. I., Prat, C., Zangl, R., Stager, C. L., Neville, H. J., & Werker, J. F. (2004). Language experience and the organization of brain activity to phonetically similar words: ERP evidence from 14- and 20-month-old infants. *Journal of Cognitive Neuroscience, 16,* 1452–1464.

Mills, D. M., Coffey-Corina, S. A., & Neville, H. J. (1993). Language acquisition and cerebral specialization in 20-month-old infants. *Journal of Cognitive Neuroscience, 5,* 326–342.

Mills, D. M., Coffey-Corina, S. A., & Neville, H. J. (1997). Language comprehension and cerebral specialization from 13 to 20 months [Special issue on origins of language disorders]. *Developmental Neuropsychology, 13,* 397–446.

Milner, B. (1995). Aspects of human frontal lobe function. In H. H. Jasper, S. Riggio, & P. S. Goldman-Rakic (Eds.), *Epilepsy and the functional anatomy of the frontal lobe.* New York: Raven Press.

Milner, B., Corkin, S., & Teuber, H. (1968). Further analysis of the hippocampal amnesic syndrome: Fourteen-year follow-up study of H. M. *Neuropsychologia, 6,* 215–234.

Molfese, D. L. (1989). Electrophysiological correlates of word meanings in 14-month-old human infants. *Developmental Neuropsychology, 5,* 79–103.

Molfese, D. L., & Molfese, V. J. (1979). Hemisphere and stimulus differences as reflected in the cortical responses of newborn infants to speech stimuli. *Developmental Psychology, 15,* 505–511.

Molfese, D. L., & Molfese, V. J. (1980). Cortical responses of preterm infants to phonetic and nonphonetic speech stimuli. *Developmental Psychology, 16,* 574–581.

Molfese, D. L., & Molfese, V. J. (1985). Electrophysiological indices of auditory discrimination in newborn infants: Bases for predicting later language development. *Infant Behavior and Development, 8,* 197–211.

Molfese, D. L., & Molfese, V. J. (1997). Discrimination of language skills at 5 years of age using event-related potentials recorded at birth. *Developmental Neuropsychology, 13,* 135–156.

Molfese, D. L., Wetzel, W. F., & Gill, L. A. (1994). Known versus unknown word discrimination in 12-month-old human infants: Electrophysiological correlates. *Developmental Neuropsychology, 3–4,* 241–248.

Molliver, M., Kostovic, I., & Van der Loos, H. (1973). Development of synapses in the human fetus. *Brain Research, 50,* 403–407.

Mondloch, C., Geldart, S., Maurer, D., & de Schonen, S. (2003a). Developmental changes in the processing of hierarchical shapes continue into adolescence. *Journal of Experimental Child Psychology, 84,* 20–40.

Mondloch, C. J., Geldart, S., Maurer, D., & Le Grand, R. (2003b). Developmental changes in face processing skills. *Journal of Experimental Child Psychology, 86,* 67–84.

Monk, C. S., Zhuang, J., Curtis, W. J., Ofenloch, I. T., Tottenham, N., Nelson, C. A., et al. (2002). Human hippocampal activation in the delayed matching- and nonmatching-to-sample memory tasks: An event-related functional MRI approach. *Behavioral Neuroscience, 116,* 716–721.

Morris, J. S., Frith, C. D., Perrett, K. I., Rowland, D., Young, A. W., Calder, A. J., et al. (1996). A differential neural response in the human amygdala to fearful and happy facial expressions. *Nature, 383,* 812–815.

Moscovitch, M., Winocur, G., & Behrmann, M. (1997). What is special about face recognition? Nineteen experiments on a person with visual object agnosia but normal face recognition. *Journal of Cognitive Neuroscience, 9,* 555–604.

Moses, P., Roe, K., Buxton, R. B., Wong, E. C., Frank, L. R., & Stiles, J. (2002). Functional MRI of global and local processing in children. *NeuroImage, 16,* 415–424.

Moses, P., & Stiles, J. (2002). Lesion methodology: Contrasting views from adult and child studies. *Developmental Psychobiology, 40,* 266–277.

Mrzljak, L., Uylings, H. B. M., VanEden, C., & Judas, M. (1990). Neuronal development in human prefrontal cortex in prenatal and postnatal stages. *Progress in Brain Research, 85,* 185–222.

Mumme, D. L., Fernald, A., & Herrera, C. (1996). Infants' responses to facial and vocal emotional signals in a social referencing paradigm. *Child Development, 67,* 3219–3237.

Murloz-Sanjuan, I., & Brivanfou, A. H. (2002). Neural induction: Default model and embryonic stem cells. *Nature Reviews Neuroscience, 3*(4), 271–280.

Nadarajah, B., & Parnavelas, J. G. (2002). Models of neuronal migration in the developing cerebral cortex. *Nature Reviews Neuroscience, 3,* 423–432.

Naegele, J. R., & Lombroso, P. J. (2001). Genetics of central nervous system developmental disorders. *Child and Adolescent Psychiatric Clinics of North America, 10,* 225–239.

Nakamura, K., Kawashima, R., Ito, K., Sugiura, M., Kato, T., Nakamura, A., et al. (1999). Activation of the right inferior frontal cortex during assessment of facial emotion. *Journal of Neurophysiology, 82,* 1610–1614.

Narumoto, J., Yamada, H., Iidaka, T., Sadato, N., Fukui, K., Itoh, H., et al. (2000). Brain regions involved in verbal or non-verbal aspects of facial emotion recognition. *NeuroReport, 11,* 2571–2576.

Nelson, C. (1994). Neural correlates of recognition memory in the first postnatal year of life. In G. Dawson & K. Fischer (Eds.), *Human behavior and the developing brain* (pp. 269–313). New York: Guilford Press.

Nelson, C. A. (1995). Ontogeny of human memory: A cognitive neuroscience perspective. *Developmental Psychology, 31,* 723–738.

Nelson, C. A. (1998). The nature of early memory. *Preventive Medicine, 27,* 172–179.

Nelson, C. A. (1999). Neural plasticity and human development. *Current Directions in Psychological Science, 8,* 42–45.

Nelson, C. A. (2000a). Change and continuity in neurobehavioral development. *Infant Behavior and Development, 22,* 415–429.

Nelson, C. A. (2000b). Neural plasticity and human development: Role of early experience in sculpting memory systems. *Developmental Science, 3,* 115–130.

Nelson, C. A. (2001). Development and neural bases of face recognition. *Infant and Child Development, 10,* 3–18.

Nelson, C. A. (2002). Neural development and life-long plasticity. In R. M. Lerner, F. Jacobs, & D. Wetlieb (Eds.), *Promoting positive child, adolescent, and family development: Handbook of program and policy interventions* (pp. 31–60). Thousand Oaks, CA: Sage.

Nelson, C. A., & Bloom, F. E. (1997). Child development and neuroscience. *Child Development, 68,* 970–987.

Nelson, C. A., & Carver, L. J. (1998). Effects of stress on brain and memory: A view from developmental cognitive neuroscience. *Development and Psychopathology, 10,* 793–809.

Nelson, C. A., & Collins, P. F. (1991). Event-related potential and looking time analysis of infants' responses to familiar and novel events: Implications for visual recognition memory. *Developmental Psychology, 27,* 50–58.

Nelson, C. A., & Collins, P. F. (1992). Neural and behavioral correlates of recognition memory in 4- and 8-month-old infants. *Brain and Cognition, 19,* 105–121.

Nelson, C. A., & Luciana, M. (Eds.). (2001). *Handbook of developmental cognitive neuroscience.* Cambridge, MA: MIT Press.

Nelson, C. A., & Monk, C. S. (2001). Use of event-related potentials in the study of cognitive development. In C. Nelson & M. Luciana (Eds.), *Handbook of developmental cognitive neuroscience* (pp. 125–136). Cambridge, MA: MIT Press.

Nelson, C. A., Monk, C. S., Lin, J., Carver, L. C., Thomas, K. M., & Truwit, C. (2000). Functional neuroanatomy of spatial working memory in children. *Developmental Psychology, 36*(1), 109–116.

Nelson, C. A., & Webb, S. J. (2003). A cognitive neuroscience perspective on early memory development. In M. de Haan & M. H. Johnson (Eds.), *Cognitive neuroscience of development* (pp. 99–125). London: Psychology Press.

Nelson, C. A., Wewerka, S., Thomas, K. M., Tribby-Walbridge, S., deRegnier, R.-A., & Georgieff, M. (2000). Neurocognitive sequelae of infants of diabetic mothers. *Behavioral Neuroscience, 114,* 950–956.

Nemanic, S., Alvarado, M. C., & Bachevalier, J. (2004). Hippocampal/parahippocampal regions and recognition memory: Insights from visual paired comparison versus object-delayed nonmatching in monkeys. *Journal of Neuroscience, 24,* 2013–2026.

Neville, H. J., Bavelier, D., Corina, D., Rauschecker, J., Karni, A., Lalwani, A., et al. (1998). Cerebral organization for language in deaf and hearing subjects: Biological constraints and effects of experience. *Proceedings of the National Academy of Sciences, 95,* 922–929.

Newman, A. J., Bavelier, D., Corina, D., Jezzard, P., & Neville, H. J. (2002). A critical period for right hemisphere recruitment in American Sign Language processing. *Nature Neuroscience, 5,* 76–80.

Nishitani, N., & Hari, R. (2000). Temporal dynamics of cortical representation for action. *Proceedings of the National Academy of Sciences, USA, 97,* 913–918.

Nissen, M., & Bullemer, P. (1987). Attentional requirements of learning: Evidence from performance measures. *Cognitive Psychology, 19,* 1–32.

Nunn, J. A., Polkey, C. E., & Morris, R. G. (1998). Selective spatial memory impairment after right unilateral temporal lobectomy. *Neuropsychologia, 36,* 837–848.

Ogawa, S., Lee, T., Nayak, A., & Glynn, P. (1990). Oxygenation-sensitive contrast in magnetic resonance image of rodent brain at high magnetic fields. *Magnetic Resonance in Medicine, 26,* 68–78.

Olesen, P. J., Nagy, Z., Westerberg, H., & Klingberg, T. (2003). Combined analysis of DTI and fMRI data reveals a joint maturation of white and grey matter in a fronto-parietal network. *Brain Research: Cognitive Brain Research, 18,* 48–57.

Olesen, P. J., Westerberg, H., & Klingberg, T. (2004). Increased prefrontal and parietal activity after training of working memory. *Nature Neuroscience, 7,* 75–79.

Onishi, T., Moriguchi, Y., Matsuda, H., Mori, T., Hirakata, M., Imabayshi, E., et al. (2004). Neural network for the mirror system and mentalizing in normally developing children: An fMRI study. *NeuroReport, 15,* 1483–1487.

Oppenheim, R. W., & Johnson, J. E. (2003). Programmed cell death and neurotrophic factors. In L. R. Squire, F. E. Bloom, S. K. McConnell, J. L. Roberts, N. C. Spitzer, & M. J. Zigmond (Eds.), *Fundamental neuroscience* (2nd ed., pp. 499–532). New York: Academic Press.

Orlich, E., & Ross, L. (1968). Acquisition and differential conditioning of the eyelid response in normal and retarded children. *Journal of Experimental Child Psychology, 6,* 181–193.

Overman, W. H., Bachevalier, J., Sewell, F., & Drew, J. (1993). A comparison of children's performance on two recognition memory tasks: Delayed non-match-to-sample versus visual paired-comparison. *Developmental Psychobiology, 26,* 345–357.

Owen, A., Roberts, A., Hodges, J., Summers, B., Polkey, C., & Robbins, T. (1993). Contrasting mechanisms of impaired attentional set shifting in patients with frontal lobe damage or Parkinson's disease. *Brain, 119,* 1597–1615.

Paetau, R. (2002). Magnetoencephalography in pediatric neuroimaging. *Developmental Science, 5,* 361–370.

Paetau, R., Ahonen, A., Salonen, O., & Sams, M. (1995). Auditory evoked magnetic fields to tones and pseudowords in healthy children and adults. *Journal of Clinical Neurophysiology, 12,* 177–185.

Parker, S. W., Nelson, C. A., & Bucharest Early Intervention Project Core Group. (2005a). Impact of deprivation on the ability to discriminate facial expressions of emotion: An event-related potential study. *Child Development, 76,* 1–19.

Parker, S. W., Nelson, C. A., & Bucharest Early Intervention Project Core Group. (2005b). Impact of early institutional rearing on the ability to discriminate facial expressions of emotion: An event-related potential study. *Child Development, 76,* 54–72.

Parkin, A., & Streete, S. (1988). Implicit and explicit memory in young children and adults. *British Journal of Psychology, 79,* 361–369.

Pascalis, O., & Bachevalier, J. (1999). Neonatal aspiration lesions of the hippocampal formation impair visual recognition memory when assessed by paired-comparison task but not by delayed nonmatching-to-sample task. *Hippocampus, 9,* 609–616.

Pascalis, O., de Haan, M., & Nelson, C. A. (2002). Is face processing species specific during the first year of life? *Science, 296,* 1321–1323.

Pascalis, O., de Schonen, S., Morton, J., Deruelle, C., & Fabre-Grent, M. (1995). Mother's face recognition by neonates: A replication and an extension. *Infant Behavior and Development, 18,* 79–95.

Pascalis, O., Hunkin, N. M., Holdstock, J. S., Isaac, C. L., & Mayes, A. R. (2004). Visual paired comparison performance is impaired in a patient with selective hippocampal lesions and relatively intact item recognition. *Neuropsychologia, 42,* 1293–1300.

Pascual-Leone, A., Grafman, J., Clark, K., Stewart, M., Massaquoi, S., Lou, J.-S., et al. (1993). Procedural learning in Parkinson's disease and cerebellar degeneration. *Annals of Neurology, 34,* 594–602.

Passarotti, A. M., Paul, B. M., Bussiere, J. R., Buxton, R. B., Wong, E. C., & Stiles, J. (2003). Development of face and location processing: An fMRI study. *Developmental Science, 6,* 100–117.

Paterson, S. J., Brown, J. H., Gsodl, M. K., Johnson, M. H., & Karmiloff-Smith, A. (1999). Cognitive modularity and genetic disorders. *Science, 286,* 2355–2358.

Paus, T., Zijdbenbos, A., Worsley, K., Collins, D. L., Blumenthal, J., Giedd, J. N., et al. (1999). Structural maturation of neural pathways in children and adolescents: In vivo study. *Science, 283,* 1908–1911.

Pelphrey, K. A., Morris, J. P., & McCarthy, G. (2005). Neural basis of eye gaze processing deficits in autism. *Brain, 128,* 1038–1048.

Peña, M., Maki, A., Kovacic, D., Dehaene-Lambertz, G., Koizumi, H., Bouquet, F., et al. (2003). Sounds and silence: An optical topography study of language recognition at birth. *Proceedings of the National Academy of Sciences, USA, 100,* 11702–11705.

Perani, D., Paulesu, E., Galles, N. S., Dupoux, E., Dehaene, S., Bettinardi, V., et al. (1998). The bilingual brain: Proficiency and age of acquisition of the second language. *Brain, 121,* 1841–1852.

Perner, J. (1993). *Understanding the representational mind.* Cambridge, MA: MIT Press.

Petitto, L. A., Zatorre, R. J., Gauna, K., Nikelski, E. J., Dostie, D., & Evans, A. C. (2000). Speech-like cerebral activity in profoundly deaf people processing signed languages: Implications for the neural basis of human language. *Proceedings of the National Academy of Sciences, 97,* 13961 13966.

Phillips, M. L., Young, A. W., Senior, C., Brammer, M., Andrew, C., Calder, A. J., et al. (1997). A specific neural substrate for perceiving facial expressions of disgust. *Nature, 389,* 495–498.

Pickering, S. J. (2001a). Cognitive approaches to the fractionation of visuo-spatial working memory. *Cortex, 37,* 457–473.

Pickering, S. J. (2001b). Development of visuo-spatial working memory. *Memory, 9,* 423–432.

Pierce, K., Muller, R. A., Ambrose, J., Allen, G., & Courchesne, E. (2001). Face processing occurs outside the fusiform "face area" in autism: Evidence from functional MRI. *Brain, 124,* 2059–2073.

Pine, D., Fyer, A., Grun, J., Phelps, E., Szesko, P., Koda, V., et al. (2001). Methods for developmental studies of fear conditioning circuitry. *Biological Psychiatry, 50,* 225–228.

Pinker, S. (1994). *Language instinct: How the mind creates language.* New York: Morrow.

Pizzagelli, D. A., Lehmann, D., Hendrick, A. M., Regard, M., Pascual-Marqui, R. D., & Davidson, R. J. (2002). Affective judgements of faces modulate early activity (~160 ms) within the fusiform gyri. *NeuroImage, 16,* 663–677.

Polich, J. (1993). Cognitive brain potentials. *Current Directions in Psychological Science, 2*(6), 175–179.

Pollak, S. D., Cicchetti, D., Hornung, K., & Reed, A. (2000). Recognizing emotion in faces: Developmental effects of child abuse and neglect. *Developmental Psychology, 36*(5), 679–688.

Pollak, S. D., & Kistler, D. J. (2002). Early experience is associated with the development of categorical representations for facial expressions of emotion. *Proceedings of the National Academy of Sciences, USA, 99*(13), 9072–9076.

Pollak, S. D., & Sinha, P. (2002). Effects of early experience on children's recognition and facial displays of emotion. *Developmental Psychology, 38*(5), 784–791.

Posner, M., & Petersen, S. (1990). Attention system of the human brain. *Annual Review of Neuroscience, 13*, 25–42.

Posner, M., & Raichle, M. (1997). *Images of mind*. New York: Scientific American Library.

Posner, M., Walker, J., Friedrich, F., & Rafal, R. (1984). Effects of parietal injury on covert orienting of attention. *Journal of Neuroscience, 4*(7), 1863–1874.

Pourtois, G., Sander, D., Andres, M., Grandjean, D., Reveret, L., Olivier, E., et al. (2004). Dissociable roles of the human somatosensory and superior temporal cortices for processing social face signals. *European Journal of Neuroscience, 20*, 3507–3515.

Puce, A., Allison, T., Asgari, M., Gore, J. C., & McCarthy, G. (1996). Differential sensitivity of human visual cortex to faces, letterstrings, and textures: A functional magnetic resonance imaging study. *Journal of Neuroscience, 16*, 5205–5215.

Puce, A., Allison, T., Bentin, S., Gore, J. C., & McCarthy, G. (1998). Temporal cortex activation in humans viewing eye and mouth movements. *Journal of Neuroscience, 18*, 2188–2199.

Puce, A., & Perrett, D. (2003). Electrophysiology and brain imaging of biological motion. *Philosophical Transactions of the Royal Society of London—Series B: Biological Sciences, 358*, 435–455.

Rafal, R., Posner, M., Friedman, J., Inhoff, A., & Bernstein, E. (1988). Orienting of visual attention in progressive supranuclear palsy. *Brain, 111*(2), 267–280.

Rakic, P. (1988). Specification of cerebral cortical areas. *Science, 241*, 170–176.

Rakic, P. (2002a). Adult neurogenesis in mammals: An identity crisis. *Journal of Neuroscience, 22*, 614–618.

Rakic, P. (2002b). Neurogenesis in adult primate neocortex: An evaluation of the evidence. *Nature Reviews Neuroscience, 3*, 65–71.

Raper, J. A., & Tessier-Lavigne, M. (1999). Growth cones and axon pathfinding. In M. J. Zigmond, F. E. Bloom, S. C. Landis, J. L. Roberts, & L. R. Squire (Eds.), *Fundamental neuroscience* (pp. 519–546). New York: Academic Press.

Raper, J., & Tessier-Lavigne, M. (2003). Growth cones and axon pathfinding. In L. R. Squire, F. E. Bloom, S. K. McConnell, J. L. Roberts, N. C. Spitzer, & M. J. Zigmond (Eds.), *Fundamental neuroscience* (2nd ed., pp. 449–467). New York: Academic Press.

Rebai, M., Poiroux, S., Bernard, C., & Lalonde, R. (2001). Event-related potentials for category-specific information during passive viewing of faces and objects. *International Journal of Neuroscience, 106*(3/4), 209–226.

Reber, A. (1992). The cognitive unconscious: An evolutionary perspective. *Consciousness and Cognition, 1,* 93–133.

Reber, A. (1993). *Implicit learning and tacit knowledge: Vol. 19. An essay on the cognitive unconscious.* New York: Oxford University Press.

Richards, J. (1994). Baseline respiratory sinus arrhythmia and heart rate responses during sustained visual attention in preterm infants from 3 to 6 months of age. *Psychophysiology, 31,* 235–243.

Richards, J. (1998). Development of selective attention in young infants. *Developmental Science, 1,* 45–51.

Richards, J. (2001). Attention in young infants: A developmental psychophysiological perspective. In C. Nelson & M. Luciana (Eds.), *Handbook of cognitive neuroscience* (pp. 321–338). Cambridge, MA: MIT Press.

Richards, J. E. (2004). Recovering dipole sources from scalp-recorded event-related-potentials using component analysis: Principal component analysis and independent component analysis. *International Journal of Psychophysiology, 54,* 201–220.

Richards, J. E. (in press). Localizing cortical sources of event-related potentials in infants' covert orienting. *Developmental Science.*

Richter, W., Somorjai, R., Summers, R., Jaramasz, M., Menon, R. S., Gati, J. S., et al. (2000). Motor area activity during mental rotation studied by time-resolved single-trial fMRI. *Journal of Cognitive Neuroscience, 12,* 310–320.

Richter, W., Ugurbil, K., Georgopoulos, A., & Kim, S.-G. (1997). Time-resolved fMRI of mental rotation. *NeuroReport, 8,* 3697–3702.

Ridderinkhof, K., van der Molen, M., Band, G., & Bashore, T. (1997). Sources of interference from irrelevant information: A developmental study. *Journal of Experimental Child Psychology, 65,* 315–341.

Ridley, A. J., Schwartz, M. A., Burridge, K., Firtel, R. A., Ginsberg, M. H., Borisy, G., et al. (2003). Cell migration: Integrating signals from front to back. *Science, 302,* 1704–1709.

Rizzolatti, G., Fadiga, L., Fogassi, L., & Gallese, V. (2002). From mirror neurons to imitation: Facts and speculations. In A. Meltzoff & W. Prinz (Eds.), *The imitative mind: Development, evolution and brain bases* (pp. 247–266). Cambridge, England: Cambridge University Press.

Rizzolatti, G., Fadiga, L., Matelli, M., Bettinardi, V., Paulesu, E., Perani, D., et al. (1996). Localization of grasp representations in humans by PET: Pt. 1. Observation versus execution. *Experimental Brain Research, 111*, 246–252.

Roberts, J. E., & Bell, M. A. (2002). Effects of age and sex on mental rotation performance, verbal performance, and brain electrical activity. *Developmental Psychobiology, 40*, 391–407.

Roberts, J. E., & Bell, M. A. (2003). Two- and three-dimensional mental rotation tasks lead to different parietal laterality for men and women. *International Journal of Psychophysiology, 50*, 235–246.

Robinson, A. J., & Pascalis, O. (2004). Development of flexible visual recognition memory in human infants. *Developmental Science, 7*, 527–533.

Robinson, D., Bowman, E., & Kertzman, C. (1995). Covert orienting of attention in macques: Pt. 2. Contributions of parietal cortex. *Journal of Neurophysiology, 74*(2), 698–712.

Roe, K., Moses, P., & Stiles, J. (1999). Lateralization of spatial processes in school aged children. *Abstracts, Cognitive Neuroscience Society, 41.*

Rossion, B., Gauthier, I., Tarr, M. J., Despland, P., Bruyer, R., Linotte, S., et al. (2000). N170 occipito-temporal component is delayed and enhanced to inverted faces but not inverted objects: An electrophysiological account of face-specific processes in the human brain. *NeuroReport, 11*, 69–74.

Rovee-Collier, C. (1997a). Development of memory in infancy. In N. Cowan (Ed.), *Development of memory in childhood* (pp. 5–39). London: University College London Press.

Rovee-Collier, C. (1997b). Dissociations in infant memory: Rethinking the development of implicit and explicit memory. *Psychological Review, 104*, 467–498.

Rowe, A. D., Bullock, P. R., Polkey, C. E., & Morris, R. G. (2001). Theory of mind impairments and their relationship to executive functioning following frontal lobe excisions. *Brain, 124*, 600–616.

Ruchkin, D. S., Johnson, R. R., Jr., Grafman, J., Canoune, H., & Ritter, W. (1997). Multiple visuospatial working memory buffers: Evidence from spatiotemporal patterns of brain activity. *Neuropsychologia, 35*(2), 195–209.

Russo, R., Nichelli, P., Gibertoni, M., & Cornia, C. (1995). Developmental trends in implicit and explicit memory: A picture completion study. *Journal of Experimental Child Psychology, 59*, 566–578.

Rutishauser, U. (1993). Adhesion molecules of the nervous system. *Current Opinion in Neurobiology, 3*, 709–715.

Sabbagh, M. A. (2004). Understanding orbitofrontal contributions to theory-of-mind reasoning: Implications for autism. *Brain and Cognition, 55*, 209–219.

Sadato, N., Okada, T., Honda, M., & Yonekura, Y. (2002). Critical period for cross-modal plasticity in blind humans: A functional MRI study. *Neuroimage, 16*, 389–400.

Sadato, N., Pascual-Leone, A., Grafman, J., & Deiber, M. P. (1998). Neural networks for Braille reading by the blind. *Brain, 121*, 1213–1229.

Sala, J. B., Rama, P., & Courtney, S. M. (2003). Functional topography of a distributed neural system for spatial and nonspatial information maintenance in working memory. *Neuropsychologia, 41*(3), 341–356.

Sasaki, Y., Hadijkhani, M., Fischl, B., Liu, A. K., Marrett, S., Dale, A. M., et al. (2001). Local and global attention are mapped retinotopically in human occipital cortex. *Proceedings of the National Academy of Sciences, USA, 98*, 2077–2082.

Sato, W., Kochiyama, T., Yoshikawa, S., & Matsumura, M. (2001). Emotional expression boosts early visual processing of the face: ERP recording and its decomposition by independent component analysis. *NeuroReport, 12*(4), 709–714.

Saxe, R., Carey, S., & Kanwisher, M. (2004). Understanding other minds: Linking developmental psychology and functional neuroimaging. *Annual Review of Psychology, 55*, 87–124.

Scaife, M., & Bruner, J. S. (1975). Capacity for joint visual attention in the infant. *Nature, 253*, 265–266.

Schacter, D., & Buckner, R. (1998). On the relations among priming, conscious recollection, and intentional retrieval: Evidence from neuroimaging research. *Neurobiology of Learning and Memory, 70*, 284–303.

Schendan, H. E., Searl, M. M., Melrose, R. J., & Stern, C. E. (2003). An FMRI study of the role of the medial temporal lobe in implicit and explicit sequence learning. *Neuron, 37*(6), 1013–1025.

Schoppik, D., Gadian, D. G., Connelly, A., Mishkin, M., Vargha-Khadem, F., & Saunders, R. C. (2001). Volumetric measurement of the subhippocampal cortices in patients with developmental amnesia. *Abstracts of the Society for Neuroscience, 27*, 1400.

Schultz, R. T., Gauthier, I., Fulbright, R. K., Anderson, A. W., Volkmar, F., Skudlarski, P., et al. (2000). Abnormal ventral temporal cortical activity during face discrimination among individuals with autism and Asperger syndrome. *Archives of General Psychiatry, 57*, 331–340.

Schwartz, B., & Hashtroudi, S. (1991). Priming is independent of skill learning. *Journal of Experimental Psychology: Learning, Memory and Cognition, 17*(6), 1177–1187.

Schwarzer, G., & Zauner, N. (2003). Face processing in 8-month-old infants: Evidence for configural and analytical processing. *Vision Research, 43,* 2783–2793.

Scoville, W. B., & Milner, B. (1957). Loss of recent memory after bilateral hippocampal lesions. *Journal of Neurology, Neurosurgery, and Psychiatry, 20,* 11–21.

Seger, C. (1994). Implicit learning. *Psychological Bulletin, 115*(2), 163–196.

Seress, L. (2001). Morphological changes of the human hippocampal formation from midgestation to early childhood. In C. A. Nelson & M. Luciana (Eds.), *Handbook of developmental cognitive neuroscience* (pp. 45–58). Cambridge, MA: MIT Press.

Shallice, T. (1988). *From neuropsychology to mental structure.* New York: Cambridge University Press.

Shallice, T., & Burgess, P. (1991). Higher-order cognitive impairments and frontal lobe lesions in man. In H. Levin, H. Eisenberg, & A. Benton (Eds.), *Frontal lobe function and dysfunction* (pp. 125–138). Oxford, England: Oxford University Press.

Shamay-Tsoory, S. G., Tomer, R., Beger, B. D., Goldsher, D., & Aharon-Peretz, J. (2005). Impaired "affective theory of mind" is associated with right ventromedial prefrontal damage. *Cognitive and Behavioral Neurology, 18,* 55–67.

Shaw, P., Lawrence, E. J., Radbourne, C., Bramham, J., Polkey, C. E., & David, A. S. (2004). Impact of early and late damage to the human amygdala on "theory of mind" reasoning. *Brain, 127,* 1535.

Shelton, A. L., Christoff, K., Burrows, J. J., Pelisari, K. B., & Gabrieli, J. D. E. (2001). Brain activation during mental rotation: Individual differences. *Society for Neuroscience Abstracts, 27,* 456–458.

Shibata, T., Nishijo, H., Tamura, R., Miyamoto, K., Eifuku, S., Endo, S., et al. (2002). Generators of visual evoked potentials for faces and eyes in the human brain as determined by dipole localization. *Brain Topography, 15,* 51–63.

Shimamura, A. (1986). Priming effects in amnesia: Evidence for a dissociable memory function. *Quarterly Journal of Experimental Psychology, 38A,* 619–644.

Shingo, T., Gregg, C., Enwere, E., Fujikawa, H., Hassam, R., Geary, C., et al. (2003). Pregnancy-stimulated neurogenesis in the adult female forebrain mediated by prolactin. *Science, 299,* 117–120.

Shors, T. J., & Miesegaes, G. (2002). Testosterone in utero and at birth dictates how stressful experience will affect learning in adulthood. *Proceedings of the National Academy of Sciences, USA, 99,* 13955–13960.

Sidman, R., & Rakic, P. (1982). Development of the human central nervous system. In W. Haymaker & R. D. Adams (Eds.), *Histology and histopathology of the nervous system.* Springfield, IL: Charles C Thomas.

Siegler, R. S. (1991). *Children's thinking* (2nd ed.). Englewood Cliffs, NJ: Prentice-Hall.

Slaughter, V., & McConnell, D. (2003). Emergence of joint attention: Relationships between gaze following, social referencing, imitation and naming in infancy. *Journal of Genetic Psychology, 164,* 54–71.

Smith, E. E., & Jonides, J. (1998). Neuroimaging analyses of human working memory. *Proceedings of the National Academy of Sciences, USA, 95,* 12061–12068.

Smith, M. L., & Milner, B. (1988). Estimation of frequency of occurrence of abstract designs after frontal or temporal lobectomy. *Neuropsychologia, 26,* 297–306.

Smith, P., Loboschefski, T., Davidson, B., & Dixon, W. (1997). Scripts and checkerboards: Influence of ordered visual information on remembering locations in infancy. *Infant Behavior and Development, 13,* 129–146.

Soken, N. H., & Pick, A. D. (1999). Infants' perception of dynamic affective expressions: Do infants distinguish specific expressions? *Child Development, 70,* 1275–1282.

Song, H., Stevens, C. E., & Gage, F. H. (2002). Neural stem cells from adult hippocampus develop essential properties of functional CNS neurons. *Nature Neuroscience, 5,* 438–445.

Sowell, E. R., Thompson, P. M., Holmes, C. J., Batth, R., Jernigan, T. L., & Toga, A. W. (1999). Localizing age-related changes in brain structure between childhood and adolescence using statistical parametric mapping. *NeuroImage, 9,* 587–597.

Sowell, E. R., Thompson, P. M., Holmes, C. J., Jernigan, T. L., & Toga, A. W. (2000). In vivo evidence for post-adolescent brain maturation in frontal and striatal regions. *Nature Neuroscience, 2,* 859–961.

Spelke, E. S. (2000). Core knowledge. *American Psychologist, 55,* 1233–1243.

Spiers, H. J., Burgess, N., Hartley, T., Vargha-Khadem, F., & O'Keefe, J. (2001). Bilateral hippocampal pathology impairs topographical and episodic memory but not visual pattern matching. *Hippocampus, 11,* 7615–7625.

Squire, L. (1986). Mechanisms of memory. *Science, 232,* 1612–1619.

Squire, L., & Frambach, M. (1990). Cognitive skill learning in amnesia. *Psychobiology, 18,* 109–117.

Squire, L., Knowlton, B., & Musen, G. (1993). Structure and organization of memory. *Annual Review of Psychology, 44,* 453–495.

Squire, L., & McKee, R. (1993). Declarative and nondeclarative memory in opposition: When prior events influence amnesic patients more than normal subjects. *Memory and Cognition, 21*(4), 424–430.

Squire, L., Ojemann, J., Miezin, F., Petersen, S., Videen, T., & Raichle, M. (1992). Activation of the hippocampus in normal humans: A functional anatomical study of memory. *Proceedings of the National Academy of Sciences, USA, 89,* 1837–1841.

Stager, C. L., & Werker, J. F. (1997). Infants listen for more phonetic detail in speech perception than in word-learning tasks. *Nature, 388,* 381–382.

Stewart, L., Henson, R., Kampe, K., Walsh, V., Turner, R., & Frith, U. (2003). Becoming a pianist: An fMRI study of musical literacy acquisition. *Annals of the New York Academy of Sciences, 999,* 204–208.

Stiles, J. (2001). Spatial cognitive development. In C. A. Nelson & M. Luciana (Eds.), *Handbook of developmental cognitive neuroscience* (pp. 399–414). Cambridge, MA: MIT Press.

Stiles, J., Bates, E. A., Thal, D., Trauner, D. A., & Reilly, J. (1998). Linguistic, cognitive and affective development in children with pre- and perinatal focal brain injury: A ten-year overview from the San Diego longitudinal project. In C. Rovee-Collier, L. P. Lipsitt, & H. Hayne (Eds.), *Advances in infancy research* (pp. 131–163). Stamford, CT: Ablex.

Stiles, J., Moses, P., Passarotti, A., Dick, F. K., & Buxton, R. B. (2003a). Exploring developmental change in the neural bases of higher cognitive functions: The promise of magnetic resonance imaging. *Developmental Neuropsychology, 24,* 641–668.

Stiles, J., Moses, P., Roe, K., Akshoomoff, N. A., Trauner, D., Hesselink, J., et al. (2003b). Alternative brain organization after prenatal cerebral injury: Convergent fMRI and cognitive data. *Journal of the International Neuropsychological Society, 9,* 604–622.

Strange, B. A., Fletcher, P. C., Hennson, R. N. A., Friston, K. J., & Dolan, R. J. (1999). Segrating the functions of the human hippocampus. *Proceedings of the National Academy of Sciences, 96,* 4034–4039.

Sur, M., & Leamey, C. A. (2001). Development and plasticity of cortical areas and networks. *Nature Neuroscience, 2,* 251–262.

Sweeten, T. L., Posey, D. J., Shekhar, A., & McDougle, C. J. (2002). Amygdala and related structures in the pathophysiology of autism. *Pharmacology, Biochemistry and Behavior, 71,* 449–455.

Tabata, H., & Nakajima, K. (2003). Multipolar migration: The third mode of radial neuronal migration in the developing cerebral cortex. *Journal of Neuroscience, 23*(31), 9996–10001.

Tager-Flusberg, H. (2001). A re-examination of the theory of mind hypothesis of autism. In J. A. Burack, T. Charman, N. Yimiya & P. R. Zelazo (Eds.), *Development of autism: Perspectives from development and theory* (pp. 173–193). Mahwah, NJ: Erlbaum.

Takahashi, T., Nowakowski, R. S., & Caviness, V. S. (2001). Neocortical neurogeneisis: Regulation, control points, and a strategy of structural variation. In C. A. Nelson & M. Luciana (Eds.), *Handbook of developmental cognitive neuroscience* (pp. 3–22). Cambridge, MA: MIT Press.

Takeichi, M. (1995). Morphogenetic roles of classic caherins. *Current Opinion in Cell Biology, 7*, 619–627.

Tantam, D., Monaghan, L., Nicholson, H., & Stirling, J. (1989). Autistic children's ability to interpret faces: A research note. *Journal of Child Psychology and Psychiatry, 30*(4), 623–630.

Taylor, M. J., Edmonds, G. E., McCarthy, G., & Allison, T. (2001). Eyes first! Eye processing develops before face processing in children. *NeuroReport, 12*, 1671–1676.

Taylor, M. J., Itier, R. J., Allison, T., & Edmonds, G. E. (2001). Direction of gaze effects on early face processing: Eyes only versus full faces. *Brain Research: Cognitive Brain Research, 10*, 333–340.

Taylor, M. J., McCarthy, G., Saliba, E., & Degiovanni, E. (1999). ERP evidence of developmental changes in processing of faces. *Clinical Neurophysiology, 110*, 910–915.

Tessier-Lavigne, M. T. (2003). Growth cones and axon pathfinding. In L. R. Squire, F. E. Bloom, S. K. McConnell, J. L. Roberts, N. C. Spitzer, & M. J. Zigmond (Eds.), *Fundamental neuroscience* (2nd ed., pp. 449–467). New York: Academic Press.

Tessier-Lavigne, M., & Goodman, C. S. (1996). Molecular biology of axon guidance. *Science, 274*, 1123–1133.

Thomas, K. M. (2003). Assessing brain development using neurophysiologic and behavioral measures. *Journal of Pediatrics, 143*, S46–S53.

Thomas, K. M., Drevets, W. C., Dahl, R. E., Ryan, N. D., Birmaher, B., Eccard, C. H., et al. (2001a). Amygdala response to fearful faces in anxious and depressed children. *Archives of General Psychiatry, 58*, 1057–1063.

Thomas, K. M., Drevets, W. C., Whalen, P. J., Eccard, C. H., Dahl, R. E., Ryan, N. D., et al. (2001b). Amygdala response to facial expressions in children and adults. *Biological Psychiatry, 49*, 309–316.

Thomas, K., Hunt, R., Vizueta, N., Sommer, T., Durston, S., Yang, Y., et al. (2004). Evidence of developmental differences in implicit sequence learning: An fMRI study of children and adults. *Journal of Cognitive Neuroscience, 16*, 1339–1351.

Thomas, K. M., King, S. W., Franzen, P. L., Welsh, T. F., Berkowitz, A. L., Noll, D. C., et al. (1999). A developmental functional MRI study of spatial working memory. *NeuroImage, 10*, 327–338.

Thomas, K. M., & Nelson, C. A. (2001). Serial reaction time learning in preschool- and school-age children. *Journal of Experimental Child Psychology, 79*, 364–387.

Thomas, K., Vizueta, N., Teylan, M., Eccard, C., & Casey, B. (2003, April). *Impaired learning in children with presumed basal ganglia insults: Evidence from a serial reaction time task.* Paper presented at the annual meeting of the Cognitive Neuroscience Society, New York, NY.

Thomsen, T., Hugdahl, K., Ersland, L., Barndon, R., Lundervold, A., Smievoll, A. I., et al. (2000). Functional magnetic resonance imaging (fMRI) study of sex differences in a mental rotation task. *Medical Science Monitor, 6,* 1186–1196.

Tomizawa, K., Iga, N., Lu, Y., Moriwaki, A., Matushita, M., Li, S., et al. (2003). Oxytocin improves long-lasting spatial memory during motherhood through MAP kinase cascade. *Nature Neuroscience, 6,* 384–390.

Trevarthen, C. (1979). Communication and cooperation in early infancy: A description of primary intersubjectivity. In M. M. Bullowa (Ed.), *Before speech: The beginning of interpersonal communication* (pp. 321–347). New York: Cambridge University Press.

Tulving, E. (1972). Episodic and semantic memory. In E. Tulving & W. Donaldson (Eds.), *Organization of memory* (pp. 381–403). New York: Academic Press.

Tulving, E., Markowitsch, H. J., Craik, F. E., Habib, R., & Houle S. (1996). Novelty and familiarity activations in PET studies of memory encoding and retrieval. *Cerebral Cortex, 6,* 71–79.

Turati, C., Simion, F., Milani, I., & Umilta, C. (2002). Newborns' preferences for faces: What is crucial. *Developmental Psychology, 38,* 875–882.

Turkheimer, E., Haley, A., Waldron, M., D'Onofrio, B., & Gottesman, I. I. (2003). Socioeconomic status modifies heritability of IQ in young children. *Current Directions in Psychological Science, 14,* 623–628.

Turner, R., Le Bihan, D., Moonen, C., Despres, D., & Frank, J. (1991). Echo-planar time course MRI of cat brain oxygenation changes. *Magnetic Resonance in Medicine, 22,* 159–166.

Tzourio-Mazoyer, N., de Schonen, S., Crivello, F., Reutter, B., Aujard, Y., & Mazoyer, B. (2002). Neural correlates of woman face processing by 2-month-old infants. *NeuroImage, 15,* 454–461.

Uhl, F., Franzen, P., Lindinger, G., Lang, W., & Deecke, L. (1991). On the functionality of the visually deprived occipital cortex in early blind person. *Neuroscience Letters, 124,* 256–259.

Vaidya, C., Austin, G., Kirkorian, G., Ridlehuber, H., Desmond, J., Glover, G., et al. (1998). Selective effects of methylphenidate in attention deficit hyperactivity disorder: A functional magnetic resonance study. *Proceedings of the National Academy of Sciences, USA, 95*(24), 14494–14499.

Vaidya, C. J., Gabrieli, J. D., Monti, L. A., Tinklenberg, J. R., & Yesavage, J. A. (1999). Dissociation between two forms of conceptual priming in Alzheimer's disease. *Neuropsychology, 13,* 516–524.

van Praag, H., Schinder, A. F., Christie, B. R., Toni, N., Palmer, T. D., & Gage, F. H. (2002). Functional neurogenesis in the adult hippocampus. *Nature, 415,* 1030–1034.

Vargha-Khadem, F., Gadian, D. G., & Mishkin, M. (2001). Dissociations in cognitive memory: Syndrome of developmental amnesia. *Philosophical*

Transactions of the Royal Society of London—Series B: Biological Sciences, 356(1413), 1435–1440.

Vargha-Khadem, F., Gadian, D. G., Watkins, K. E., Connelly, A., Van Paesschen, W., & Mishkin, M. (1997). Differential effects of early hippocampal pathology on episodic and semantic memory. *Science, 277*(5324), 376–380.

Vargha-Khadem, F., Salmond, C. H., Watkins, K. E., Friston, K. J., Gadian, D. G., & Mishkin, M. (2003). Developmental amnesia: Effect of age at injury. *Proceedings of the National Academy of Sciences, USA, 100*(17), 10055–10060.

Verfaellie, M., Koseff, P., & Alexander, M. P. (2000). Acquisition of novel semantic information in amnesia: Effects of lesion location. *Neuropsychologia, 38*(4), 484–492.

Vingerhoets, G., de Lange, F. P., Vandemaele, P., Deblaere, K., & Achten, E. (2002). Motor imagery in mental rotation: An fMRI study. *NeuroImage, 17,* 1623–1633.

Volpe, J. J. (1995). *Neurology of the newborn* (3rd ed.). Philadelphia: Saunders.

Volpe, J. J. (2000). Overview: Normal and abnormal human brain development. *Mental Retardation and Developmental Disabilities Research Reviews, 6,* 1–5.

Waber, D. P., Carlson, D., & Mann, M. (1982). Developmental and differential aspects of mental rotation in early adolescence. *Child Development, 53,* 1614–1621.

Waber, D., Marcus, D., Forbes, P., Bellinger, D., Weiler, M., Sorensen, L., et al. (2003). Motor sequence learning and reading ability: Is poor reading associated with sequencing deficits? *Journal of Experimental Child Psychology, 84*(4), 338–354.

Walden, T. A., & Baxter, A. (1989). Effect of context and age on social referencing. *Child Development, 60*(6), 1511–1518.

Walden, T. A., & Ogan, T. A. (1988). Development of social referencing. *Child Development, 59,* 1230–1240.

Warkany, J., Lemire, R. J., & Cohen, M. M. (1981). *Mental retardation and congenital malformations of the central nervous system.* Chicago: Year Book Medical.

Webb, S. J., Monk, C. S., & Nelson, C. A. (2001). Mechanisms of postnatal neurobiological development in the prefrontal cortex and the hippocampal region: Implications for human development. *Developmental Neuropsychology, 19,* 147–171.

Webb, S., & Nelson, C. (2001). Neural correlates of perceptual priming in human adults and infants. *Journal of Experimental Child Psychology, 79,* 1–22.

Weiss, E., Siedentopf, C. M., Hofer, A., Deisenhammer, E. A., Hoptman, M. J., Kremser, C., et al. (2003). Sex differences in brain activation pattern during a visuospatial cognitive task: A functional magnetic resonance imaging study in healthy volunteers. *Neuroscience Letters, 344,* 169–172.

Werker, J. F., Cohen, L. B., Lloyd, V. I., Cassaola, M., & Stager, C. L. (1998). Acquisition of word-object association by 14-month-old infants. *Developmental Psychobiology, 34,* 1289–1309.

Werker, J. F., Fennell, C. E. T., Corcoran, K. M., & Stager, C. L. (2002). Infants' ability to learn phonetically similar words: Effects of age and vocabulary size. *Infancy, 3,* 1–30.

Werker, J. F., & Lalonde, C. (1988). Cross-language speech perception: Initial capabilities and developmental change. *Developmental Psychology, 24,* 672–683.

Werker, J. F., & Tess, R. C. (1984). Cross-language speech perception: Evidence for perceptual reorganization during the first year of life. *Infant Behavior and Development, 7,* 49–63.

Werker, J. F., & Vouloumanos, A. (2001). Speech and language processing in infancy: A neurocognitive approach. In C. A. Nelson & M. Luciana (Eds.), *Handbook of developmental cognitive neuroscience* (pp. 269–280). Cambridge, MA: MIT Press.

Whalen, P. J., Kagan, J., Cook, R. G., Davis, F. C., Kim, H., Polis, S., et al. (2004). Human amygdala responsivity to masked fearful eye whites. *Science, 306,* 2061.

Whalen, P. J., Shin, L. M., McInerney, S. C., Fisher, H., Wright, C. I., & Rauch, S. L. (2001). A functional MRI study of human amygdala responses to facial expressions of fear versus anger. *Emotion, 1,* 70–83.

White, T., & Nelson, C. A. (2004). Neurobiological development during childhood and adolescence. In R. Findling & S. C. Schulz (Eds.), *Schizophrenia in adolescents and children: Assessment, neurobiology, and treatment.* Baltimore, MD: Johns Hopkins University Press.

Wimmer, H., & Perner, J. (1983). Beliefs about beliefs: Representation and constraining function of wrong beliefs in young children's understanding of deception. *Cognition, 13,* 103–128.

Windischberger, C., Lamm, C., Bauer, H., & Moser, E. (2003). Human motor cortex activity during mental rotation. *NeuroImage, 20,* 225–232.

Wong, R. O., & Lichtman, J. W. (2003). Synapse elimination. In L. R. Squire, F. E. Bloom, S. K. McConnell, J. L. Roberts, N. C. Spitzer, & M. J. Zigmond (Eds.), *Fundamental neuroscience* (2nd ed., pp. 533–554). New York: Academic Press.

Woodruff-Pak, D. (1993). Eyeblink classical conditioning in H. M.: Delay and trace paradigms. *Behavioral Neuroscience, 107,* 911–925.

Woodruff-Pak, D., Logan, C., & Thompson, R. (1990). Neurobiological substrates of classical conditioning across the lifespan. In A. Diamond

(Ed.), *Development and neural bases of higher cognitive functions* (Vol. 608, pp. 150–173). New York: New York Academy of Sciences.

Woodruff-Pak, D., Papka, M., & Ivry, R. (1996). Cerebellar involvement in eyeblink classical conditioning in humans. *Neuropsychology, 10*, 443–458.

Wynn, K. (1992). Addition and subtraction by human infants. *Nature, 358*, 749–750.

Wynn, K., Bloom, P., & Chiang, W. C. (2002). Enumeration of collective entities by 5-month-old infants. *Cognition, 83*(3), B55–B62.

Yancey, S. W., & Phelps, E. A. (2001). Functional neuroimaging and episodic memory: A perspective. *Journal of Clinical and Experimental Neuropsychology, 23*, 32–48.

Yang, T. T., Menon, V., Eliez, S., Blasey, C., White, C. D., Reid, A. J., et al. (2002). Amygdala activation associated with positive and negative facial expressions. *NeuroReport, 13*(14), 1737–1741.

Zacks, J. M., Gilliam, F., & Ojemann, J. G. (2003). Selective disturbance of mental rotation by cortical stimulation. *Neuropsychologia, 41*, 1659–1667.

Zago, L., & Tzourio-Mazoyer, N. (2002). Distinguishing visuospatial working memory and complex mental calculation areas within the parietal lobes. *Neuroscience Letters, 331*, 45–49.

Zola, S. M., Squire, L. R., Teng, E., Stefanacci, L., Buffalo, E. A., & Clark, R. E. (2000). Impaired recognition memory in monkeys after damage limited to the hippocampal region. *Journal of Neuroscience, 20*, 451–463.

Index

Visual priming, 93–94
Visual recognition memory,
    80–81
Visuospatial module, 117–118
Visuospatial working memory,
    145–148
Voltage plots, 48

W

Williams syndrome, 117, 118
Wisconsin Card Sorting Task
    (WCST), 152–153

Word processing/word learning,
    64–65
Working memory, 148–149

X

X-linked lissencephaly, 20–21